956
Gol

Golan, Matti   MIDDLE
                EAST

The secret
conversations of
Henry Kissinger

Date Due

CONGREGATION RODEF SHOLOM
KOLB LIBRARY

956
Gol

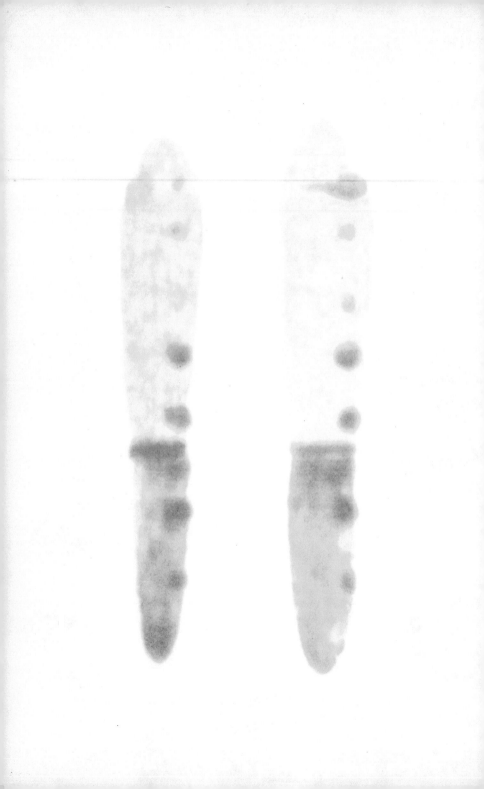

THE
SECRET
CONVERSATIONS
OF
HENRY KISSINGER

THE
SECRET
CONVERSATIONS
OF
HENRY KISSINGER

Step-by-Step Diplomacy in the Middle East

by Matti Golan

Translated by Ruth Geyra Stern and Sol Stern

Quadrangle/The New York Times Book Co.

Copyright © 1976 by Matti Golan. All rights reserved, including the right to reproduce this book or portions thereof in any form. For information, address: Quadrangle/The New York Times Book Co., 10 East 53 Street, New York, New York 10022. Manufactured in the United States of America. Published simultaneously in Canada by Fitzhenry & Whiteside, Ltd., Toronto.

Library of Congress Cataloging in Publication Data

Golan, Matti.
    The secret conversations of Henry Kissinger.

    Includes index.
    1. Israel-Arab War, 1973—Armistices. 2. Kissinger, Henry Alfred. 3. Israel—Foreign relations—United States. 4. United States—Foreign relations—Israel. I. Title.
DS128.18.G64 1976   956'.048   75-36262
ISBN 0-8129-0608-X

To my late father Schmuel and my mother Shoshana
To my wife Neitza and my children Lee-Schmuel
and Tamar-Leah-Dean

CONTENTS

THE
SECRET
CONVERSATIONS
OF
HENRY KISSINGER

Prologue

It was an all too familiar scene at the council hall of the Palace of Nations in Geneva. The date was Thursday, September 4, 1975, one month short of two years since the outbreak of the Yom Kippur War. In the center of the hall were three desks arranged in a U shape. A single TV crew was waiting to start filming the event. In the gallery were dozens of journalists who traveled from all over the world to witness the signing ceremony of another interim agreement between Israel and Egypt.

Several minutes before 5:00 P.M. the familiar figure of Major General Ensio Siilasvuo, commander of the UN Emergency Force, entered the hall. He took his place in the center next to his black American assistant, James Jones.

At exactly 5:00 P.M. the Egyptian delegation—three officers and a civilian diplomat—paraded into the hall and took its place at the table to the right of the UN group. Three minutes later the Israeli delegation—two civilians and an army man—entered the hall.

In a gloomy monotone the Finnish general recited the formula that had been agreed upon ahead of time with the two delegations:

Honorary delegates. I am happy to welcome you to
the Palace of Nations. I understand that the agreements to be signed today are the following: an
agreement between Israel and Egypt; an addendum;
maps added to the agreement. I propose that we
proceed with the signing.

The bulky documents were put on the table, and
exactly fifteen minutes later the agreement between
Israel and Egypt was signed.

I sat in the first row in the journalists' gallery with
a sense of déjà vu. As a diplomatic correspondent and
a columnist for the Israeli newspaper *Haaretz*, I had
covered all the negotiations and agreements that had
followed the Yom Kippur War. This was the third
time I had been in that hall. There was the Geneva
conference in December 1973, the disengagement-of-
forces agreement between Israel and Syria in May
1974, and now the second interim agreement with
Egypt.

Precisely because it was such a familiar scene I felt
a sudden chill. Nothing had changed. There was the
same cool, even hostile atmosphere at this ceremony
as at all the others.

The members of the two delegations were riveted
to their chairs as if held by the devil. Their eyes
wandered in all directions—to the walls covered with
large murals, to the carpet, the ceiling, to Siilasvuo.
The only direction they did not look was toward the
opposite delegation. On entering and leaving they
shook hands only with the representatives of the UN.

As the signing ceremony took place, the architect
of the agreement was on his way back to Washington.
After many months of tiring negotiations, Henry Kissinger was being feted for taking another step toward
peace and accomplishing an important political victory. And there were millions who shared this view,
not only in the United States, but in Israel and Egypt.

I too had felt that way at the time of the disengagement-of-forces agreement between Israel and Egypt in 1974. Like most of the people in Israel, I saw Kissinger as a peace angel who had come to minister to a Middle East tired of war and suffering. But then slowly during my work as a reporter I started hearing things. The more I heard the more nervous I became. There was a terrible contradiction between what I was hearing and the public declarations of the American secretary of state and the Israeli government. What was really behind the shining external diplomatic facade? The need to answer this question became almost an obsession for me.

Fortunately I was given access to sources of information that enabled me to see beyond the curtain of public relations that surrounded the process of negotiations in the Middle East. I decided to write a book that would reveal what had been going on behind the closed doors in Washington, Jerusalem, and Cairo as Kissinger developed his step-by-step diplomacy, starting with the outbreak of the Yom Kippur War and continuing right up to the latest negotiations for an interim agreement with Egypt.

I worked on this book feverishly for seven months and when I finished it I breathed a great sigh of relief. But there was one more hurdle to cross—the Israeli military censor. When I handed the manuscript to the censor in Tel Aviv on March 25, 1975, it never occurred to me that there would be more than routine and minor changes requested. I certainly did not expect a four-month nightmare during which my book was banned, I was turned into a media commodity, the book was made a focus of high political intrigue, and the Israeli government behaved in a bizarre fashion. The story of the banning of the book is worth telling in itself. It is also inextricably linked to the political events described throughout these pages. It thus serves as a most appropriate prologue to the book itself.

As I turned over the manuscript to the censor, Colonel Itzhak Shani, I asked how long it would take him to check it.

"If it's a problematic book, between four and six weeks," he said. "If not, maybe even two weeks."

After two weeks there was no word from the censor. I went down to Tel Aviv from my home in Jerusalem in order to meet Shani. He was polite and amiable. "The book is certainly unusual," he said, "and the checking takes time."

"How long?"

This time he wouldn't commit himself. "One has to check and it takes time." When I pressed a little harder he replied that, according to the law, the censor can hold a book for examination for a period of three months.

"But," I protested, "this book is not a romance or poetry. This is a political book that is linked to current developments and time is a crucial factor."

"We are doing, and we will do, our best to finish quickly," the polite censor promised me.

Another week passed, and not a word. I called Shani.

"What's happening?"

"Nothing special. A routine check."

"When will it end?"

"Soon."

"What is 'soon'? A week? Two weeks?"

"It is hard to say."

"Is it possible to meet you?"

"Absolutely. The door is always open."

Polite, smiling, and amiable. Always willing to meet—even though he had nothing to tell me.

Another week, and another appointment with Shani. Nothing new since the previous meeting, but many calm smiles. The "routine check" continued. Three more similar meetings during which all attempts to elicit more specific details met with evasive smiles.

However, I still believed that since this was a political and not a military book, it had a good chance even if they cut some parts.

I saw the red light for the first time on Monday, May 5. I called Shani, but he still did not have an answer. In an angry voice I said, "This is not possible." I said I would like to meet him a day later. He replied that he would contact me. At 5:00 P.M. he called: "The chief censor wants to see you tomorrow at 12:00 noon."

I finally began to understand that this was no longer a "routine check." But I was still thinking in terms of partial deletions—a section here, a section there. Or perhaps a rewriting of this or that chapter.

At 11:30 P.M. there was another call from Shani. He said he was sorry but he had just received a message from the chief censor that he had to postpone the meeting to Wednesday at 9:00 A.M.

"What is the nature of our meeting with the chief censor?" I asked.

"Very simple. He wants to meet you."

"Isn't this irregular?"

"Absolutely not."

"Does this raise the possibility of the banning of the whole book?"

"Not necessarily. Things like this have happened before."

On Wednesday, May 7, at 9:00 A.M. I walked into the chief censor's office. Brigadier General Walter Bar-On was expecting me. Tall, with silver hair and limpid, light blue eyes, Bar-On courteously invited me to sit down, instructing his secretary to bring black coffee. I certainly needed it.

"What I am about to say now is strictly official," Bar-On began with a stern expression on his face. Sounding like someone reciting a part written by someone else he continued: "I have decided to ban the book from beginning to end, on the grounds of damage to the security of the state. In my opinion the publication of the book would create a situation where no state would agree to negotiate with Israel. The relationship with the United States would also be severely damaged. The publication of the book could cause the cutting off of military aid."

After he read the sections of the law authorizing the prohibition of publication of material damaging the security of the state, Bar-On read a declaration, which was sent me in a letter a day later:

1. On March 25, 1975, you delivered for the scrutiny of the censor a rough draft of your book *Confrontation and Separation* or *Kissinger in the Middle East.*

2. I read the draft version and examined it pursuant to the authority vested in me by my position, and conveyed to you my conclusion in our conversation that took place on May 7, 1975, in the presence of the publishers. Since the book is almost entirely based on secret and top secret information and also cites classified documents, I prohibit the publication of the book, all of it or part of it, completely or as a series, in the country or outside the country, in Hebrew or in translation, since its publication, in my opinion, would damage the defense of Israel.

3. In light of the nature of the material submitted by you to the censor, as herein described, and also in light of the book being replete with literal quotations of secret and top secret documents, you were directed, in our conversation of May 7, 1975, to hand to me every copy of a draft that was prepared by you and every copy of the secret and top secret documents that were quoted by you in the book, or upon which you relied in your writing, and this shall be not later than noon, May 8, 1975. A similar demand was given to the publishers.

When Bar-On finished I looked around to convince myself that this was no nightmare from which I would awake in a cold sweat.

The first to break the silence was Bar-On. He was now at ease, looking quite relieved. "That was the official part," he said. "Unofficially I want to tell you that in all my years as a censor I have never run into such an accumulation of restricted material." Lowering his eyes he continued sadly: "Such material can come only from very senior personalities. And this thought fills me with deep sorrow."

In the meantime I had managed to recover. "Is it not possible to omit several sections from the book?" I asked. Bar-On's face turned stern again.

"No," he said, "every word in the book could damage the security of the state."

"But," I said, raising my voice, "I know this book. And I know that in it there are sections and full chapters that have nothing to do with the security of the state."

"I do not agree with you," was his laconic answer. And that, in his view, was the last word since the law grants the censor exclusive discretion.

"Perhaps it is possible to rewrite a few sections and chapters?" I tried again. Bar-On did not rule this out in principle. "If you submit a new book, of course I will carry out my responsibility and examine it," he said. But, he said, it would be possible to speak of this only after I had turned in all handwritten copies, the documents in my possession and in the possession of others. I replied that there were no documents in my possession, only copies of the draft. "I hope," stressed Bar-On, "that there is no copy of the book outside the country."

I reassured him that this was the case. Before we parted, Bar-On added a few words about how decent he was being in not demanding the copies of the manuscript immediately, allowing me the grace of delivering them the following day, "in order to enable you to take counsel if you desire." I replied that, given the fact the censor had waited six weeks while I had the copies, this abrupt ultimatum was rather strange. But basically I didn't dispute the point. I was still in shock.

What I didn't know at the time was that all my arguments with Bar-On were totally pointless. The matter was already out of his hands and being dealt with at the highest governmental levels—taking up a good deal of the valuable time of the prime minister himself.

From the censor's office I went to the offices of *Haaretz*. There was a short conversation with Gershom Schocken, the editor of *Haaretz* and my publisher. I gave him the details of the meeting with Bar-On. Schocken expressed amazement at the censor's action and asked what I intended to do. I said I would wait for legal advice.

Driving back to Jerusalem, I considered whether to release the story of the banning of the book to the press. On the one hand, I thought, there is a chance that the release would embarrass the censor and prompt him to reconsider. But there was also the possibility that publicity would turn it into a contest of prestige and make it harder for the censor to back off. Naively I still thought there was room for compromise. The second consideration carried more weight and I decided not to break the story.

Therefore I was truly stunned when upon returning home, at 6:00 P.M., I received a call from a member of the Knesset who asked:

"What do I hear, Matti? They banned your book? Is everything all right with you?"

"How do you know?" I replied.

"What do you mean? Are you joking with me?"

"No. Very seriously. Whom did you hear it from? I told no one about it."

"What are you prattling about? The whole city is talking about it. In the Knesset they didn't talk about anything else today."

And then he told the following story—which even on that extraordinary day sounded utterly fantastic. At 8:00 A.M. Prime Minister Itzhak Rabin instructed Cabinet Secretary Gershon Avner to summon all the ministers to a secret and urgent cabinet meeting that would start in two hours. In order to ensure secrecy the ministers were asked to arrive at the meeting in taxis and not in their official cars.

A few ministers later recalled that when they entered the conference room in the prime minister's office they were convinced that a war was about to break out. Their fears were further aroused when they saw the legal adviser to the government, Attorney General Meir Shamgar; the head of intelligence, Major General Shlomo Gazit; and the chief censor, Bar-On. The prime minister opened the meeting. After a few sentences many ministers couldn't believe their ears. He was reporting not about an imminent war, not a state of emergency—but a book by Matti Golan! The book, the prime minister said, is based on top secret documents—or to be more precise, the protocols of conversations between the American secretary of state and the Israeli negotiating team during the negotiations for disengagement of forces agreements with Egypt and Syria. If the book were published, said Rabin, Kissinger would be forced to resign and relations with the United States would be disrupted irrevocably. After the prime minister read a few excerpts from the book, Attorney General Shamgar gave a legal briefing explaining the sections of the law which provide for the banning of the book.

Very few ministers asked to speak, and those who did expressed no reservations. They only demanded that a thorough investigation be conducted to reveal the source of the leaks. The prime minister reassured them that the investigation was fully under way and that the culprit would be brought to trial regardless of his public position.

The length of time that this meeting remained secret was even shorter than that of routine secret meetings of the government. Within hours several cabinet ministers were continuing their discussions at a table in the Knesset cafeteria. Someone sitting close to the illustrious table was, of course, eavesdropping and heard a few sentences of the conversation. After a few minutes he got up and told several journalists that the topic of the high-powered conversation was Matti Golan. The rumor quickly spread from mouth to mouth in the cafeteria and in the corridors: There was a government meeting at which they discussed Matti Golan. And at 1:00 P.M. the Foreign Affairs and Security Committee of the Knesset would convene for a special and urgent meeting on the same subject!

But what had Matti Golan done to merit such an honor? The guessing games among the Knesset regulars began to flourish, getting wilder and wilder. Someone remembered that he heard something about the capture of a spy network, and my name was even mentioned in connection with the ring. Journalists jumped to the phone to call my house. But I was running around Tel Aviv, not suspecting that the big show was in Jerusalem, without my presence.

At 2:00 P.M. several of the Knesset journalists finally found out that the subject of the government meeting had been the banning of my book. In the meantime the Knesset committee meeting adjourned. Two of the journalists picked up a ride to Tel Aviv with a member of the committee, General (Res.) Avraham Yoffe. What had happened in the committee? they pressed the general. He refused to give them even a hint, so the journalists began to freely tell each other what they knew about the banning of the book.

Yoffe was astounded. "Those scoundrels!" he exclaimed, his face turning red with anger. "As soon as I get to Tel Aviv I'm going to call Rabin" (Yoffe's brother-in-law). "He comes to us and makes us swear that we won't even reveal the existence of the book, and you already know everything."

The government's campaign against my book was not yet over for the day. After the committee meeting Prime Minister Rabin and several aides traveled to Tel Aviv to brief the committee of editors of the Hebrew newspapers on the banning of the book. No details concerning its contents were given, and the editors exhibited no special curiosity about it. The only debate was about whether to publish the censor's decision to ban the book. Rabin and Shamgar were strongly against publication. They claimed that even revealing the censor's decision could hurt the security of the state. Two editors of *Haaretz* demanded that at least the fact of the ban be released. Surprisingly, Bar-On joined this demand. After some discussion it was decided that the newspapers could write dispatches concerning the ban but should submit them to the censor. If these were approved they could be published. But Rabin turned to the chief censor in anger: "What is this? What are you doing?" It was clear that the prime minister was out to keep the very existence of the book a secret.

That evening the editor of *Haaretz* wrote a short item on the banning of the book. The item was sent to the censor but was rejected and sent back. Schocken called Bar-On: "What happened?"

Bar-On replied, "I had second thoughts, and decided to prohibit it."

On the evening of that incredible day I first asked myself a question which I have never satisfactorily answered. I had enough experience to understand the possible political considerations in banning the book, but why had the government acted in such a panicky, heavy-handed way? Why didn't anyone call me beforehand in order to try to find an honorable way out? Why didn't the prime minister or Shamgar or Bar-On try to reach a compromise with me to exclude sections? Why didn't they try postponing the publication of the book before they took such drastic steps?

When the material on which I based the book was first offered to me, I assumed that someone in the Israeli government, someone in a crucial position, was interested in having the material publicized. And since the material was made available to me in its most authentic form, clearly that person was interested in having the material revealed with great impact.

If I was right, I had thought to myself, then the book would be okayed by the censor, perhaps with slight omissions. Even if I were mistaken then at most there would be more serious deletions, and I would be asked to rewrite a few of the sections in order to conceal the sources.

Neither of the two happened. Yet even after the unprecedented treatment the book was given I believed that there was originally an intention at the highest level for the material to see the light of day. Because of the banning of the entire book and the government's lame explanations, I guessed that someone, that very person, had now gone back on his original intention—perhaps because of changing political circumstances in the area of relations with the United States.

However, all this was speculation. It is just as possible that the Rabin government was so intimidated by Kissinger that it banned the book out of sheer panic.

At the time I couldn't afford too much concern about the government's motives. My main task was to try to figure out how to get the book released by the censor. Even more immediately, I had to decide whether to comply with the government's demand to turn over the copies of the manuscript within 24 hours. The attorneys I consulted were unanimously of the opinion that legally there was no precedent for the government demand that I surrender the manuscript.

But there were obviously other than legal questions involved in this strange affair. The other considerations were brought home to me forcefully by Schmuel Tamir, one of Israel's top courtroom attorneys. Tamir is also a member of the Knesset and was on the Security and Foreign Affairs Committee when Rabin reported to it on my book. Meeting me on the sidewalk outside his office Tamir told me: "Matti, I did not examine the law regarding the turning in of the manuscript, but I suggest that you do everything that is demanded of you without asking many questions. Regardless of what the law says, they are determined to arrest you if you do not hand in the manuscript."

I was surprised. I argued that if I handed over the manuscript without the law requiring me to do so, there would be implications that went far beyond this specific case—affecting the whole press.

"Do you want to be a martyr?" he asked. "Do you want to fight the war of the press?" Holding my arm, he said very excitedly, "Matti, I was there in the committee. I heard them. Such a battery of big wheels I haven't seen even on the eve of the war. They mean business. Listen to me. These are the kinds of waves that when they approach the best thing to do is dive under and wait until they pass. Afterward raise your head and we'll see what can be done."

My publisher, Gershom Schocken, and I decided to obtain the services of Itzhak Tunik, president of the Israeli Bar Association. Tunik immediately got in touch with Attorney General Shamgar, who told him that if I did not accede to the government's demand I would be prosecuted and a search warrant would be issued for myself and my relatives; the manuscript would be confiscated in any event.

It was the first time I heard officially that I might be arrested. "Is there or isn't there a legal basis for the censor to demand the manuscript?" I asked Tunik.

"To the best of my judgment and on the basis of my examination—no," he replied. He explained that the censor can confiscate documents, but not manuscripts.

"So that is what counts," I said.

"Not exactly," replied Tunik. "The question is whether you want to focus your battle specifically on the issue of handing over the manuscript." And then Tunik asked a question that caught me unprepared: "What, actually, do you want? Do you want the book or do you want to fight the battle of the press?"

I did not know. The truth was that during the past two days I had had no time to think about it. But I knew very clearly what I didn't want: "I'm not willing to hand over the manuscript if I am not obliged to do so by law."

Tunik was thinking. "The trouble is," he said, "that we are being forced to do things under pressure. I would have liked the three of us—Schocken, you, and myself—to be able to consult." He went to the phone, dialed, and finally reached the attorney general at his home.

"Is it possible to receive an extension, another 24 or 48 hours?" Tunik was listening and nodding his head, murmuring from time to time, "Yes, yes." Finally he put down the receiver. "There is nothing to talk about," he said. "I have known Shamgar for many years. He is a sober and rational man, but I have never heard him so excited. He told me that he is already being approached with complaints that he is being too soft-handed about the matter." The government would not give me one extra minute.

That evening, with the promise of full support from Schocken, I decided that I would not turn over the manuscript. I called Shani to tell him. "Every word that I tell you now you can report to those above you," I said to him. "I decided not to turn over the

manuscripts—primarily because no one found it necessary to talk to me before they confronted me with the
power of the law. The prime minister engaged in discussions with me many times on matters of state and
he never doubted that my concern and loyalty to the
security of the state was any less than his. The fact
that he did not find it necessary to speak to me before
he went to the cabinet and the other forums makes
me rebel and dictates my decision. I find support in
the opinion of attorney Tunik that the law does not
obligate me to turn in the manuscripts."

"I think you are mistaken in your interpretation
of the law," Shani answered.

"You receive your interpretation from Shamgar,
and that's okay," I said. "I accept the interpretation
of Tunik."

The next morning Schocken was on the phone to
me. He had spoken to Tunik again and after hearing
his views on the advisability of fighting on the issue
of turning over the manuscript he changed his own
mind. "I think it is better for you to hand over the
manuscript," he said to me.

On the basis of this conversation, it was clear to me
that I couldn't begin to contemplate taking on the
government. And so at about 12:00 noon I walked
into the censor's office in Jerusalem and turned over
a briefcase full of manuscript copies to Lieutenant
Colonel Yehuda Katz, not knowing when or if I would
ever see them again. Katz counted the pages of the
manuscript, very precisely, one by one. When he finished he gave me two documents to sign. One of them
was a receipt for the manuscript. The second document was a declaration:

> I, who have signed below, Matti Golan, hereby
> declare that:
> 1. I do not retain any copy, or copies, or photo-

copies of the manuscript, or any part of it, and I do not have protocols, telegrams, or any such material, or copies or photographs that were used for the writing of the book.

2. The above detailed material also is not in the hands of any other person who received the material from me or on my behalf.

After I signed, I told Katz that Schocken had a copy of the book. He said they would call the publisher right away to get it and added a note to the declaration: "Another photocopy is with the editor of *Haaretz*, Gershom Schocken."

However, no one from the censor's office called Schocken that day. After threatening me with arrest if I did not keep the deadline, the government allowed a copy to remain with the editor of *Haaretz* for nine days.

The confiscation of the entire manuscript, not just the documents, was an unprecedented act in a democratic society—even one in a state of war—an act that, if successful, would pose ominous threats to freedom of speech and expression. Of even greater concern was the fact that the authorities were prepared to arrest me. The section of the law that Shamgar quoted to Tunik as a basis for a possible bill of particulars against me was section 23(c) of the penal code: "Whoever acquires, collects, prepares, writes, or holds secret information without being so authorized is subject to 7 years' imprisonment; if he intends to hurt the security of the state he is subject to 15 years' imprisonment."

This is so broad that it could be used against any diplomatic and military correspondent every day of the week. There is almost no document or piece of information of diplomatic or military significance that could not be labeled secret. Certainly no document that fails to meet that test would be of interest to the public.

Never before had this section been used against a journalist in Israel—even as a threat. That was so because of the democratic character of Israel's various governments but no less so because of some small print in the same section of the law: "It would be a proper defense to a person accused of violation of subsection (c) if he did not violate the law to acquire information that is secret, and that he acquired it, collected it, prepared it, wrote it, or held on to it innocently and for proper purposes." Meaning that whoever receives secret information innocently and for a reasonable purpose will be acquitted—unless it is proved that he acquired that information in an illegal way, such as through theft or breaking in. It was clear to all—including Rabin and Shamgar—that the information in my hands was received in a legal way. Shamgar knew he had no case against me, which is precisely why he implored me to turn in the manuscript voluntarily. On the other hand, he intended to prosecute me if I did not do so. It was a classic use, not of the law itself (which I did not violate), but of the mere threat of prosecution. Shamgar knew that I understood the agony, the expense, the length of a trial of this kind, in which the accused could never be the winner even if ultimately acquitted. The only exception was the sensationalist newsweekly *Haolam Hazeh*, which decided it would try to break the government censorship in its issue that was to come out Tuesday night, May 13.

For me the silence was crushing. Is it possible, I asked myself, that in the state of Israel a book can simply disappear as if it never existed?—that not one person will say, "What the hell is in this book that caused it to be totally banned by the state?"

Every day that went by made it clear that it was

not only possible but was actually happening. From the committee of editors, a body capable of raising such issues, there was complete silence. None of them asked to read the book. It did not occur to anyone to demand that a representative of the committee be allowed to read the book and convey his opinion to the other editors. The editors were simply content to take the word of the prime minister that the whole book could hurt the security of the state.

Not surprisingly, the silence was broken by a foreign journalist. Terence (Terry) Smith, *The New York Times* Jerusalem correspondent, learned of the banning of the book. He immediately wrote up the story and submitted it to the censor. He was then told that his entire dispatch was prohibited, but Smith refused to accept the verdict. He told the censor that the story of the banning was not of a military nature. Therefore he would defy the censor and file the story. Then, getting on the special international telephone line reserved for journalists, he called the foreign editor of *The Times* in New York. Knowing that the censor's office was listening in, Smith deliberately told his editor that he would be filing a story later that evening on the banning of the book, and that he would be defying the censor. He said that if they were cut off or if he was prevented from making the call he would leave the country and file from Greece or Cyprus.

Faced with a direct confrontation with a foreign journalist the censor backed off. Smith filed his story from Israel and it appeared the next day in *The New York Times*. The fact that Smith wasn't expelled or even reprimanded shows that the censors knew that state security was not involved—that the censorship was totally political. The real damage that was done was not to state security but to the credibility of the whole military censorship system and to the government.

The evening that Smith filed his story, I was listening to the radio at midnight. At the end of the hourly news bulletin the following short announcement was made:

> In response to a question, the army spokesman said that Mr. Matti Golan presented a book for preliminary examination by the military censor and after it was clear to the censor that the book was full of secret and top secret material and that its publication would hurt the security of the state, the censor decided to forbid the publication of the book.

It is not necessary to add that the question the army spokesman supposedly answered was never asked. The government knew that *The Times* was about to publish the story and wanted to make it seem that it had released the news on its own initiative.

On Tuesday morning there were already detailed reports on the banning of the book in the Israeli press, with *The New York Times* story providing the main source. This of course is the customary way of circumventing censorship in Israel. To write something independently is forbidden, but to quote foreign reports is acceptable.

From that moment my phone never stopped ringing. There was hardly a broadcasting network or newspaper that did not ask for interviews or answers to questions, the main one being: "What's in the book?" In return for a little quote from the book I was offered interviews with the biggest TV networks and travel all over the world. I refused to divulge anything about the contents of the book.

Another repeated question was my opinion of Israeli censorship. And once more a disappointment was awaiting the journalists. Instead of the devastating attack on the state and the censorship which they were expecting, they heard me give a lecture on the special situation of Israel, surrounded by enemies, and of the authorities' understandable sensitivity on the matter of security.

Phone calls also started coming from the largest and most respectable publishing houses in the United States. "If you are willing to smuggle the book to us, money won't be a problem," said one excited executive. On the spot he offered $250,000. I made it clear to everyone that the book would see light only after it was cleared by the censors.

I realized that I needed a high-powered lawyer to handle the case in all its ramifications. I was recommended to Arie Marinsky of Tel Aviv. In addition, I took on a college friend, Abraham Goren of Jerusalem.

The immediate problem was whether to approach the High Court of Justice to appeal the decision to ban the book. After checking the law and precedents we reached the conclusion that such a direct appeal had almost no chance. The court had in the past tended to accept the censor's decisions with almost no argument. We therefore decided on another line— to ask that I be allowed to rewrite the book. Marinsky sent a letter to the chief censor, on behalf of Schocken and myself, in which he suggested that I be given a copy of the book for rewriting. In order to make it easy on Bar-On, we said the rewriting would be done in the censor's office with his cooperation.

Bar-On's reply to Marinsky on June 3, 1975, came as a shock. "My legal advisers have expressed their opinion," he wrote, "that since the book is packed with secret material that is the property of the state, your client has no right according to any law to read it." But he then went on to say that "in these conversations you have stressed that your client is interested in an early and quick publication and that publishers from outside the country have offered your

client $100,000 as a starting sum for the publication
of the book."

Contrary to all custom, this letter was sent to all
the newspaper editors. The intention was very clear:
to present me as someone willing to steal state secrets
for profit. This really hurt. The truth is that I could have
become rich overnight. But during all the days of the
affair it never occurred to me to act in violation of the
law for any sum of money and I rejected any suggestion to smuggle out the book or parts of it. This,
I thought, was the reward for abiding by the law.

The refusal to let me rewrite the book was unequivocal. Should we now turn to the High Court of Justice?
Should we reply to Bar-On's letter? Marinsky thought
that we should answer it as sharply as possible.

Instead I managed to do a revised version of the
book on my own, and on June 17, 1975, I submitted
the new version to the censor. Together with the
manuscript Bar-On received Marinsky's reply to his
last letter. It said:

> Regarding the nature of the considerations that
> caused you to ban the publication of the book com-
> pletely: you must know very well from your conversa-
> tions with the prime minister that the anxiety over
> the publication of the book does not derive only from
> the fear of revelations of secret information. The
> prohibition was imposed primarily in order to prevent
> the revelation of the true image of the American
> secretary of state, Dr. Kissinger, to the public in
> Israel and outside of it. And this is because of the
> fear of your superiors that the publication of precise
> facts of the slips of the tongue, of the true style, of
> his undisguised opinions, of the ambitions and the
> aims of Dr. Kissinger—would hurt the political line
> that is now taken by them in fateful problems which
> involve the existence and the nature of Israel as a
> sovereign state.
> Our client, on the other hand, maintains that it is

his right and his duty to remove the mask which is
reflected in the polished formulas of the American
secretary of state to the media, and to penetrate the
curtain of selected leaks that are brought to the
knowledge of the public by an anonymous "senior
official" in Dr. Kissinger's party.

Of the affair of the $100,000, Marinsky wrote:

> Your words are very simply slanderous. I did not
> tell you in our conversations that publishers from
> outside the country offered my client the starting sum
> of $100,000 for the publication of the book. I told
> you that my client, Matti Golan, rejected in disgust
> the proposal to leak information from the book,
> while taking precautions to hide the source of the
> leak, for a financial reward of $100,000. Your trans-
> parent attempt to damage the good name of Mr.
> Matti Golan and to present him as a money grabber
> demonstrates that you are a victim of considerations
> and methods that do not become your position and
> your role. Let us suggest that you search for more
> fitting targets to teach morals on hurting national
> and state principles in reward for money.

The messenger who gave Bar-On the manuscript
and the letter told him that for the time being the
letter would not be released for publication. We decided to hold it in order not to hurt the chances of
the rewritten manuscript.

I was still afraid that too much publicity could
turn the whole affair into a contest of prestige. Goren
supported me. But Marinsky argued that silence by
us would be interpreted by the authorities as a sign
of weakness, making it easier for them to reject the
rewritten book, too. After arguing among ourselves we
decided to give the authorities a chance to make their
decision in a calm atmosphere.

Though we were completely silent the affair began
to surface elsewhere. I was told that the prime minister

had reported to a group of Israeli officials that during his recent visit to Washington he was asked by Kissinger to send him a copy of the book. According to Rabin, Kissinger argued that he had the right to know what was in it so that he could prepare a defense by the time the book was published. Rabin also said that Kissinger told him that a copy of the book was in Cairo.

This report worried me greatly. From the moment I handed in the manuscript I feared various dirty tricks—for example, that the book would be leaked outside of the country, and that I would be accused of leaking it without having the chance of proving the contrary. I did not believe the story about a copy being in Egypt. Knowing how Kissinger operated, I assumed almost with certainty that this "revelation" was aimed at making Rabin believe that the book had been leaked in any event—and what's more to the enemy—and thus convince him to send a copy to Washington.

I then received information that a well-known Washington figure close to Kissinger was telling people that he had been allowed to see the manuscript of my book. He also claimed to have checked out the legal possibilities of publishing the book without my permission but stressed that he would not do it if it could harm me or the security of Israel.

I called the prime minister's office immediately and asked for an urgent meeting with Rabin. Mordechai Gazit, the director of the prime minister's bureau, agreed to meet me right away. I told him of the information that had reached me and then said, "I relay this information to you for two reasons. First there is a danger that Kissinger will leak parts of the manuscript that are convenient to him, while accusing the Israeli government of doing it. Therefore, if a copy of the manuscript has been transferred to Kissinger, and only the prime minister knows that, then I think

Kissinger should be informed right away that we are aware of the possibility of a leak by him and the seriousness with which the Israeli government would see such an act. The second reason is that I refuse to let someone build a frame-up around me that I leaked the contents of the book. A week ago I gave the censor a rewritten book and this is the only book I am interested in publishing."

Gazit promised to pass on the contents of the conversation to the prime minister that night. But I still could not calm down. At 1:00 A.M. I phoned Washington and asked a friend of mine to relay a message to the Washington "source" that unauthorized publication of the book would cause heavy damage to myself and the state. My friend calmed me down by telling me that the person in question had already changed his story. This time he was saying that in order to see a copy of the book he had to come to Israel.

What was going on here? My friend expressed a hypothesis that seemed logical: Kissinger was acting through this person to find out if it was my intention to smuggle the book out and publish it despite the censorship. I phoned Gazit and gave him the new information. He told me that he was 98 percent convinced that a copy of the book had not gotten to Kissinger, but he had still not checked with the prime minister.

The following morning I phoned Marinsky and Goren and told them of the developments. That day, June 25, we sent the prime minister the following letter:

> According to reliable information that our client, Mr. Matti Golan, is in possession of, you were asked by the American secretary of state, Dr. Kissinger, during your last visit to Washington to reveal to him the contents of the book that was banned from publication by the military censor in Israel. Accord-

ing to the information in our client's possession, Dr.
Kissinger argued that he has to prepare for the coming revelations if and when the manuscript or parts
of it are cleared for publication. Our client does not
have confirmed information about your reaction to
this request of the secretary of state. But it is claimed
by a source close to Dr. Kissinger that it is possible
for the secretary of state or someone acting for him to
read the copy of the manuscript that was confiscated
by the military censor.

And furthermore this person is now making inquiries among Israelis who are in Washington in order
to find out the expected reaction of Mr. Matti Golan
and/or the authorities in Israel if selected parts of
the book were to be leaked to the media in the
United States as a preventive act.

In order to remove any possibility of doubt, misunderstanding, or mistaken interpretation in the
future it is our duty to inform you, in the most
unequivocal way, that our client did not relay a copy
of the original manuscript, all of it or some of it,
written or orally, directly or indirectly, to anyone
outside of the country.

It is clear, therefore, that in case of publication of
the manuscript, all of it or some of it, outside of
Israel, the responsibility will fall entirely on the
Israeli government. Our client, Mr. Matti Golan,
reported yesterday orally and in detail to the director
of the prime minister's bureau, Mr. M. Gazit, on the
matters that are described in our letter, and asked him
to bring his report to your attention. We found it
necessary to put these things in writing for good
order and, as has been said, in order to prevent the
possibility of misunderstanding or mistaken interpretations in the future.

At noon I called Gazit again. He had already
spoken with the prime minister and informed me that
he was 100 percent convinced that a copy of the book
had not been sent to Kissinger.

We continued to wait. The days crawled by. On

June 27 Marinsky received a letter from the chief censor replying to our last letter. Bar-On dealt with the rewritten manuscript curtly: "I am now examining the second manuscript that was given to me. When I have finished the manuscript I will inform you of my decision."

Immediately after receiving the letter Marinsky called me. "It cannot go on like this. He is laughing at us. We must prove to him that we also have teeth; otherwise he won't move."

We were in agreement that the censor apparently intended to delay the book for the full period permitted by the law—three months. Marinsky proposed that we call a press conference where I would reveal the details of the whole affair, kill the rumors that the book deals with political gossip, and speak of the main lines of the book. He suggested that I accuse the authorities of using political censorship of the worst kind. I agreed and also suggested that we give copies of the revised version to various members of the Knesset on the political left and right.

In addition to Schmuel Tamir of the right-wing opposition, copies were given to Arie Eliav and Yosef Sarid, dovish members of the Labor party. One copy also went to Shlomo Rosenfeld, the editor of the newspaper *Maariv*. All were agreed that there was nothing in the manuscript that could harm the security of the state.

We then called a press conference for July 9 but announced it a week early to give the government time to reconsider its position. A day before the press conference I initiated a conversation with a very senior cabinet minister. "The behavior of the censor is unclear to me," I told him. "Maybe he wants to hint to me that now, after the publicity that was given to the book, he cannot pass the book, but if I publish it outside the country without his permission he will look the other way. Or maybe he wants to pass the book only after the conclusion of an interim agreement with Egypt. Until now I was willing to wait. But the trouble is that he does not say anything and therefore I will have to attack him at the press conference."

The minister's reply was laconic: "Call Bar-On tomorrow morning before the press conference."

"Would you speak to him before then?"

"I cannot add a thing. Call him."

I was doubtful. A day later, Tuesday, July 8, at 10:00 A.M., I sat in my study preparing notes for the press conference that was to begin in an hour and a half. I called Bar-On.

"Good morning, Mr. Golan," said Bar-On, very friendly. "I just finished talking with Marinsky. I told him that within a week I would conclude the examination of the book and that it would be largely accepted."

My heart stopped beating. Is it possible? I asked, "What do you intend to cut out?"

"Mr. Golan," Bar-On calmed me, "I promise that you will have no reason for dissatisfaction. And another thing: I followed you from the beginning of the affair and I want you to know that I appreciate the fact that you acted honestly and honorably."

When I got to the press conference I was shocked. The hall was full. There was not an Israeli newspaper or important foreign newspaper that was not represented. I sat at the head of a table with a battery of microphones in front of me and five TV cameras pointed at me. Strange, I thought, to be on this side of the table. One of my colleagues whispered to me, "Matti, what's happening here? Did you come to announce the fall of the government?"

I opened by saying that the press conference was supposed to have an entirely different nature. The change, I explained, was caused by a dramatic development in the last two hours. After I spoke of my conversation with Bar-On, someone asked me half seriously: "Why didn't you have the press conference two weeks ago? They would have confirmed the book then."

One week later I was in Bar-On's office in Tel Aviv for the second time. Bar-On looked like someone who had just had a great weight lifted off his shoulders. "Mr. Golan," he opened, smiling, "the first time you were here a surprise was also awaiting you. This time it is a good one."

As if he were reading my thoughts, he said quickly, "I excised only one word which appears in five places."

One word! After all these months. I wanted to jump out of my seat. Only with difficulty did I control my joy. Bar-On handed Marinsky a letter addressed to me:

> Re: your book *Kissinger in the Middle East*.
>
> 1. Hereby returned to you are the drafts of the manuscripts of your second book confirmed by us, except for pages 25, 26, 27, 36, and 39 where we have signified corrections.
>
> 2. You are hereby reminded that any additional material to be published in your book, such as introduction and preface, additional chapters, conclusion, titles, subtitles, photos, titles to photos, etc., must be handed to the censorship.

Iced coffee and cookies were brought to the table and the conversation moved toward a discussion of the problems of censorship. After Bar-On said once more that he had no claims against me, I asked, "Mr. Bar-On, why couldn't this have been done before all the guns were put into action?"

He thought for a moment. "I am not free to refer to the subject," he said, "but I can only assure you that I had nothing to do with the way in which the book was banned. In any event," he added smilingly, "I don't think you have reason to complain."

The nightmare was over. The book was in my hands once more. As I left the censor's office I felt liberated.

Yet the bitter struggle with the censor and the government had left its mark. In order to justify his arbi-
trary action, the prime minister had said that the
book, if published, would force the American secretary
of state to resign.

I never had any such expectations or aims. My
purpose in writing what follows was rather simple
and old-fashioned. As a reporter I wanted to set the
record straight. There are revelations in what follows
that will be embarrassing to Henry Kissinger, but
others will be just as damaging to the reputations and
public images of other political leaders. The point is
to get beyond the public images, the public relations,
the deliberate obfuscation that has been so much a part
of the step-by-step diplomacy of the past two years. In
the Middle East, as elsewhere, one must know what
happens after the doors close behind the diplomats.

I

The Airlift:
Israel's Agony, Kissinger's Opportunity

In Washington, New York, and Jerusalem it all began in utter confusion.

On Friday morning, October 5, 1973, Mordechai Shalev, the Israeli chargé d'affaires in Washington, was about to leave his home for the embassy building. Filling in for Ambassador Simcha Dinitz, who was on leave in Israel mourning the death of his father, Shalev wanted to get to his office early on this last working day before Yom Kippur. Before he could get out of the door, however, the bell rang and a messenger handed him a telegram. It was from Jerusalem and the message was anything but routine.

Shalev was instructed to ask for a very urgent meeting with the American secretary of state. But Jerusalem was not sure of Kissinger's whereabouts and Shalev was told that if Kissinger was in New York, Foreign Minister Abba Eban should also participate in the meeting. The telegram was signed by Mordechai Gazit, director general of the prime minister's office and Golda Meir's political adviser. There was not even a hint of why Shalev should ask for the meeting with Kissinger, but the telegram did say that he should stand by for a clarifying telegram or phone call.

Knowing that Kissinger was in New York for the

UN General Assembly session, and that Eban was there as well, Shalev immediately called Eban's political secretary, Eytan Bentsur, to alert the Israeli foreign minister. Two hours later Shalev called Bentsur again to say that the appointment with Kissinger was set for 4:00 P.M. in New York.

But Eban had other plans. He had previously scheduled an appointment for the same hour with the Nigerian foreign minister. (At the time rumors were floating that Nigeria intended to break relations with Israel.) Affronted by Gazit's telegram, and since he had not been informed of any reason for urgency, Eban decided to keep his appointment with the Nigerian and put off Kissinger.

Acting on Eban's instructions, Bentsur informed Shalev that the foreign minister would not be present at the four o'clock meeting with Kissinger. But at that moment in Washington the harried Shalev had more serious concerns. It was already past noon, but clarification had not arrived from Jerusalem; without instructions Shalev could not leave for New York. He waited until 2:00 P.M., then called the State Department to tell Kissinger's personal assistant that instructions from Jerusalem had not yet arrived. He asked to have the meeting postponed to a later hour. This, he was told, was impossible—the secretary of state had a crowded schedule for the rest of the day. Shalev was told, however, that after receiving his instructions from Jerusalem he could deliver a message to Brigadier General Brent Scowcroft, deputy chairman of the National Security Council, who maintained constant contact with Kissinger. Shalev agreed. He reported back to Gazit in Jerusalem and began a nervous vigil, waiting for the clarifying telegram.

To Eban, back in New York, the whole incident was just one more blow to his pride. He, the foreign minister of Israel, had been asked to be present at a meeting with Kissinger only if the U.S. secretary of state was in New York! In Washington the prime minister would have been satisfied with the mere presence of the chargé d'affaires.

Not that Eban had any illusions left about Golda Meir's appreciation of him. She had long since stripped him of his authority in the most important domain of Israeli policy—relations with the United States. Telegrams and phone calls from the Washington embassy were routinely sent direct to the prime minister—not to the foreign office. If Eban wished to read them, he had to literally drag himself over to her office—though with less sensitive messages he was permitted to send an aide to bring back copies.

Frustrated senior foreign office officials pressed Eban to fight for his authority, but they were usually answered by a shrug. In time he learned to live with the crumbs the prime minister left him. He was not going to risk the trappings of public office in a conflict with the tough old leader. Thus, as the 24-hour countdown to war began in the Middle East, Israel was represented in the United States by a superfluous and disgruntled foreign minister and a confused junior official.

In Israel, there was deep complacency as well as confusion. Indeed, in the hours while Mordechai Shalev waited for his clarifying telegram in Washington, the primary preoccupation of most Israelis was not with the Arab armies on the borders but with the Jewish chancellor of Austria, Bruno Kreisky. Under the pressure of Arab terrorist blackmail, Kreisky had recently decided to close Vienna's Schonau Castle—used by Israel as a transfer camp for Jewish immigrants arriving from the Soviet Union.

In a well-publicized gesture, Golda Meir had flown off to personally try to persuade Kreisky to change his mind, but she only met with a crude rejection. Upon her return to Israel, three days before Yom Kippur, she complained publicly that the chancellor hadn't even offered her a cup of tea. And that was the dramatic story being given banner headlines in the Hebrew newspapers right up to the day before Yom Kippur.

The Kreisky affair broke at the height of the national election campaign, and it provided Mrs. Meir with a superb opportunity for emotionally bombarding the public. On Thursday, October 4, before thousands at a campaign rally in the Givataim basketball stadium, she devoted much of her speech to a vivid description of her trip to Vienna and a vitriolic denunciation of the Austrian chancellor—all to thunderous applause. As for the Arabs, she repeated a line that had become an integral part of all of her speeches, as well as those of other government leaders, since the Six-Day War: "For as long as peace does not come we will remain in place where we are today—in the north, in the south, and in the east."

The day before, the chief of staff, Lieutenant General David (Dado) Elazar, had spoken even more confidently. At a ceremony commemorating Israeli paratroopers, Elazar declared grandiosely: "The enemy must know that Zahal [the Israeli defense force] has a long arm, and when this arm reaches the depth of his territory it turns into a fist!"

On the day that the chief of staff was speaking of Israel's "long fist" both he and the prime minister received information on Egyptian and Syrian troop concentrations near the borders. At a cabinet meeting convened by Golda Meir that day, however, she did not bring it up. The only subject on the agenda, Wednesday, October 3, was her visit to Kreisky.

The information on movements of the Egyptian and Syrian armies continued to flow in, however, and Mrs. Meir began to worry. On Friday, October 5, she was inclined to convene the cabinet, but the army people calmed her with an intelligence evaluation that there was no reason to expect a war. Still, Mrs. Meir decided on some action. She instructed Cabinet Secretary Michael Arnon to summon those ministers who were in Tel Aviv, where she was scheduled to spend the day, but not to bother the ministers who were out of town.

An ad hoc group of seven ministers heard a report on Egyptian and Syrian army movements. The chief of staff emphasized, however, that both armies were arranged in defensive positions of the kind which indicate maneuvers. He acknowledged that with the Russian system used by both armies they could immediately move over to the offensive, but the chief of intelligence expressed the view that these were only maneuvers—and added that American intelligence shared this evaluation.

Defense Minister Moshe Dayan also reported that in the last few hours information had been received about the landing of Russian transport planes at Damascus Airport. There could be many explanations for this, Dayan said, but one possible explanation troubled him: the transport planes might be intended for the evacuation of Soviet civilians in Damascus. If so, Moscow had clear information on imminent military activities.

Dayan and the chief of staff reported that despite the relatively reassuring evaluations they had ordered a high state of alert on all fronts. The meeting authorized the prime minister and the minister of defense to draft the reserve forces if and when the need arose. Following the meeting and further high-level consultations, consensus was reached on the contents of a telegram to be sent to Washington, where Shalev was still waiting.

At 5:00 P.M. Washington time, the anxiously awaited clarifications arrived for Shalev to be relayed to Kissinger. It was a document that reflected the confusion prevailing in Jerusalem. The military preparations of Egypt and Syria, the telegram stated, could be the result of Arab fears that they were about to be attacked by Israel. Or the military preparations might indicate that Egypt and Syria—both or either—planned to attack Israel.

Shalev was instructed to ask Kissinger, on behalf of the prime minister, to assure Egypt and Syria that Israel had no aggressive intentions. On the other hand, Shalev should make it clear to Kissinger that if Israel were attacked she would react forcefully and massively. The prime minister asked that these words in particular be brought to the attention of Egypt, Syria, and the Soviet Union by the secretary of state.

If the telegram to Shalev had ended there, it is possible that events would have taken a different course. But Shalev was asked to transmit an additional message to Kissinger only—the Israeli intelligence evaluation that the Syrian army movements reflected Damascus's expectation of an Israeli preventive strike. As for the Egyptian army, Israel's evaluation was that it was engaged in large maneuvers that would conclude on October 7.

Shalev was told to go ahead and relay the entire contents of the telegram to Kissinger through Scowcroft—and he did so immediately. When General Scowcroft received the message, Kissinger's experienced deputy noticed the discrepancy between the main body of the telegram and the intelligence evaluation. Only in the main body was the possibility of an attack on Israel by the Arab countries mentioned, and then only as a second possibility, after the primary evaluation that the Arabs feared Israel's intentions. There was no stress on a possible Arab attack in the Israeli intelligence evaluation. As an army man who appreciated the high level of Israeli intelligence, Scowcroft had no hesitation about which of the two versions to favor, and he did not urge the busy secretary of state to deal with the message immediately. Kissinger, in fact, did not read the telegram until Saturday morning, when it was too late.

For Foreign Minister Eban and his political secretary Bentsur, Yom Kippur was to be a day for sleeping very late at the Plaza Hotel. The officials needed the rest after a tiring trip from Israel and hectic sessions with delegation heads and foreign ministers at the UN General Assembly. After bolting the shutters to keep the sunlight out of his room, Eban took the phone off the hook, just in case someone, somewhere, forgot the holiness of the day. Before that, however, he did remember to call his wife Susie in Herzliya, promising not to let anything disturb his Yom Kippur rest.

Bentsur was the first to learn that the cherished day of rest would not materialize. Close to 7:00 A.M. he was awakened by the sound of loud knocking on his door.

"Mr. Bentsur! Mr. Bentsur!" came the demanding, insistent voice.

"Who it is?" the sleepy secretary managed to mutter.

"An urgent telegram from Israel."

Bentsur's mind began to function. An urgent telegram? On Yom Kippur? He could not recall any pending business that might require a telegram. Someone in Jerusalem was exhibiting a rather exaggerated devotion to duty he thought as he dragged his heavy legs slowly to the door.

Bentsur, who had no knowledge of the arrival of the clarifying telegram to Shalev on the previous day, gave a tip to the messenger and took the telegram. It was from Israel Galili, a cabinet minister, and it read: "We have clear information Egypt and Syria are about to launch a war at 6:00 P.M."

Still wearing his pajamas, Bentsur sprinted down the corridor to Eban's room. Panting heavily, he knocked on the door. There was no answer. The foreign minister apparently was keeping his promise to sleep soundly. Undeterred, Bentsur started kicking violently at the door, causing startled heads to poke out of rooms in the plush hotel. Finally he managed to rouse the foreign minister out of bed.

Eban read the telegram sitting on the living-room couch in his pajamas. He instructed Bentsur to make immediate contact with Kissinger at the Waldorf Towers. Within ten minutes Bentsur handed Eban the telephone with the American secretary of state on the other end of the line. It was 6:30 A.M. New York time, 12:30 P.M. Israel time.

Eban read Kissinger the telegram he had just received. Kissinger, who had already received a similar message from U.S. Ambassador to Israel Kenneth Keating, promised to do some checking and call back. The return call came in ten minutes. In a voice that betrayed little tension Kissinger said that he had just spoken with the Egyptian ambassador, who charged that the Israeli navy was attacking in two places. Though he stressed his own disbelief, Kissinger asked Eban to ascertain whether there was any truth in the Egyptian claim.

Thus Eban now had to call the Foreign Office in Jerusalem, where he was able to talk to the ministry's director general, Mordechai Kidron. "The Egyptian claim is baseless," the director general quickly responded. Then Kidron suddenly interrupted the conversation and asked Eban to wait on the line. After a few tense seconds, the voice of the director general came back, halting and worried: "Just this minute a note was given to me. The war has broken out."

For Kissinger the hour before the outbreak of war was consumed in frantic but perfunctory diplomatic contacts. His first move was to call President Nixon at the Florida White House in Key Biscayne. A second call went to the Soviet ambassador in Washington, Anatoly Dobrynin. Kissinger asked that Moscow do all in its power to restrain Egypt and Syria. He also proposed that the two superpowers agree to "keep their hands off" in case a war does break out. Dobrynin promised an answer after consultation with the Kremlin. He soon called back. The Soviet Union, he assured Kissinger, accepts both requests and will act accordingly. Kissinger would remember Dobrynin's words vividly in the days to come—when Russian Antonov transport planes brought enormous amounts of arms to Cairo and Damascus, and when the deep involvement of Moscow in the war preparations came to light.

Next Kissinger got a cable off to King Faisal in Saudi Arabia asking him to exert his influence with Presidents Sadat and Assad. He then called UN Secretary General Kurt Waldheim and briefed him on the situation.

Till the very outbreak of the fighting, however, Kissinger remained more concerned with the possibility of an Israeli preemptive strike than an Egyptian-Syrian attack. At the last moment he called Shalev requesting that he relay to his government "a presidential entreaty" not to start a war. At the same time he instructed Ambassador Keating to relay a similar message personally to Golda Meir.

All this despite the fact that Kissinger had already received intelligence reports indicating that the Arab "defense formations" were moving over to offensive dispositions—reports which also stressed the tranquillity on the Israeli side of the borders. Nevertheless, Kissinger was now suddenly taking very seriously the part of Friday's telegram warning that Israel "would react forcefully and massively" if Egypt and Syria began hostilities. Kissinger assumed that Israel was ready for war and he was thinking of two possibilities: despite its disclaimers Israel would strike first, something he certainly did not want; or Israel was preparing a trap for the Arab armies. He was not much worried about the outcome of the war and estimated it would last at most three or four days, leaving the Egyptian and Syrian armies destroyed.

In this Kissinger was mistaken, but the real blunder was that the foreign ministers of both Israel and the United States were taken completely by surprise. For the 24 hours before the outbreak of war they were within a mile of each other in the center of Manhattan, but they did not consult until it was too late. For very different reasons neither was aware of the rising concern of the Israeli government as expressed in the telegram transmitted through Shalev a day earlier.

It is difficult to know what the results might have been if Kissinger had been appraised of the Israeli message as soon as it was sent to his hotel in the late afternoon hours of Friday. Certainly he would have transmitted the Israeli warning to the Soviets and the Arabs. It can be assumed that he also would have added, especially for Moscow, a severe American warning on the consequences of aggression—for the aggressors and to the policy of détente.

It is equally difficult to guess the reaction of Cairo, Damascus, and Moscow. But some assumptions can be made on the basis of facts known today. The most important element in the Egyptian-Syrian attack was the element of surprise. If they knew that this element had been removed, might they not have canceled their plans or at least postponed execution to a later date? Is it not also reasonable to assume that on Friday it was possible through a vigorous and swift diplomatic action to prod Moscow to restrain its allies?

For Israel it was not necessary to rely entirely on Scowcroft's discretion. The Israeli foreign minister also happened to be in New York. If Mordechai Gazit had sent the message directly to Eban on Friday, as Galili did in fact on the following day, Eban would have had no difficulty in seeing Kissinger or at least talking to him on the phone. But routinely, and particularly during emergencies, Eban was the last person the prime minister would turn to. She made it a custom, enforced on her own staff as well as personnel in the Washington embassy, that Eban was the last person to be informed of anything important.

Shalev could have, perhaps should have, taken the initiative and informed Eban of the message as soon as it arrived. After all, Eban was technically his boss. But this did not even occur to the chargé d'affaires, who had learned from his direct superior, Ambassador Dinitz, that all communications with Israel should be directly with the prime minister's office. Since that was the case, and since Dinitz was in Israel, the fateful contacts were left in the hands of a junior diplomat. Thus 14 hours that could have been used to prevent or at least postpone the war were wasted because of an overly optimistic intelligence evaluation, and because of the years of hostility of the prime minister toward her foreign minister.

The last precious hours in Tel Aviv were taken up with discussion of options that no longer existed. At 7:00 A.M. on Saturday the prime minister summoned Dayan, Galili, the chief of staff, and the head of intelligence to her Tel Aviv office. Deputy Prime Minister Yigal Allon was also invited, but he was at his kibbutz in the north of the country. When Allon asked the cabinet secretary if he should come by helicopter, he was told: "There is no urgency, you can come by car."

Nevertheless, war was already a certainty and drastic options were discussed at the meeting. Chief of Staff Elazar demanded an immediate general call-up of reserves. Davan was opposed, saying that such a move would be considered a provocation and Israel would be accused of starting a war. He recommended a limited call-up—an opinion accepted by the prime minister. The chief of staff also suggested that Israel not wait for the Arab attack but launch a preventive strike. He said that he had already checked with Brigadier General Binyamin (Benny) Peled, commander of the air force, and was told the air force could be ready for a strike at 1:00 P.M. Dayan and Mrs. Meir were convinced, however, that such a step would not be countenanced by Israel's main ally, the United States, and they vetoed Elazar's proposal.

When Mrs. Meir and Dayan decided against a first strike they were operating on what then seemed to be reasonable political calculations. They did not know that their discussion of options was already academic. Only later was it discovered that the ground forces along the line were too meager to carry out any successful action, not to mention a preemptive strike. The air force would only have been ready by 1:00 P.M. This, as it turned out, was less than an hour before the outbreak of the war and not the five hours upon which the Israelis were mistakingly basing their discussion of this option.

To this day no one knows where the assumption of a 6:00 P.M. Arab attack came from. It is not mentioned in any intelligence report and no one remembers who said it first. But from the moment it was mentioned it was accepted as a fact.

Thus, when Mrs. Meir and Dayan decided against a preemptive attack, they innocently believed they were making a great military sacrifice for the sake of their friendship with the United States. Mrs. Meir made sure that Henry Kissinger understood this right away. As soon as the Saturday morning meeting was over, she called in U.S. Ambassador Kenneth Keating. She gave him a message for Kissinger: Egypt and Syria are about to attack Israel; Israel has decided not to launch a preemptive strike.

It was in the middle of a full-dress cabinet meeting, at exactly 12:55 P.M. Israel time, that Mrs. Meir was informed the war had started. From that moment the main focus of the discussions with Kissinger shifted to the crucial question of resupply. Cabinet-level discussion soon took place in Israel on what items to request from the United States. At one meeting several days after the war began, Defense Minister Dayan reported that Israeli tanks were fighting with their last shells. In addition, he said, there was a serious shortage of clothing, especially winter underwear. At that point Treasury Minister Pinchas Sapir could no longer restrain himself. Pounding on the table with a clenched fist, he shouted, "What is that? You don't have underwear? You mean the Galaxies [the American transport planes] have to bring underwear?"

And indeed the Galaxies eventually did bring underwear, along with the shells. But not as quickly as Israel had hoped. For Israel the need for supplies was an agony of life-and-death proportions. For Henry Kissinger it was a golden opportunity, and provided the leverage to achieve his political objectives—or so he thought.

Ambassador Dinitz returned to Washington on Sunday evening, October 7. He immediately went to see Kissinger and told him that the United States was the main factor behind Israel's difficult decision not to preempt. Therefore he felt justified in suggesting that the United States had a special responsibility to its ally in the matter of military resupply.

Surprisingly, however, the first list of requested items handed over by Dinitz was very modest—and illustrated the optimism that still prevailed in Tel Aviv. The United States was asked for approximately 200 tons of equipment. Israel even said that the shipment had to go by air only if "an emergency comes up."

Kissinger did not try to brush off America's moral responsibility for the needs of Israel. But for several reasons he had no intention of fulfilling those needs. And the modest initial list of Israeli requests only served to confirm Kissinger's evaluation that within three days after the call-up of reserves Israel would deliver a decisive blow to end the war in triumph.

Kissinger calculated that the military aid to Israel, while not making the crucial difference in the field, could damage the still hoped-for cooperation with Moscow and future relations with the Arab countries. And this was a consideration not merely for the future. The Arab oil-producing countries had already begun threatening an oil embargo against the United States if it provided military aid to Israel. At this time there was complete concurrence on this point between Kissinger and Defense Secretary James R. Schlesinger. And President Nixon, busy listening to the Watergate tapes, was leaving all the initial moves to his secretary of state.

But nothing of this was said to Dinitz. On the contrary, in telephone conversations and endless meetings Kissinger fed the ambassador expressions of solidarity and empty promises that gained him time. Kissinger was convinced that if he could carry Dinitz along for another few days the war would end and the United States would come out of it unstained in the eyes of the Arabs—and détente with the Soviet Union would be preserved.

What Kissinger kept from Dinitz, however, he openly communicated to Dobrynin. He willingly told the Soviet ambassador of the pressures put upon him by Israel to rush military supplies and that he was holding his ground. In return, he asked that Moscow exert its influence for a cease-fire and prevent an escalation of the war by holding back supplies to its own allies. And here is where Dobrynin seduced Kissinger— just as Kissinger seduced Dinitz—by feeding him with promises of the Soviet Union's willingness to cooperate. Dobrynin of course was also playing for time. Every additional day that went by without military supplies to Israel brought clear profits for Egypt and Syria—and for Soviet diplomacy.

On the evening of the third day of the war, Golda Meir was very worried. Earlier that day fragmentary reports coming in to the general staff had raised the hope of an Israeli breakthrough to the west bank of the Suez Canal. But in a few hours it became clear that the Israeli task force had hardly reached the eastern bank before being thrown back. The whole venture had cost dearly in casualties without any military gain.

The news from Washington was even more ominous. Ambassador Dinitz continued to feed Tel Aviv reports that Kissinger was willing to cooperate on arms supplies but was being sabotaged by the Pentagon. Dinitz could only offer the hope that in a short time Kissinger would overcome the stalling of the Pentagon.

If the Israeli envoy in Washington had been anyone other than Dinitz he would surely have received a severe reprimand from the prime minister, who should have been demanding results, not explanations. Dinitz, however, was like a favorite child of Golda Meir. During her years as foreign minister and afterward as prime minister, he was her shadow and right arm, first as her political adviser and then as director general of the prime minister's bureau. But Dinitz had feared the day when the old leader would retire, and he hoped to stake out a position of his own before then. As a reward for his loyal service, against the advice of the foreign ministry, she appointed him to the coveted post of ambassador to Washington a few months before the war.

Despite their cozy relationship, as the situation turned grave Mrs. Meir realized that Dinitz was failing in Washington. On Monday evening she sent him an extraordinary telegram saying that she would personally fly to Washington to try to get the question of supplies taken care of. She instructed Dinitz to inform Nixon and Kissinger and coordinate the visit with the American officials. Asking Dinitz to inform her as soon as a suitable date was agreed upon, she admonished him not to allow it to be put off too long. She stressed to Dinitz, however, that everything must be kept secret so as not to reveal Israel's desperation to the Arabs.

A visit by Israel's leader in the middle of the war would, of course, have been both dramatic and unprecedented, and it is unclear whether Mrs. Meir intended to go through with it or just meant the telegram to serve as a prod to Washington. But it certainly had its effect in stirring up the State Department.

Kissinger let Dinitz know that a visit by Mrs. Meir was the last thing he needed at this time. Maintaining diplomatic niceties, he did not exactly say that Washington opposed the visit—he only mentioned considerations that cast doubt on its advisability. Dinitz's telegram to the prime minister reported Kissinger's objections as follows:

• The visit might be made public by Israel later, when its timing could embarrass the United States.

• There was no practical way of keeping the visit a secret. Undoubtedly Arab and Soviet intelligence, as well as the media, would discover it.

• A visit in the midst of the war would illustrate in the most dramatic way the American identification with Israel. Such a development would be interpreted at once as a provocation by the Soviet Union and the Arab countries.

The final point was the most important. There was no need for a visit, Kissinger now argued, because the business of Israel's resupply needs would be taken care of within a few hours.

Kissinger was on the defensive because senators

such as Henry Jackson, Walter Mondale, Hubert Humphrey, Jacob Javits, Birch Bayh, and Abraham Ribicoff were beginning to stir about aid to Israel. The result was a meeting between Nixon and Kissinger at noon, Tuesday, October 9, after which Kissinger was able to tell Dinitz that the president had decided "in principle" to comply with Israel's requests and to replace the arms it had lost so far in the war. But at the same time, Kissinger reported, the United States was not prepared to transfer the equipment directly to Israel in military planes. He suggested two possibilities: transferring the equipment all the way from the United States in Israeli aircraft; or transferring the supplies to the Azores in leased civilian planes where they could be picked up by Israel. Kissinger added, as was his ritual those days, that as a true friend of Israel he had taken the initiative with Nixon on the resupply decision.

To put it mildly, that was an inaccurate description of what actually happened in Nixon's office on October 9. Several American Jewish leaders discovered the truth during a meeting with Nixon on June 4, 1974, before the president left for his trip to the Middle East. According to Arthur Hertzberg, president of the American Jewish Congress, the revelation came out this way:

> Nixon found an opening in the conversation to say to Kissinger in front of us: "It should be known that it was I and not you who gave the order on the fourth day of the war to give Israel all the arms." He turned to Kissinger and added, "Henry, do you remember that on that fourth day you came and suggested that I send five planes?—and I said if it's all right to send them five, let's send them fifty. Isn't that what I said, Henry?"—and Kissinger confirmed it.

But Dinitz did not know on October 9 of the conversation in Nixon's office. Delighted with what he believed were positive developments, and more convinced of Kissinger's friendship, the ambassador reported the presidential decision to Tel Aviv. He didn't notice the trap hidden between the lines of that decision. There was no date, no timetable—only a decision "in principle." Those who received Dinitz's telegram in Tel Aviv also didn't notice the catch. It didn't even occur to the Israelis to insist that American planes fly the equipment all the way to Israel.

In any event Kissinger never had any notion of actually implementing the "in principle" decision. It was in his power to control the matter and he proved it in the days that followed. Nixon, in over his head in the Watergate affair, was still leaving all the details to his secretary of state. The presidential decision deliberately did not mandate Kissinger to carry it out by any precise date. In fact, Nixon left Kissinger with total discretion on the timing of the airlift—in order to allow him room for further maneuvering.

For Kissinger, blocking aid to Israel was not done out of ill will but strict political calculation. In that respect the presidential intervention and the decision "in principle" (even though it was more generous in the matter of the planes than he expected) actually served Kissinger's purpose. It helped keep Mrs. Meir in Tel Aviv, it pacified Ambassador Dinitz and Israel's supporters in the United States, and thus it gave Kissinger a few more days.

Kissinger could not have carried out the great charade if it had not been for the unconscious collaboration of the Israeli ambassador. The key to the Kissinger-Dinitz relationship was the Israeli ambassador's ego. Moving from provincial Jerusalem to Washington had profoundly affected Dinitz. Here, in the center of world power, he was master of his own house and not just Mrs. Meir's assistant. He was not only the sole link between Washington and Jerusalem, but his position made him the uncrowned leader of U.S. Jewry. And he had no intention of sharing this power. Other embassy personnel were kept from contacts with the White House or the State Department. Only he moved in the high circles and, above all, close to the number one superstar—Henry Kissinger.

Kissinger, supreme artist of personal diplomacy, sensed what Dinitz was like from the moment the ambassador arrived in Washington. He started massaging his ego. Dinitz surrendered completely to Kissinger's solicitations and personal charm. He was flattered that the powerful, brilliant Kissinger called him frequently, consulted him, and invited him to official and private social events. Without desiring it, without even being conscious of it, Dinitz turned into Kissinger's man.

No doubt as he pleaded with Kissinger for the arms shipments Dinitz uttered some harsh words. But ultimately he believed that Kissinger was pure; that the wolves were in the Pentagon. Dinitz thus never mustered the powerful weapons at his disposal.

On the second day of the war several American Jewish leaders sent a letter to Nixon which included a request for urgent aid to Israel. Other Jewish leaders met with Kissinger and several senators. But all these were private meetings, and they were no cause for concern to Kissinger.

The only thing Kissinger feared was public protest. If there had been an outcry by senators, Jewish leaders, and journalists, Nixon would have been forced to respond and come out of his Watergate cocoon. Kissinger would not have been able to continue his stalling tactics.

But for that to happen Dinitz had to give the signal. From time to time he actually threatened to "go public," but in a remarkable performance Kissinger made sure that he never moved. He never left Dinitz alone. He spoke to him at least six or seven times a day. Each time he promised that the arms were coming, the arms were coming. And Dinitz, with his trust in Kissinger unshaken, agreed to wait.

All that time Foreign Minister Eban remained in New York to deal with possible cease-fire initiatives at the Security Council. Dinitz never reported to him about the negotiations for the airlift, nor did the ambassador think of calling the foreign minister to Washington to aid in the negotiations.

Kissinger encouraged this tendency. Keeping everything in Dinitz's hands served his own aims. At one point when Dinitz mentioned the possibility of inviting Eban to Washington, Kissinger replied, "What for? Let's leave the discussion at our level." More balm for the ego of the Israeli ambassador, who of course accepted the suggestion.

Intercession by Eban might not have changed anything. Possibly Kissinger would not have let anyone move him. But Eban, with his diplomatic rank and experience, might have been able to speak differently to Kissinger. He might have developed a more objective analysis of Kissinger's tactics. Thus he might have made Kissinger's life more difficult and by so doing speeded the airlift by a day or two.

In any event, developments at the Security Council over cease-fire negotiations eventually required Eban to see Kissinger. Before doing so he met with Dinitz, who told him of a conversation he had that day with Schlesinger. The secretary of defense, he recounted, suddenly did not present excuses about technical and bureaucratic difficulties. Schlesinger bluntly acknowledged that the airlift delay was a result of political considerations—the United States did not want to burn its bridges to Moscow and the Arab states. Despite Kissinger's warning not to admit the connection between politics and military supplies, Schlesinger told Dinitz that Israel could not hope for more than 20 leased planes to transfer equipment plus 16 Phantoms at the rate of two planes every three days. In the condition Israel was in at the time this was like beggaring the poor.

Dinitz reminded Schlesinger of the presidential decision of October 9. Schlesinger did not react, merely repeated his previous words. He did not deny, did not confirm, did not try to blame anyone. In other words, Schlesinger knew things that were hidden from Dinitz, who along with Mrs. Meir knew only of the presidential decision "in principle."

With this fresh information Eban, accompanied by Dinitz and Shalev, entered Kissinger's office on the seventh floor of the State Department. It was Friday, October 12, at a very late night hour. The two foreign ministers immediately turned to the situation in Israel with regard to supplies, especially tanks and planes. The slow pace of the supplies, Eban stressed, is the main reason preventing Israel's advances on both fronts. Expressing his disappointment, Eban said that after the presidential decision of October 9, the hope in Israel was that the supply would be immediate. And it never occurred to anyone in the government that the results would be so meager.

Kissinger was still trying to put on a show for Eban and Dinitz. He put the responsibility on "other factors in the administration" who were sabotaging the presidential decision. As a demonstration of his concern Kissinger called Scowcroft on the spot and instructed him to verify that C-130 transport planes would leave for Israel the very next day. Putting down the phone, he added that if this order were not carried out, Deputy Secretary of Defense William Clements should be sent back to Texas. Kissinger had chosen Clements, the Texas oil magnate, as the scapegoat—claiming that Clements was sabotaging the airlift because of his interests in the Arab oil-producing countries. (Clements himself would deny it all in a meeting with Defense Minister Dayan the following

January. Clements told Dayan not to believe that the
Pentagon held back the supplies. It was only political
considerations, he said.)

Nothing more clearly illustrates Kissinger's cynical
political manipulation of Israel's arms needs than
his dealings with American Jewish leaders during the
first week of the war. At the same time that Kissinger
was attempting to buy the goodwill of Moscow by
holding up arms shipments to Israel, he was dangling
the same arms over the Jewish leaders' heads to get
them to help liquidate his number one domestic alba-
tross—the Jackson amendment.

The legislation which came to bear Henry Jackson's name was first presented to the U.S. Senate on
October 4, 1972. Its main feature was that the U.S.-
Soviet trade agreement granting the Soviets most-
favored-nation status would be conditioned on free
emigration from the Soviet Union. Nothing was said
in the amendment about Jews, but since it was presented at the peak of agitation on the Soviet Jewry
issue, it was obvious what the intent was.

At first Nixon and Kissinger did not take the Jackson initiative too seriously. But as the list of supporters of the legislation grew to include a majority
of the House of Representatives and the Senate, they
began to fear that their whole policy of détente was
in danger.

Kissinger campaigned against the proposed legislation not only in the Senate itself, but with the Israeli government and U.S. Jewry. The American Jewish leadership absorbed most of the pressure. Wherever
possible it had tried to be forthcoming with the Nixon
administration expecting there would be reciprocity—
especially where the interests of the state of Israel
were involved. Strong entreaties to come out against
the Jackson amendment were repeatedly directed at
the Jewish leadership by Kissinger. But these de-

mands went beyond acceptable limits even for the generally accommodating Jewish leadership. It was too much to expect a Jewish leader to publicly come out in opposition to a measure designed to aid other Jews in distress.

Finally an unwritten understanding was worked out. The Jews would not oppose the Jackson amendment but would not go out of their way to rally support for it. This arrangement received the blessing of the Israeli government and was observed until the Yom Kippur War.

Now with Israel in dire straits, Kissinger recognized the chance that had come his way, or so he thought, to deliver the *coup de grace* to the Jackson amendment. He knew that the Jewish leadership would come to him to speed up military aid to Israel. And he was preparing a warm reception.

What went on in Kissinger's office during the first few days of the war was revealed in a secret meeting of the Zionist Executive in Jerusalem on November 21, 1973. Professor Allen Pollack described the predicament of the American Jewish leadership. Pollack told the other members of the executive that before the war they "could not afford to appear to make a choice between Nixon or Congress. We need both. This was our position and this was the delicate line we have been walking for months and months."

According to Pollack this neutrality changed under pressure from Kissinger:

> Precisely because of the crisis and because we're first and foremost concerned with Israel, when the secretary of state directly and indirectly came and said this is what he wants, we agreed, whether rightly or wrongly, that if the survival of Israel is at stake, we're not going to sit there maintaining our own positions. So we agreed we would go and do what he asked.
>
> And first he said he would go and speak to the

Congress and we should support it, and we agreed. Then he came and said that's not enough, he didn't go and they didn't go and we should go for him, and we agreed. In other words, what I want you to realize is that we did go for the sake of Israel, we changed the line and we kept going and going and going . . .

Pollack's account was confirmed by Rabbi Israel Miller, the chairman of the "Presidents' Club" (the Conference of Presidents of Major American Jewish Organizations) . Here is how he explained the decision of the Jewish leaders:

We're dealing with political judgments of a very difficult nature and sometimes they change in the course of time. The judgment that we can make now after a cease-fire, such as it is, is a little different from the judgment that one could make in the first day of the war, or the second day of the war, when the Egyptians were on the other side of the canal and when we, who were listening to different reports, were not so certain that they would be stopped at that point or that the Syrians would be stopped in the Golan, despite the fact that we had all kinds of faith in Israel. We were faced with a difficult decision. The secretary of state took advantage of this because it doesn't matter whether détente is good for us or not, good for the Jews or bad for the Jews, at this point we needed the president and the secretary of state and we needed them desperately.

There is no doubt then that Kissinger offered the Jews, in the first and most difficult days of the war, a cynical arms deal in return for active support in defeating the Jackson amendment. Kissinger's maneuver almost succeeded. The Jews were so anxious about the fate of Israel that they actually approached Jackson directly and asked him to withdraw his legislation.

Jackson, however, understood only too well what was behind the sudden approaches of the Jewish leaders, and refused to back down. Also operating against Kissinger was the quickening pace of events. Before Kissinger's moves managed to achieve any momentum, the day approached when it was no longer possible to put conditions on the resupply of arms to Israel. Kissinger abandoned his pressures on the Jewish leaders when he began to understand that soon the sole authority over supplying the arms would be taken from him.

All of Kissinger's maneuvers over the arms supply to Israel rested on the assumption that the Russians would act with some restraint, and he occasionally threw out a warning to Moscow to that effect. In a speech to the Center for the Study of Democratic Institutions on October 8, he said: "We shall resist aggressive foreign policies. Détente cannot survive irresponsibility in any area, including the Middle East." But he was basically hopeful, thinking of new diplomatic initiatives which depended to a large extent on the goodwill of the Soviet Union. In that same speech he spoke of the "need to move from a preventive diplomacy to a creative diplomacy."

But Moscow apparently was not impressed with either Kissinger's warning or his vision. The leaders of the Kremlin had their own ideas about "creative diplomacy," and they intended to carry them out.

At first Leonid Brezhnev's tactic was to cover up the Russian involvement in the war through soothing declarations. Most of them were conveyed to Kissinger through Dobrynin. Brezhnev made his own contribution during a reception in the Kremlin for Japanese Prime Minister Kakuei Tanaka on October 8, when he declared that his country supports "a just and fair peace in the Middle East and a secure existence for all the states and people in the area."

That was the last pacific declaration from Brezhnev during the war. From then on Moscow did not even try to hide the depth of its involvement. There is no clear explanation for this shift, but one reason undoubtedly was that with Washington still stuttering through its dialogue with Israel, the Kremlin thought that a weakened President Nixon would not dare come out decisively on Israel's side. Moscow's evaluation was that a president busy listening to Watergate tapes would not risk an involvement that carried the potential of another Vietnam, not to mention the risk of an oil embargo.

The Soviet Union then stepped up its own open and active involvement. On Tuesday, October 9, Brezhnev sent a message to Houari Boumediene in which the Algerian president was requested to "take all the required steps with a view to supporting Syria and Egypt in the difficult struggle imposed by Israel." That day both American and Israeli intelligence discovered increased Soviet arms shipments to Egypt and Syria by sea and a buildup of Soviet naval presence in the Mediterranean.

The Soviet airlift to Cairo and Damascus began a day later, Wednesday, October 10. Israeli and American intelligence had no doubts about this escalation. But though Kissinger now knew the Russians were spitting at him, he chose to disregard it. He was still clinging tenaciously to his assumption of Soviet moderation. Thus, that day State Department spokesman Robert McCloskey said that he could not confirm that the Soviet Union had even begun an airlift. He added that if it were confirmed that Moscow is engaged in a "massive" airlift it would change the entire situation.

If there was only a "light" airlift, presumably there would be no change in the picture and Israel would not get much military aid. But the real catch was that the interpretation of what was massive and what was light would be left to Kissinger.

Later that day word came in that the Soviet Union had put three of its airborne divisions in Eastern

Europe on alert. Kissinger would later claim that this was the point at which he abandoned his hopes in Moscow's moderation and opened all the taps to pour equipment into Israel. Marvin and Bernard Kalb's book *Kissinger* presents the secretary of state's version:

> During the night [Wednesday] Kissinger had reached a major decision: Russia had to be stopped—not only to save Israel, but, in his mind, to spare the world from the possibility of a big-power confrontation. The Soviet airlift and alert had changed his attitude about Israel's capacity to win a quick victory. Just as he had misjudged prewar intelligence, so too had he misjudged the will and capability of the Arabs and the duplicity of the Russians. He was not determined to open a massive airlift of American military supplies to Israel. . . .
>
> "We tried to talk in the first week," Kissinger later explained. "When that didn't work, we said, fine, we'll start pouring in equipment until we create a new reality."

After this dramatic description of Kissinger's decision, there is an equally dramatic version of how Kissinger fought the obstructionism of Schlesinger:

> Kissinger told Dinitz to see Schlesinger about getting the equipment. He implied that this time Schlesinger would be more accommodating.
>
> Later in the afternoon, Kissinger argued forcefully with Schlesinger about the need to correct the military imbalance in the Middle East. He again urged his colleague to charter twenty American transport planes to fly emergency supplies to Israel. Schlesinger resisted Kissinger's appeal. The Defense chief argued just as forcefully that even a limited American airlift to Israel would so infuriate the Arabs that they would impose an oil embargo on the United States. The argument was resolved only after Kissinger had won the president to his point of view. Nixon ordered Schlesinger to charter twenty transport planes.

That description does not even stand the test of Kissinger's own public statements. Not only did he not read the Russian moves correctly on October 11, but a day later he was still full of hope. In a press conference at the State Department on Friday, October 12, he was asked: Given the Soviet Union's behavior, do you intend to make sure that the United States will preserve the military balance?

Referring to Brezhnev's letter to Boumediene, Kissinger replied:

> We did not consider the Soviet statement to the president of Algeria helpful. We also did not consider the airlift of Soviet military equipment helpful. We also do not consider that Soviet actions as of now constitute the irresponsibility that on Monday evening I pointed out would threaten détente.
>
> When that point is reached, we will in this crisis, as we have in other crises, not hesitate to make a firm stand. But at this moment we are still attempting to moderate the conflict.
>
> As of this moment, we have to weigh against the actions of which we disapprove, and quite strongly, the relative restraint that has been shown in public media in the Soviet Union and in the conduct of their representative at the Security Council.

Kissinger did have a problem, but it was not with Schlesinger. It was entirely personal: the difficulty of convincing himself that the Russians were not keeping the rules of détente, the diplomatic project he was so intensely involved with. Thus, even on October 11 he continued the charade with Dinitz, speaking of a total number of 6 planes when the president had already cleared 50 planes in principle. The only accurate point in the Kalbs' description is Kissinger's admission that in the first week of the war he "tried to talk," and did not think of sending equipment to Israel. But that was not what he had been telling Dinitz with such persuasive force.

The situation began to be taken out of Kissinger's hands on Friday, October 12. Mrs. Meir's patience was at an end. Kissinger's stalling tactics were now plain to see and on that day she sent a desperate message to Washington pleading for an immediate, direct, and massive American airlift of arms and equipment. This time the message was not sent to Kissinger —it went directly to President Nixon.

Nixon was also now ready to move, having begun to understand what the Russians were up to. His desk was covered with intelligence reports on the unprecedented Russian airlift. All his approaches to Moscow, directly and through Kissinger, to "keep hands off" had been answered with soothing words, but he now realized that he was being played for a fool. The Russians simply wanted to gain time; they believed they could go on discounting the president, who in addition to his Watergate troubles had now just lost his vice-president in a scandal.

Nixon had also just received two greetings from King Faisal of Saudi Arabia. Both warned that if an airlift to Israel were launched Faisal would carry out his long-standing threat and embargo oil to the United States.

This time the threats fell on deaf ears. Nixon saw that the situation was now endangering not only his own position but the very foundations of U.S. policy in the Middle East. If the war ended in Israel's defeat or even its weakening, the Soviet Union would become the dominant, permanent influence in the Arab countries.

This realization stirred Nixon's combative spirit. On Saturday, October 13, he summoned the National Security Council and this time his order was clear and unambiguous: an immediate and massive military resupply effort, without any restrictions, using American military transport planes direct to Lod Airport.

And miraculously all the bureaucratic wolves in

the Pentagon that Kissinger had conjured up during the past seven days disappeared. All of a sudden Schlesinger and Clements went into action with striking efficiency. The point is that they never did have the power, authority, or will to violate an unambiguous presidential directive. It is equally clear that up to then they had acted consistently with the instructions of the president as brought to their attention by his loyal adviser.

And so, on late Saturday afternoon, the secretary of state was able to call Eban in New York to inform him that all obstacles had been removed. According to Kissinger, 67 transport planes were now in the air and on their way to Lod Airport. A similar message was relayed to Ambassador Dinitz, who immediately passed it on to Jerusalem.

A few hours later citizens in the Tel Aviv area could hear the drone of the giant jets above their heads. No one complained about the noise. Cars stopped on the roads, windows opened in apartments. People went out into the blacked-out streets, their eyes turned to the skies—to the approaching flickering lights. Some people were crying. Many others, knowing nothing of leased planes, the Azores, or wolves in the Pentagon, were murmuring, "God bless America."

II

The Battle for the Cease-Fire

The maneuvering over a cease-fire began almost as soon as the first shots were fired. Abba Eban was thinking about it even before the hostilities began. On Yom Kippur, at 7:30 A.M. New York time, Eban was on the phone to Golda Meir asking if he should move for an immediate cease-fire resolution at the UN when the war started. Mrs. Meir said she would give him an answer later.

Five hours later Eban received instructions that reflected the early optimism at general staff headquarters. The dispatch said:

> Do not agree to a cease-fire until there is a return to the status quo. The aim is to hit the enemy on the two fronts and it is our intention to throw every last Syrian and Egyptian back behind the cease-fire lines. The spirit of Zahal [Israeli defense forces] is strong. The government is assembling now to hear a report.

Optimism also prevailed in Key Biscayne, Florida. On Sunday, October 7, President Nixon saw no need to return to Washington, though his spokesman announced that the president was "very concerned." The secretary of state summoned the National Security Council but it made no major decisions. Immediately afterward Kissinger invited in Soviet Ambassador Anatoly Dobrynin. Kissinger handed him a letter from Nixon for Brezhnev suggesting a UN Security Council meeting to try and achieve a cease-fire. Nixon's letter was based on earlier agreements that the two super-powers would act to stop local conflicts that threat-ened the peace. Within a few hours the Soviet leader had agreed to convene the Security Council.

But these were only pro forma diplomatic gestures. Moscow was not interested in stopping a war that had been so long and so meticulously planned. The aim of the war was to capture large chunks of territory in the Sinai and on the Golan Heights. There was thus no point in talking of an early cease-fire. Washington also had no illusions on this matter. Kissinger under-stood that only when Israel managed to disrupt the aims of the Arabs would it be possible to talk. He had no doubt that Israel would do just that and speedily.

After getting the consent of U.S. Ambassador John Scali and Soviet Ambassador Yakov Malik, the stand-ing president, Sir Laurence McIntyre of Australia, called the Security Council into session on the third day of the war, October 8. He too had no illusions. He knew that the only chance for passage of a cease-fire resolution lay in a joint Soviet-American draft—which did not yet exist.

As expected, the members of the council went through a well-known and banal script. Scali called upon the sides to return to the cease-fire lines (mean-ing the prewar status quo) and stop the fighting. Representatives of the People's Republic of China and the Soviet Union opposed any return to the pre-war situation, and together with the representatives of Egypt and Syria poured fire and brimstone on the Israeli "aggressors." After an hour and a half the council adjourned with no decision. Everyone now waited for the battlefield developments which would ultimately set the timing and conditions of a cease-fire.

On the fifth day of the war, October 10, Egypt, Syria, and the Soviet Union reached the conclusion that the goals they had set for themselves had been in large measure achieved. Yakov Malik called John Scali. The Soviet ambassador said that his country now agreed to present a joint draft to the Security Council for a cease-fire "in place." Scali immediately relayed the Soviet proposal to Kissinger and asked for instructions. Kissinger relayed the offer to Dinitz who in turn called Golda Meir. Even though the battlefield situation was grim her reply was an unequivocal no. Israel would agree to a cease-fire only on condition of a return to the prewar situation.

Dinitz relayed the Israeli position to Kissinger, who concurred completely. He too understood that a cease-fire "in place" at this point would be a death-blow to any attempt to achieve an acceptable political agreement after the war.

Kissinger informed Dobrynin that the United States would not be a partner to any initiative under the conditions offered. The United States would agree to cosponsor a cease-fire initiative that would provide for a return to the prewar lines. But he made the proposal more for the record than out of any hope the Russians would consider it seriously—which they did not.

The entire picture changed drastically on October 12, the seventh day of the war. In Tel Aviv there was still no sign of the American airlift. The Egyptian army was powerfully dug in along the canal, and showed no willingness to come out of its missile umbrella. The Israeli counterattack on the Golan Heights was moving slowly with heavy losses. In this atmosphere the Soviet Union once more offered a cease-fire "in place." Mrs. Meir's reaction this time would shock many people in Washington, Americans and Israelis alike. She was willing to accept the very proposal she had rejected just two days before.

Kissinger summoned Dinitz to discuss the tactical question of who would offer the cease-fire resolution at the UN. The secretary of state suggested that someone else, preferably Britain, propose the cease-fire. Kissinger would inform the Soviets that an Israeli condition to the cease-fire was an immediate exchange of prisoners. The resolution should also stipulate that the cease-fire would take effect 12 hours after its adoption. Kissinger, thinking mainly of the Syrian front, believed that Israel could use the time to improve its position. He had no great hopes for a meaningful change on the Egyptian front.

Mrs. Meir's response was indicated in a telegram sent to Eban and Dinitz:

> In Syria a small advance continues, and the resistance has become tougher because of the intervention of the Iraqis. Therefore, one should agree with the scenario offered by Kissinger even without the time extension.

Eban and Dinitz couldn't believe what they were reading. Even without the 12-hour reprieve? They quickly realized that the leadership in Israel did not believe it could improve its situation in 12 hours, that they feared every additional hour would just make the situation worse.

In fact, at that moment in Tel Aviv, Mrs. Meir, Dayan, and Chief of Staff Elazar were so tired and pessimistic that they were ready to throw in the towel. The three had decided on the cease-fire themselves. They were prepared to inform the cabinet of their action only after the green light came from Kissinger on the British initiative. Fortunately for Golda Meir and Israel she never did have to inform the cabinet. In fact till this very day her desperate telegram has not been entered into the official records of the government.

Once the okay came from Tel Aviv for the cease-fire, Eban, together with Shalev and Dinitz, went to see Kissinger at 10:30 P.M. But now there was a new problem. Kissinger told the Israelis that the British had foolishly asked Sadat ahead of time for his reaction to their cease-fire proposal. And Sadat, once confronted with the question in a formal way, had to reiterate the official Egyptian position, which was that the cease-fire resolution had to include an Israeli retreat to the borders of June 4, 1967. Now, said Kissinger, the British were unsure whether they should go ahead as planned.

It took the British another day to make up their minds. On October 13 they informed Kissinger they had decided not to present the resolution because of Egypt's opposition. Kissinger then suggested to the Soviets that Australia might introduce the resolution, but the Soviets opposed this. Kissinger asked Eban whether Israel was interested in having the United States offer the resolution.

Eban cabled Jerusalem for clarification. Is the breakdown in the British initiative for a cease-fire critical from Israel's point of view? he asked. Further, does Israel agree to an American initiative for a cease-fire?

The replies Eban received on Sunday, October 14, reflected a sudden and dramatic turning point in the war. The answer to the first question was no; an emphatic no was the answer to the second. The reason for the opposition to the American initiative was clear. Such an initiative, coming from the ally of Israel, would have been interpreted as a clear sign of weakness.

But more importantly Israel was now no longer

so sure it even wanted a cease-fire, because new facts were starting to accumulate in the field. On the southern front the Egyptians had just emerged from their missile umbrella and launched a massive attack with three divisions. It was the very move that everyone was waiting for at general staff headquarters in Tel Aviv. Golda Meir now decided to stall until she had the results of the Egyptian attack and the counterattack of the Israeli task force on its way to "Africa" (the west bank of the Suez Canal).

The results of the Egyptian attack were clear by the end of the day. They were hurled back with a loss of about 240 tanks. But news of the counterattack was slow coming in. The forces led by Major General Ariel (Arik) Sharon had found a gap between the Egyptian Second Army and Third Army which enabled them to reach the canal without much difficulty. The troubles began when they reached the water's edge. The bridges that were thrown across the canal started collapsing and precious time was taken up by repair work. Therefore, by October 16 only a few tanks from Sharon's division had reached the west bank of the canal. The Egyptians did not understand what was happening. They were convinced that it was only a showy spectacle by a small force that would be destroyed or would return quickly to its base.

That day Golda Meir mounted the rostrum of the Knesset to deliver a special address on the military and political situation. She began with the following announcement: "At this hour, while we are gathered in the Knesset, Zahal forces are operating on the west bank of the canal."

The words went through the heavy air of the packed hall like an electric current, and there was a stunned silence. Afterward it became clear that when she made the announcement neither Mrs. Meir nor the general staff had any assurance that the bold military operation of Sharon would be successful. But she decided to take a risk, moved by the human yearning to be able to report some success to the dispirited people of Israel.

It was an error that could have led to a military disaster. At that hour the Egyptians were still convinced that Sharon's breakthrough was not serious. Mrs. Meir's statement in the Knesset might have opened their eyes. Luckily the Egyptians refused to wake from their calm sleep. They were so sure of their own achievements that they fell into the same trap of overconfidence that had brought disaster upon the Israelis just ten days earlier. The military commentator of Radio Cairo reported to his listeners that Zahal "attempted" to penetrate with a tank unit west of the canal "in order to enable Golda Meir to announce in her speech to the Knesset that Israeli forces are fighting west of the canal. The aims of Israel are political, not military."

Mrs. Meir of course did not find it useful to inform the Knesset of the various negotiations regarding a cease-fire. She was content to say that "so far the Israeli government has received no proposal from any political factor for a cease-fire." Technically that was the truth because the prime minister meant an "official" proposal and the negotiations had not gotten to that stage.

And now she was also able to contemplate the conditions for a cease-fire free from the pessimism that characterized her telegram of October 13. She concluded:

The Egyptians and the Syrians, so it seems, have not been hurt enough to show any desire to stop the shooting. I am certain that when we shall succeed in bringing our enemies to the verge of collapse the "volunteers" will not delay to appear, representatives of states who would tempt our attackers with a cease-fire.

At the very hour she was speaking, the first volunteer was on his way from Moscow to Cairo. What the eyes of Cairo did not see, the electronic eyes of the Soviet spy satellites picked up. When the findings of the satellite were analyzed in Moscow, in addition to the reports of the size of the American airlift to Israel, Brezhnev sent Premier Alexei Kosygin immediately to the Egyptian capital. The Soviet Union now launched its own active drive for a cease-fire.

Publicly of course the Soviet Union and Egypt continued to insist that the cease-fire include a complete Israeli retreat from the Sinai, the Golan Heights, Judaea, and Samaria (including east Jerusalem). But they did not repeat this demand in the unofficial negotiations, which now picked up again.

On October 17, the twelfth day of the war, Brigadier General Scowcroft called Dinitz to report that the Russians had just asked for the American position on a cease-fire "in place" which would be linked to UN Security Resolution 242. The Americans replied that they did not oppose it in principle but they asked for a specific proposal.

Since the adoption of Resolution 242 on November 22, 1967, it had become the basis for all political initiatives for a solution to the Middle East conflict. It was accepted as such by all the nations including Israel and the Arab states. The basic principle of the resolution was that the Arab states recognize the right of Israel to live in peace within secure and recognized boundaries in return for an Israeli retreat from territories it had captured in the 1967 war. But in effect the two sides accepted the resolution with their own interpretations.

These rival interpretations focused on section 1 (a), which discusses the "withdrawal of Israeli armed forces from territories of recent conflict." The key word is "territories." The Arabs and their allies add "the," and read it "from the territories," meaning from *all* the territories. Israel reads the clause as it is: "from territories"—meaning from *most* territories but not all. And what is "most"? In the Israeli view this will be determined in negotiations between the parties.

Israel's fear was that any discussion of a cease-fire resolution that included reference to Resolution 242 would give the Soviet Union a chance to win support for incorporation of the Arab interpretation. This fear was well founded because the majority of the council members, including Britain, which had originally introduced Resolution 242, tended by now to accept the Arab interpretation.

In any event, in the conversation with Scowcroft, Dinitz was asked to solicit Mrs. Meir's reaction to the Soviet initiative. The Israeli ambassador immediately reported his conversation with Scowcroft to Mrs. Meir and Eban. Eban then also communicated some considerations to Mrs. Meir on the cease-fire issue, raising the points he thought Kissinger would demand clear Israeli responses to:

1. Is Israel ready for a cease-fire in place?
In the light of our agreement to the previous scenario [of October 12] and the subsequent big improvement I assume we shall answer positively in principle.
2. Are we ready for reference to Resolution 242?
In my opinion there is no realistic possibility of preventing a specific reference, because in the light of our declared positions the matter would be taken for granted by the Americans. In fact, the Americans have already accepted this point in their reply to the Russians, and insisted only on the question of how the reference would be worded. I propose that our answer shall be that we do not oppose the phrase "negotiations for a peace agreement on the basis of Resolution 242," but we do oppose any added detail.

Eban then suggested the following Israeli reply to the United States:

> Israel is prepared in principle to accept a cease-fire proposal in place but wants to gain time to become stronger.
>
> Israel agrees to the reference to Resolution 242 with no additional detail, and firmly insists on including the phrase "negotiation" in any resolution that would refer to Resolution 242.
>
> Israel opposes British sponsorship, and suggests American-Soviet or Australian sponsorship.
>
> Israel requests American resistance to the point of a veto [in the Security Council] to any amendments that Israel opposes.
>
> Israel reminds the Americans that prisoner exchange is a condition for a cease-fire agreement.

But with things now going so well for the Israeli task force in "Africa" the prime minister was no longer in a hurry. She sent Eban a telegram saying that she had promised the cabinet that she would not accept any decision regarding a cease-fire without a prior discussion. (This was a promise she had been willing to ignore only five days before.) Reference to Resolution 242 in the cease-fire resolution was also not acceptable to her. Finally she asked Eban to return immediately to take part in the cabinet meeting that would discuss the cease-fire. Eban's travels would be a ploy to gain the time that was now needed to improve the situation on the fronts.

It was clear to Mrs. Meir that it would not be long before the Security Council would start getting proposals for a cease-fire. Seemingly then the foreign minister's presence would be required in New York. But precisely because Eban supported reference to Resolution 242 she wanted him out of town. As she explained to those close to her: "He will cause less damage here than in the United States."

Before leaving for Israel on October 20, Eban had his last conversation with Kissinger. There would be a cease-fire, Kissinger said, but he didn't know what political price would have to be paid. Eban suggested a formula that would establish a cease-fire in place, with no further details, as in the formula for a cease-fire ending the 1967 war. Kissinger replied that Anwar Sadat would never agree. The Egyptian president had said several times that the '67 agreement was a disaster to Egypt in that it froze the situation created by the war.

Kissinger wanted to know how Israel saw the time factor now. Eban replied that a time delay before a cease-fire no longer worked to the disadvantage of Israel and hoped that this fact would also influence U.S. moves. Kissinger replied that Eban could inform the prime minister that the principle guiding U.S. policies during the war would continue to guide it now.

It was a conversation of two experienced diplomats. Kissinger did not need a translation to understand that Israel hoped he would not hurry too much in arranging a cease-fire. Eban in turn was allowed to assume that Kissinger had made a commitment along these lines. But nothing was official.

Before leaving his hotel for his plane to Israel, with his suitcases already packed, Eban received a call from Dinitz. The ambassador said he had been called for an urgent appointment with Kissinger and he expected developments. Could Eban delay his departure a half hour?

Eban promised to wait. But the half hour passed with no word from Dinitz. Eban was forced to go to the airport. There a message was waiting for him. It said that Dinitz had sent a telegram that would be given to him at Orly Airport in Paris by someone from the Israeli embassy there.

When Eban stopped at Orly Airport the journalists were faster than the man from the embassy. "What can you say about Kissinger's trip to Moscow?" they asked the Israeli foreign minister. Eban's long diplomatic experience helped him keep his cool without admitting that he knew nothing of Kissinger's mission to Moscow, which at that hour was already airborne. He managed to mutter something about the need for consultation between the two superpowers and sneaked away. Only afterward did he receive Dinitz's telegram with the news about the "new development."

It had become clear to the Kremlin that Egypt was facing a military disaster, greater perhaps than that of the Six-Day War. The Israeli army was standing close to Cairo, and there seemed to be nothing that could prevent it from outflanking and destroying the two Egyptian armies encamped on the east bank of the Suez Canal. Kosygin, who had come from Cairo a few days earlier, brought with him an agreement in principle from Sadat for a cease-fire. But this agreement had been given only in return for a Soviet promise to guarantee the carrying out of the cease-fire by Israel —a promise that would have great import in the days to come.

In the early morning hours of Saturday, October 20, the fifteenth day of the war, Ambassador Dobrynin suddenly relayed to Kissinger an invitation from Brezhnev to fly immediately to Moscow for urgent consultations. If Kissinger could not get away, Brezhnev said he would send Foreign Minister Andrei Gromyko to Washington.

After consulting the president, Kissinger informed Dobrynin that he would be en route to Moscow in his special plane that very evening. Only those of his closest aides who would accompany him were let in on the secret operation. The pool of reporters joining him on the trip were also briefed, but not for publication.

Later that afternoon Kissinger called in Dinitz to tell him of the trip. The Israeli ambassador was shocked. He reminded Kissinger of Israel's desire to gain time in order to finish the job on the west bank of the Suez Canal, adding that this also was in the American interest. Kissinger calmed him. He said he didn't believe that any agreement would be achieved in Moscow. Why then had he accepted the Soviet invitation? Dinitz wanted to know. Kissinger listed two reasons:

• Turning down the Soviet invitation could harden the position of the Kremlin perhaps to the point of direct military intervention in order to enforce a cease-fire.

• The trip would give Israel two or three precious days.

But if the Soviets are so hungry for a cease-fire, Dinitz asked, why was Kissinger so sure he wouldn't reach agreement with them? The secretary explained that the Soviet Union still insisted that the cease-fire be linked to an obligation for immediate Israeli retreat from all territories conquered in June 1967. It was clear to Kissinger that this was a fantastic demand, which one could not expect Israel even to consider— certainly not after the turnabout on the battlefield.

Kissinger then wanted to know what the Israeli government would accept. What kind of agreement would be considered positive? Dinitz had no new instructions in that matter. The government had not yet decided on its conditions for a cease-fire. Dinitz had in hand only the views of the prime minister, and he offered those to Kissinger: A cease-fire "in place," with a provision that would speak generally of direct negotiations for peace; absolutely no reference to Security Council Resolution 242, especially if the agreement were to be formulated in Moscow, because that would give extra weight to the Arab-Soviet interpretation of section 1 (a) of the resolution.

Kissinger did not comment on this and only repeated his assurances that Israel had nothing to fear; no big news would come from the meeting in the Kremlin, and he, Kissinger, would do all he could to slow down the talks. He even went so far as to let Dinitz in on one of his delaying tactics: upon his arrival at Vanukov Airport near Moscow he would tell his Soviet hosts that he was tired from the trip and wished to begin the discussions only on the following day. In keeping with that spirit Dinitz wished Kissinger a safe voyage but not a fruitful one.

Later that day Kissinger attended a dinner at the Mayflower Hotel for the Chinese representative, Huang Chen. Kissinger paid his respects to the guests and left directly for the airport and his special Boeing 707. Only when he was airborne was the official announcement of the trip released.

Close to 8:00 P.M. the following day Kissinger's plane landed in Moscow. The reassuring promises he gave Dinitz were forgotten the moment he stepped on Soviet soil. The discussions in the Kremlin began two hours after touchdown.

Dinitz had reported to Israel that on the basis of his last conversation with Kissinger they could safely assume they had enough time to achieve their military objectives.

Upon his arrival in Israel on Saturday evening, October 20, Eban was confronted by more journalists probing for a reaction to the Kissinger mission to Moscow. He told them: "Kissinger's trip to Moscow is a continuation of contacts between the two powers, but we are not facing any initiative, dispute, or clarification regarding the conditions to be agreed upon for a cease-fire."

On Sunday, October 21, while Kissinger was conversing in Moscow, Deputy Prime Minister Allon was calming down General Sharon in the Israeli salient west of the canal. Sharon was worried that there wouldn't be enough time to destroy the Egyptian armies. Allon reassured him: "You don't have to hurry. You have all the time you need."

That evening at 9:00, when Kissinger was almost wrapping up the talks in Moscow, Eban was reporting to the Knesset Foreign Affairs and Security Committee that the talks in the Kremlin did not involve more than an exchange of opinions. There should be no worries that a cease-fire would emerge from that forum. While he was speaking a messenger came in and handed Eban a note. It read: "The material is beginning to arrive. I suggest that you stop the meeting of the committee. [Mordechai] Gazit."

The "material" was two messages brought to the prime minister by Ambassador Kenneth Keating immediately after he received them from Washington. After studying them just before 10:00 P.M., Mrs. Meir instructed the cabinet secretary to alert all the ministers for a meeting at 12:00 midnight.

One message was from Kissinger; it included the conditions of a cease-fire that he had already agreed to in Moscow. The other was from President Nixon asking the Israeli government to make an immediate announcement consenting to the Moscow agreement.

Mrs. Meir was shocked and furious. The reports of Eban and Dinitz had given her a firm basis for believing that the Moscow talks would end inconclusively. The last thing she expected, particularly after Kissinger's reassurances to Eban and Dinitz, was that he would put his own signature on an agreement without even consulting her. Mrs. Meir never said flatly that Kissinger had betrayed Israel, but this idea was obviously uppermost in her thoughts. At no time, however, did she suggest rejection of the agreement.

As if to pour salt on her wounds, at a few minutes past midnight she received an urgent phone call from the British ambassador. She took the call during the cabinet meeting. The ambassador told her that a very urgent telegram from Sir Alec Douglas-Home had just arrived in which the British foreign minister implored the prime minister to consent to the Moscow agreement. Mrs. Meir said, "Thanks," making it sound more like a curse, and slammed down the receiver. She and the other ministers now realized that not only did Kissinger not consult her, but he informed her of the agreement after he told the British foreign minister—a conclusion reached by simply allowing for the time necessary for the British to route the message to Israel.

Rage, however, was not a policy. After the massive airlift, even though it had come late, the government recognized it was in no position to refuse an explicit request from Nixon. Everyone knew, as well, that the need for U.S. aid would not end with the cessation of hostilities.

A major dilemma facing the ministers, however, was the problem of prisoners of war. Should Israel insist on its previous absolute condition that a prisoner exchange be part of any cease-fire agreement? Mrs. Meir and Dayan knew that abandoning this condition conceded to the Arabs a very powerful bargaining card. They also had no illusions about the Arabs' willingness to respect the Geneva convention, signed by Egypt and Syria, requiring an exchange of prisoners immediately after any cease-fire. But it was clear that sticking to the demand now would be tantamount to a refusal to accept the Moscow agreement. That is how Nixon and Kissinger would have seen it, which was the decisive factor. The government decided unanimously to accept the Moscow agreement.

Militarily Israel needed a few more days to surround the two Egyptian armies on the east bank of the canal and to capture the town of Suez. There was full intention to respect the cease-fire, but if it was violated by the Egyptians, even in the smallest way, Israel would not content itself with a local reaction. It would continue the offensive—if possible to the point of destroying the Second and Third armies, or at least encircling them.

Close to 3:00 A.M. Mrs. Meir sent a message to Nixon informing him of Israel's acceptance of the cease-fire agreement on condition that the Arab nations which took part in the war also accepted. Her distaste for the timing and the proceedings behind the agreement could be detected only in the additional message: "The Israeli government requests that the secretary of state, on his way from Moscow to Washington, stop in Tel Aviv to transmit explanations and clarifications."

In New York on Sunday, October 21, at 2:00 P.M. local time, the phone rang in the office of Israel's UN Ambassador Yosef Tekoah. On the line was the standing president of the Security Council, Australian Ambassador McIntyre. He said that the United States and the Soviet Union had just informed him that they wished to convene the Security Council immediately to present a jointly sponsored resolution for a cease-fire in the Middle East. The council meeting was set for 4:00 P.M.

Tekoah thought quickly. As a veteran of such maneuvers he understood that if the United States and the Soviet Union had reached an understanding regarding a cease-fire, it meant that the military situation for the Arabs was very bad. In that case the best service he could perform for his country was to play for time.

Tekoah told McIntyre truthfully that this was the

first he had heard about the cease-fire resolution. Therefore he needed time to contact Jerusalem and receive instructions. The Australian expressed his doubts. Both powers were demanding an immediate session. But Tekoah stuck to his guns. He could not participate in the meeting before receiving instructions from home, and he did not believe that he could possibly receive them by 4:00 P.M. The polite Australian didn't promise anything but said he would try to accommodate the Israeli. A half hour later he called again. Instead of 4:00 P.M. the council would convene at 4:30. Tekoah thanked him politely but expressed his doubts about the possibility of meeting the new deadline.

In the meantime Tekoah contacted Tel Aviv. He was told to wait for instructions. At 4:30 there was no word from Tel Aviv. Tekoah sent one of his assistants to the UN building to tell McIntyre that the Israeli ambassador was in the midst of his contacts with Tel Aviv and could not come yet. Not having any other choice, the Australian was forced to postpone the meeting repeatedly until 10:00 P.M.

The sponsors of the resolution, Ambassadors John Scali and Yakov Malik, moved for adoption of the following procedure: first a vote on the proposal, and then a debate. This procedure was not unprecedented, especially in situations where the time factor was so critical. Tekoah took the floor, however, and announced that he could not agree to such a procedure. He asked to speak because he had important things to say. Israel, he argued, has a special status as a belligerent and it is not customary to refuse such a request.

Tekoah had assumed that if he spoke the Arabs would do so too. Within five minutes ambassadors of the Arab countries had put their names on the list of speakers, with the other council members not far behind.

The first speaker was the Chinese ambassador. After his customary terse denunciation of the imperialist and aggressive Israelis he moved on, to the surprise of all, and gave the Soviet Union a thorough and slanderous going-over. He put the blame on Moscow for all the disasters to hit the world and the Arabs. As he spoke, the face of Ambassador Malik turned red with fury. Finally the Russian shouted at the Chinese ambassador: "Look what you're doing. You assist the aggressive Israelis in gaining time." At that point Tekoah made his own dilatory contribution, shouting to Malik that every time he spoke of "aggressors" he should clarify that he meant Egypt and Syria. Malik turned back to Tekoah and shouted epithets. The Chinese ambassador screamed at Malik. The Australian chairman felt he was losing control and declared a recess. At the very moment the gavel was banged down the TV cameras caught Tekoah with a half smile of satisfaction on his face.

During the recess Malik and the Arab ambassadors gathered for strategy consultations. The Soviet ambassador was asked to let the Chinese ambassador get on with his speech without interruptions so as not to waste time. Malik consented.

Finally Tekoah delivered the speech sent him from Tel Aviv. He announced Israel's agreement to the American-Soviet resolution on condition that it would also be accepted by all the states which took part in the war. He added several items which Israel regarded as essential to the agreement:

• Acts of hostility against Israel by other Arab forces, such as Iraq, which operate from the territories of countries neighboring Israel, must stop.

• All acts by the terrorists must cease.

• Full and immediate exchange of prisoners.

• Interpretation of Resolution 242 as in the past, meaning Israeli retreat from "territories" and not from "the territories."

On October 22 at 12:52 A.M. New York time, the Security Council, by a vote of 14 to 0 (with the abstention of the People's Republic of China) adopted the American-Soviet Proposal, originally formulated in Moscow, that became Security Council Resolution 338:

> The Security Council (1) calls upon all parties to the present fighting to cease all firing and to terminate all military activity immediately, no later than 12 hours after the moment of the adoption of this decision, in the positions they now occupy; (2) calls upon the parties concerned to start immediately after the cease-fire the implementation of Security Council Resolution 242 in all of its parts; (3) decides that immediately and concurrently with the cease-fire, negotiations start between the parties concerned under appropriate auspices aimed at establishing a just and durable peace in the Middle East.

It was most unusual that the resolution did not specify who would supervise its implementation. No one brought the subject up, certainly not Ambassador Tekoah, who had received precise instructions not to say a word about it.

A few hours later Kissinger arrived in Israel to a mixed reception. The hundreds of ordinary people who came to Lod Airport to thank the secretary of state greeted him with a sustained round of applause, expressing the war-weariness of the Israeli public and their ignorance of the behind-the-scenes maneuvering. Kissinger knew that he could expect a different reception at the prime minister's office.

As he shook hands with Eban in front of his plane Kissinger whispered to him: "I presume she is wild with anger at me." Eban confirmed Kissinger's suspicion. He said that the agreement was totally unexpected and very serious in its implications for future relations. After the airport ceremony Eban and Kissinger entered the black bulletproof Cadillac that accompanies the secretary of state wherever he goes. During the ride into the city Kissinger gave Eban the following explanation of what happened in Moscow:

When he arrived at Moscow on Saturday night, Kissinger recalled, he made some attempt to postpone the discussions by feigning fatigue as he had promised Dinitz. But his hosts insisted that the discussions start right away, and it was impossible to refuse without arousing their suspicions and anger. Throughout the initial conversations on Saturday night and Sunday morning the Soviets insisted on their original position: a cease-fire must include the obligation of Israel to withdraw to the June 4, 1967, borders. They first demanded that the retreat start immediately with the cease-fire and be completed in accordance with a clear and detailed timetable. Afterward they agreed to settle for just an obligation, without an immediate implementation, and with no timetable—and presented this as a big concession.

Kissinger said that he had flatly rejected the Soviet proposal and listed two conditions for a cease-fire agreement: First, a cease-fire "in place." Second, the Soviet Union must agree that every time Resolution 242 is mentioned in the agreement, reference must also be made to "negotiations" because, he told the Russians, "it has been proved that Resolution 242 is useless without negotiations."

The Soviet turnabout from complete rigidity to acceptance of the U.S. position came suddenly, without any preliminary haggling, Kissinger recounted. This is typical of negotiating methods of Communist regimes, he explained, drawing an analogy from his negotiations with North Vietnam and China.

After agreement was reached, however, there was little cheerfulness in the Kremlin. Kissinger described the mood of his hosts as "ugly." Perhaps in order to justify his disregard of Israel and perhaps because it was the truth, Kissinger told Eban: "If I had not wrapped it up immediately they would have passed over to intimidation and threats; and they would have convened international bodies where I would not have gotten what I got from them directly."

Kissinger argued that a week earlier it was not conceivable that Israel could have gotten a cease-fire under such favorable conditions. Eban commented that the new military situation—an achievement for which Israel had paid dearly—justified the improved conditions, so it was not a matter of Kissinger's diplomatic talent. Kissinger did not argue with this but claimed that Israel had to focus more on the positive substance of his efforts and not on his unorthodox procedures.

Nevertheless, Eban asked, why didn't he consult? Or why, at least, didn't he send some warning signal of what to expect so that Israel could speed up its military activities? Kissinger's answer would later turn into a cynical joke in Israel, but he said it with a completely straight face: the Russians engaged in electronic jamming which disrupted the communications system in his special plane and in the U.S. embassy. "Whoever conducts negotiations in Moscow has to pay a price," he said to Eban.

Golda Meir was not willing to swallow this tale so easily. If they were jamming, she asked when Kissinger got to her office, how did he manage to communicate with the president so many times? And if it was possible to relay a message on the agreement to Douglas-Home, why was it impossible to relay a message to Tel Aviv? Kissinger was not willing to go into details. He stuck to his version while calling her attention to the positive aspects of the agreement.

But Mrs. Meir had another question for him: Why did he consent to the reference to Resolution 242 in the agreement when he knew that Israel opposed it? Here Kissinger offered an explanation which was to become very familiar in the months to come: it was a presidential decision. He consulted, he said, with President Nixon, who instructed him to agree to the Soviet demand.

Mrs. Meir then wanted to know about the prisoners. Why didn't the agreement provide for an immediate prisoner exchange? Kissinger called it a very complicated problem. Linking the prisoner issue explicitly to a cease-fire would have torpedoed the agreement and pushed Moscow against the wall. There would have been threats and possibly active intervention. However, he assured Mrs. Meir there was no need for concern. "Prisoner exchanges will be implemented immediately after the cease-fire," he promised, citing a personal commitment from Brezhnev.

At an expanded meeting in which Dayan, Eban, Allon, and Galili took part, specific clauses of the agreement were discussed. "Negotiations toward peace," for example. What kind of negotiations? In the message from Nixon to Mrs. Meir a day earlier direct negotiations were mentioned, but "direct" didn't appear in the agreement, the prime minister complained. Kissinger calmly explained that the intent was "direct negotiations" even though it was not explicitly stated. The wording of the agreement, he emphasized, made that self-evident, because it called for negotiations under "appropriate auspices."

The Israelis didn't find it so self-evident, but they didn't press the point. They suspected that direct negotiations had been discussed in Moscow; that Nixon even received a draft that included the word "direct," but the Soviets changed their minds at the last moment.

Where would the negotiations take place? Here, for the first time, Kissinger mentioned a Geneva conference. He said it should be convened soon. Mrs. Meir opposed it. She said that politically she could not go to such a conference before the Israeli elections, meaning not before December 31. Kissinger argued it was important to strike while the iron was still warm. If the conference did not convene early, he said, it might not convene at all. But he did understand Mrs. Meir's political problems and suggested an early ceremonial opening session with the substantive discussions to be held after Israel's election. Golda Meir was more amenable to this but did not commit herself.

It was not because he attached any practical significance to Geneva that Kissinger insisted upon an early opening. On the contrary, he was convinced that it would only be a hollow demonstration. He already was explaining that it was not possible to move quickly and directly to a general agreement. Therefore one should try for partial agreements, step by step. The main effort, he said, should be invested in Egypt, to try to break the logjam there.

The meeting was then expanded to allow the chief of staff and some of the commanders to come in and brief Kissinger on the military situation. Only then did Kissinger fully realize how close Israel was to a smashing rout of the Egyptian army. While explaining the situation the Israelis continued to complain about not being allowed to finish the job. Stung by the criticism Kissinger finally asked how many days the army needed to complete the encirclement of the two Egyptian armies on the east bank of the Suez Canal. Chief of Staff Elazar put it at around seven days, but the air force chief, Brigadier General Peled, excitedly argued that now, without their air defense umbrella of SAM missiles, it was possible to destroy the two armies in two or three days. Kissinger responded: "Two or three days? That's all? Well, in Vietnam the cease-fire didn't go into effect at the exact time that was agreed on."

Perhaps it was only a chance remark, but Kissinger's hosts did not ask for further clarification. The words sounded to them like an indirect go-ahead for the continuation of the fighting—perhaps not for as long as Elazar was speaking of, but certainly for the two or three days Peled contemplated.

That impression was strengthened when the question of supervision of the cease-fire was discussed. Eban declared that when the Security Council ordered a cease-fire in 1967 it delegated a general of the UN Emergency Force to supervise its implementation. He expressed amazement that this time there were no similar arrangements. Under Secretary Joseph Sisco interjected that perhaps it was possible for the UN truce observers' staff in Cairo to be given the job of supervision. But Kissinger interrupted his aide and said brusquely: "We won't handle the damned thing." Apparently Kissinger didn't want to deal with the complicated issue of supervision just then, but the Israelis could not help but interpret this remark as an indication that he would not be so unhappy if for some reason the fighting went on past the cease-fire deadline.

The talks concluded with mutual promises to continue cooperation. On the way to the airport Kissinger asked Eban again to implore the prime minister to agree to the opening of the Geneva conference soon, "if possible by the end of November." He knew that there was a problem with the elections, but after all, he said, "the Israeli public will certainly look with favor on pictures of Arab and Israeli foreign ministers sitting around one table." Kissinger already saw the electoral advantage which the opening of the Geneva conference before the election would provide for the ruling Labor party. He could see that to a political animal like Golda Meir this would be a most important consideration. As it turned out, he was right.

At 6:55 P.M. on October 22, the deadline set for the cease-fire, the northern front was more or less quiet. On the southern front, a strange, tense silence also replaced the sound of explosions. But about two hours later shots began to be heard from the direction of the Third Army. The commander of the Egyptian force decided to try to break out of the partial siege he was under. The Israelis had no difficulty in smashing the attempt right away, but they had no intention of stopping at that. The army had been waiting for this opportunity. The war on the southern front flared up again, with the Israeli forces moving with speed on the city of Suez. Capturing it would complete the encirclement and possible destruction of the Third Army—the elite of the Egyptian forces.

Kissinger never intended to let Israel finish off the Egyptian Third Army. That would have frustrated his own plans to be the mediator after a stalemated military situation. It was also apparent that his offhand comparison of the Vietnam cease-fire situation to that in the Middle East was ill placed. In the Middle East, unlike Vietnam, the Soviet Union was riding the losing horse and Kissinger was soon feeling heat for it. From the morning of October 23 he was under constantly mounting pressure by the Soviets, accompanied by warnings and threats of dire consequences. With every additional meter taken by the Israeli army Kissinger feared that all his achievements were in danger, the policy of détente would be disrupted, and he would lose his chance of regaining the good will of the Arab countries.

In Israel, in response to the pressure of criticism, he had irresponsibly encouraged the Israelis. Now in order to pacify the Soviets and the Arabs he began to threaten Israel. He called in Ambassador Dinitz and was blunt and brutal. "You want the Third Army? We won't go to a third world war for you," he warned Dinitz. Dinitz could tell Mrs. Meir, if the war continued as a result of Israeli actions, not to count on military aid from the United States.

During that day Israeli army forces reached the outskirts of the city of Suez. But there they were stopped. The resistance in the city was greater than expected, and the house-to-house fighting was slow and costly.

In the meantime, Kissinger together with Dobrynin asked for the convening of the Security Council to propose another cease-fire resolution. But another obstacle had surfaced in Egypt. President Sadat was in a rage. He felt cheated by the Israelis, by the United States, and also by the Soviet Union—which had promised to prevent any Israeli movement forward after the cease-fire. As a condition for agreeing to the second cease-fire resolution, he demanded that the safety of the Third Army be guaranteed, this time by both powers. He was satisfied only after a secret message from President Nixon promised him that the Third Army would not be destroyed or starved.

On October 24, by a vote of 14 to 0 (with the usual abstention of the People's Republic of China) the council adopted Resolution 339, which tied up the loopholes that had remained in Resolution 338. This time arrangements for the supervision of the cease-fire were clearly determined. Another new element was a demand that the forces return to where they stood at 6:55 P.M., October 22—a demand that could apply only to Israel.

In the afternoon hours of October 24 the first group of UN observers—12 of them—left from Cairo. At approximately 7:00 P.M. the advance party met with Israeli units at an axis on the Cairo road. They planted the blue UN flag in the ground—and so established the first border point between the two armies.

But the shooting had not yet stopped, and the temperature in the international political arena soon reached the boiling point. Sadat now firmly demanded from Brezhnev payment of the bill that Kosygin had signed during the war. He also demanded payment from Nixon. The key to payment of the bills was in the hands of Israel. However, events now were moving at top speed. Reports soon reached Washington of a high alert of Soviet units in Eastern Europe, with seven Soviet airborne divisions on standby. Direct Soviet military intervention in the Middle East loomed as a real possibility.

At the UN an initiative of the so-called neutral countries was developing. It would have authorized the dispatch of a Soviet-American force to supervise the cease-fire. Dobrynin told Kissinger that Israel was continuing to violate the Security Council resolution, and therefore he would support the initiative and might even lead it. Kissinger told Dobrynin that the United States would veto it. A joint force of the two superpowers, he argued, was a time bomb that could lead to a superpower conflict.

In the evening hours a telegram from the Kremlin arrived at the White House. It contained two major points:

• The cease-fire must be implemented immediately, and in order to ensure it the dispatch of a joint U.S.-Soviet force was necessary.

• If that was not acceptable, "we would be forced to consider urgently taking one-sided steps in order to stop the violations of the cease-fire by Israel."

Kissinger was in a delicate position. On the one hand he wanted the same thing as Moscow. He opposed the encirclement of the Third Army and the continuation of the war and was angry about Israel's continuing offensive. But he was constrained by two factors: having encouraged them, he could not now stop the Israelis or erase their achievement with the kind of brutal speed Moscow was urging, and he was absolutely unwilling to countenance any one-sided action by the Soviet Union.

He had to act simultaneously on two levels. To

the Israelis there were more threats that they would lose the protection and support of the United States if the offensive continued. The Russians he answered in their own coin. With the concurrence of the president he ordered an alert of U.S. units, including the nuclear-supplied Strategic Air Command.

In order to stress the determination of the United States "to go to the brink" over a direct Soviet intervention in the Middle East, Kissinger went on TV and mentioned the possibility of nuclear war:

> We possess, each of us, nuclear arsenals capable of annihilating humanity. We, both of us, have a special duty to see to it that confrontations are kept within bounds that do not threaten civilized life.

Both threats worked. The Kremlin instructed Malik to drop the proposal for an American-Soviet force. The alternative emerged as Security Council Resolution 340, which established a UN Emergency Force "to be combined of units of member nations of the UN except for permanent members of the Security Council." UN Secretary General Waldheim immediately ordered the UN force in Cyprus—900 Australian, Finnish, and Swedish soldiers—to leave for Cairo. He appointed Finnish Major General Ensio Siilasvuo commander of the force.

The tension evaporated, and with it the danger of a conflict between the superpowers. A day later, October 26, the alert of U.S. army units was lifted. Calm was also noticeable in Soviet army units.

Israel also took Kissinger's warnings seriously and its offensive stopped—though the Third Army was now effectively encircled. On October 25 only a few shots were heard from some Egyptian soldiers trying to reach their forces on the west bank of the canal. Soon there was silence on the southern front.

In the United States the press and the administration's critics started a post mortem on Kissinger's nuclear alert. In the Watergate atmosphere they were deeply suspicious of the authenticity of the claimed Soviet threats. But Kissinger was looking ahead. Seeing the map of the Israeli and Egyptian armies locked together on both sides of the Suez Canal, he was already contemplating the first step toward a new U.S. Mideast policy.

III

Kilometer 101: The First Step

After the shooting stopped, the two sides closely examined the three UN cease-fire resolutions. It was clear that further negotiations were necessary to implement the resolutions. Israel immediately took its traditional position—direct negotiations on the political level. Kissinger rejected this proposal out of hand, saying the Egyptians would obviously refuse. He suggested that the UN serve as intermediary.

The first contacts with the Arabs after the war might determine the character of all that followed, and therefore Israel opposed an intermediary, certainly the UN, which had demonstrated both its ineffectiveness and bias in the past.

It was Mordechai Gazit, director general of the prime minister's bureau, who came up with the idea of direct negotiations between military representatives under the "auspices" (as distinct from mediation) of the UN. His assumption was that the Egyptians would not reject this format since it had been used for the armistice talks between the two countries after the 1948 war. Kissinger was less optimistic. He believed Egypt was still not ready, psychologically or politically, for direct negotiations at any level. But since there was no better suggestion available he decided that "it won't hurt to propose it."

It was not the first or last time that Kissinger was mistaken in his evaluation of Israel's bargaining power. Sadat's positive answer reached Washington on Saturday, October 27, hours after the Israeli proposal was received in Cairo. A surprised Kissinger reported the Egyptian answer immediately to Jerusalem.

Israel had also proposed Kilometer 105 on the Cairo-Suez road as the site of the meeting. Egypt agreed and suggested that the first meeting take place without delay. It was set for Monday, October 29, at 3:00 P.M. and Israeli army units frantically began to prepare the site. After measurements were taken and the precise location settled upon, four tents were put up.

At the agreed time an army helicopter deposited Major General Aharon Yariv, the head of the Israeli delegation, at the site. But there was no trace of the Egyptians. A half hour passed, then an hour. Yariv contacted the command post of the UN Emergency Force and asked what had happened. They replied that they could not make contact with the Egyptians.

In the meantime Tel Aviv received an urgent message from the State Department: Why don't the Israelis show up for the meeting? The nervous Egyptians are waiting. In the query was the implicit suspicion that Israel was up to something.

Only after further clarification did everyone realize that the Israeli army surveyors had made a mistake and put the tents at Kilometer 101 instead of 105. The two delegations were waiting four kilometers apart, each suspecting the worst of the other.

A new starting time was set for 1:45 A.M. Tuesday, October 30, this time at Kilometer 101. Once more the Israelis were the first to arrive. The UN personnel reported that the Egyptians were on their way. Major General Yariv, a short, handsome man in his late forties, waited outside the tent in the darkness, alone with his thoughts.

Just three months earlier Yariv had retired from the army after a long and distinguished career, his last post being chief of intelligence. Of the many civilian jobs that were offered to him, he accepted the prime minister's invitation to serve as her special adviser against Arab terrorism. Then the Yom Kippur War came and Yariv was reactivated into service as a special assistant to the chief of staff. He distinguished himself by his cool handling of various assignments under great pressure. Mrs. Meir then appointed him head of the Israeli delegation to the Kilometer 101 talks. Now he contemplated the odd stroke of fate that had brought him here in the desert to meet face to face with an Egyptian general. How should he greet him? And how would the Egyptian react?

Yariv's thoughts were disturbed by the beams of approaching vehicles. The Egyptian convoy stopped close to the central tent and the head of the Egyptian delegation, Lieutenant General Abdel Ghany el-Gamasy, was the first to step out—a tall, thin man with a mustache and a serious bearing. As head of the operations branch of the Egyptian general staff, Gamasy was responsible for the planning of the war, especially the crossing of the Suez Canal, and he now enjoyed immense prestige both in and outside of Egypt.

Yariv and Gamasy walked toward each other. Spontaneously Yariv cocked his arm and saluted. Gamasy returned the salute, and then extended his arm in a handshake. They led the two delegations and the UN officials into the large tent. The Egyptians and Israelis sat facing each other on two sides of a long table, at the head of which sat a UN officer—Lieutenant Colonel Auliss Kemplenen from Finland.

Speaking in English, Yariv opened the first meeting. He welcomed the cease-fire, expressing his hope that the talks would be fruitful and that the war had been the last in the area. He then announced that Israel would allow one convoy of food to be transferred to the besieged Third Army. After that concession he moved to Israel's demands: an immediate prisoner-of-war exchange; lifting the Egyptian blockade of the straits of Bab el Mandeb; return of the bodies of soldiers killed in enemy territory. As for an Israeli retreat to the October 22 lines, he had a counterproposal: a disengagement of forces by trading banks of the canal—in effect the return of the two armies to the lines before October 6.

Gamasy, on the other hand, wanted to discuss the principles of UN Security Council resolutions 338 and 339. He claimed that Egypt had stopped shooting at the hour agreed upon in the first resolution, but in the two days following October 22 changes occurred in the positions of the two sides.

Interestingly, Gamasy did not raise the question of specific Israeli cease-fire violations. He never said that Israel improved its position on October 23 and 24. He spoke only of a general change in positions and the implementation of resolutions 338 and 339, requiring a return to the October 22 lines.

This was no coincidence. He had received clear instructions not to admit the extent of the Israeli advance on the twenty-third and twenty-fourth, with the encirclement of the Egyptian Third Army. President Sadat did not want to allow anything to undermine the euphoria of victory which still prevailed in Cairo. Sadat's gambit was made clear in his press conference of October 31:

> The Israelis say that the Third Army is encircled. But you must know that the major part of this army is west of the canal and not east. The story of the encirclement was used according to the methods of Goebbels. They [the Israelis] have put me in a dilemma: Should I wipe out their force, which is

squeezed between the two parts of the [Third] army?
Or should I obey the cease-fire?

At Kilometer 101, however, they weren't discussing
supplying food and water to the Israeli force but to
the Egyptians. Yariv was only willing to discuss arrangements for the one convoy of supplies to the
encircled army. Gamasy insisted on speaking about
regular, ongoing supply arrangements, which he
claimed was provided for in the cease-fire agreements.
Finally, however, Gamasy agreed to discuss the technical arrangements for the one convoy of trucks which
Israel had offered.

After this problem was disposed of, Yariv demanded
that Egypt hand over a list of Israeli prisoners at the
next meeting. Gamasy couldn't promise anything but
said he would check.

The two generals then started to bargain like mer-
chants at an oriental bazaar. Yariv asked that Israeli
army units be allowed to search for bodies in territory
being held by Egypt. Gamasy said he would have to
wait until the establishment of a line of UN posts
on the Cairo-Suez road. In other words, Israel would
get nothing until regular supplies were arranged for
the soldiers of the besieged army and the city of Suez.

When Gamasy asked whether Red Cross planes
would be allowed to fly over Israeli territory to take
out the wounded soldiers of the Third Army, Yariv
replied by inquiring about the fate of the wounded
Israeli soldiers. Gamasy claimed there was a difference
between the wounded soldiers of the Third Army and
the wounded Israeli prisoners. His wounded soldiers
were not prisoners of war, he said. But Yariv insisted
that the issue required mutuality—wounded for
wounded.

Yariv and Gamasy clearly needed further instructions and also more authority to explore possibilities.
They decided to adjourn the first meeting without

making any decisions. The horde of journalists waiting outside the tent were given the following announcement at 3:50 A.M.: "The UN proposed a meeting between representatives of the Israeli and Egyptian armies under the auspices of the UN. Both sides agreed and the meeting took place."

Three hours later the first convoy of Egyptian trucks arrived. In accord with procedures agreed on by Yariv and Gamasy the cargo started to move to the Third Army. Israel also decided that day to answer Red Cross requests and transferred 200 containers of plasma to the hospital in Suez.

At the second meeting, that afternoon, Gamasy began to explore the Israeli reaction to a more comprehensive disengagement of forces. Egypt was not insisting on a precise drawing of the October 22 lines, provided that movement of the Israeli army would open up a free path to the Third Army and the city of Suez. The Egyptian scenario was as follows: First step, an Israeli retreat more or less to the October 22 lines. Second step, an Israeli retreat from the west bank of the canal to a line in the Sinai, probably to the Mitla and Gidi passes. Third step, an additional Israeli retreat in the Sinai to the El Arish-Ras Muhammed line.

Gamasy's argument was that in any event, Israel would sooner or later have to retreat into the depths of the Sinai. Why then, he asked Yariv, move the Egyptian army from the east bank to the west only to have to move it back again?

Israel on the other hand obviously saw its presence on the west bank of the canal as a bone in Egypt's throat. The price of removing that bone would be as high as possible.

Time was pressing on Egypt. The Egyptian general staff was flooded with urgent pleas from the Third Army commanders and the city of Suez for food, water, and medical supplies. Egypt was in no position to force Israel back militarily; therefore, it soon gave up on a retreat to the October 22 lines. Instead, at the second meeting, Gamasy was urgently demanding a corridor through the Israeli lines to the Third Army and the city of Suez. To emphasize the seriousness of the situation, Egypt started making threats. If there was no supply corridor, then, feeling itself pushed into a corner, it would be forced to open the war again.

Yariv had no authority to agree to Gamasy's demand but he was able to tell Gamasy that whether the discussion was about October 22 lines, a corridor, or a more comprehensive disengagement, nothing could happen before the problem of the prisoners was dealt with.

The Israeli government was under intense domestic pressure on the prisoner issue. Israel had given Egypt the list of prisoners it held, had allowed the Red Cross to visit them, had transferred medicines and plasma to the city of Suez and the Third Army. In return Egypt had given nothing. Israel had more than 6,000 Egyptian prisoners. Egypt had only a couple of hundred Israeli prisoners. Logic demanded that Egypt be even more interested than Israel in a quick settlement of this issue, but the Egyptians were using it as a bargaining card for its other demands.

Therefore, Israel had been forced to declare that it would allow no wounded Egyptian soldiers to be evacuated from the Third Army until Egypt met the following minimal conditions: turning over the list of Israeli prisoners and allowing them Red Cross visits, a quick release of all wounded prisoners, and a firm timetable for the exchange of all prisoners.

Gamasy continued to insist on the distinction between the wounded Israeli prisoners of war and the wounded soldiers of the besieged Third Army, who, he said, deserved preferred treatment. It was a distinction that Yariv could not see. The Egyptians were refusing, he argued, an exchange of wounded prisoners of war. On the other hand they were demanding that Israel should agree to the evacuation of wounded Egyptian soldiers still on active status.

Gamasy soon had to acknowledge the absurdity of his position; he and Yariv then agreed on a draft proposal:

1. Israel would allow the evacuation of wounded soldiers of the Third Army, would return wounded Egyptian prisoners of war, and allow a supply of medical supplies to the city of Suez.

2. Egypt would release all wounded Israeli prisoners of war, hand over a list of all prisoners, and allow Red Cross visits to Israeli prisoners.

After a long session the generals became hungry. Yariv and Gamasy left the tent together to take a break. One of the guards eavesdropped on the following conversation:

> Yariv: I suggest that we have something to eat or else we will starve.
> Gamasy: I'm not hungry. I'll only have something to drink.
> Yariv: If you don't eat you'll get tired.
> Gamasy: I'm used to it. I don't eat much. That's why I'm so skinny.
> Yariv: That way you'll live longer.
> Gamasy: On the other hand, I drink coffee and smoke cigarettes and that's very bad.
> Yariv: Why don't you stop? I smoke only cigars. It's better for the health.
> Gamasy: I gave up already. I tried a few times to stop but didn't succeed. So be it. I'm reconciled that I will live till the end of my days with this sin.

Jerusalem approved the draft proposal except for one point: instead of evacuation of all wounded soldiers of the Third Army, it would only allow out the severely wounded. (According to the Red Cross there were 75 severely wounded soldiers in the Third Army area.) Israel demanded that Egypt also immediately return an Israeli pilot, Dan Avidan, who had been in Egyptian captivity since he was shot down during the fighting along the Suez Canal in 1970.

That night Egypt relayed to Israel, through the UN, its agreement in principle to the proposal that had been worked out in the tent. The details, said Egypt, should be finalized between Yariv and Gamasy in the meeting scheduled for October 31.

Before the next meeting Lieutenant General Gamasy was appointed to the additional post of assistant for political affairs to the minister of war. Yariv realized that Gamasy's new appointment was not merely a pat on the back. The intention was to bestow political authority upon Gamasy, and by extension the whole Egyptian delegation. At the previous meeting Yariv had said that a separation-of-forces agreement should be handled at the political level. Egypt obviously hoped that by giving Gamasy a political title the separation-of-forces issue could be discussed at Kilometer 101. Israel had made it clear that "political level" meant at least the involvement of cabinet ministers, but Yariv was authorized to discuss the subject, and they had already been doing so in general terms.

Egypt now had another concrete proposal: an Israeli retreat to 35 kilometers east of the canal with the Egyptian front line established 10 kilometers east of the canal. Between the two lines would be a UN buffer zone. On either side of the buffer zone would be demilitarized areas whose depth would be determined by negotiations.

Yariv could not make an official response but it was nonetheless a significant development. It was the first time that Egypt agreed to the principle that its forces on the east bank of the canal would be thinned out. In fact, Egypt at this stage demonstrated greater generosity than President Sadat would show at the beginning of the Kissinger shuttle in January 1974. Gamasy even said it would be possible that there would be no tanks and missiles on the east bank of the canal—only mechanized infantry. There was only one thing which Egypt regarded as non-negotiable—an Egyptian presence on the east bank. Egypt would have found it impossible psychologically and politically to reconcile itself to giving up its presence in the Sinai after its soldiers had fought their way across the canal.

It was then back to the subject of the wounded prisoners. They had an agreement in principle, but there was still quibbling on details. They argued about the definition of the "seriously" wounded and whether they should be certified by Red Cross doctors. Finally they agreed and asked the UN to establish a timetable for the exchange.

Then Gamasy announced that he had brought along a surprise for Yariv. It was the Israeli pilot Dan Avidan, who was turned over in an emotional ceremony.

During one of the breaks Yariv and Gamasy took a short walk in the desert. Strolling side by side like two tourists enjoying the view, their conversation turned to friendly bantering. The Egyptian general suggested that they wrap it all up right there. There could be a Geneva conference, but the real negotiations would be between them, Gamasy said. But Israel had to retreat, to evacuate the whole of Sinai.

What about Sharm el Sheik? asked Yariv.

Gamasy said: maybe something international, and then there will be peace.

Yariv, who knew the nuances of the Arab language, wanted to know if Gamasy meant *sulkh* or *saalam*. (*Sulkh* means a peace of reconciliation and forgiveness. *Saalam* means a state of no war, or nonbelligerency.)

Gamasy smiled and told Yariv that he meant

saalam. The *sulkh* would come only after many years. On the spot Yariv suggested a meeting between Sadat and Golda Meir. Gamasy did not oppose it in principle but said they should first finish the business at Kilometer 101 and afterward that would be possible. The two generals then returned to the tent, disagreeing cordially all along the way.

At the next meeting at Kilometer 101 Yariv was absent. He was with the prime minister in Washington.

The initiative for the visit to Washington had come from the prime minister. The main purpose was to give President Nixon a substantial list of military items needed to put the army back on its feet. Though she did not expect the Americans to give her everything, she did not expect insurmountable difficulties. After all, the man in the White House was someone with whom she had established a good relationship in recent years. And as a moral justification for her requests she still had the Israeli decision, practically dictated by the United States, not to start the war first.

Kissinger also had an interest in talking to the prime minister, but on an entirely different matter. He knew the purpose of Mrs. Meir's visit and he expected a quid pro quo. The situation at Kilometer 101 was causing him great concern and he wanted more give in the Israeli position.

Kissinger needed the Israeli concessions, he believed, to protect his growing investment in President Sadat. Kissinger perceived that the Egyptian president held the keys that would open doors for the United States in the Middle East. During the negotiations for the cease-fire Kissinger had heard pleasant tunes from Sadat, proclaiming his honest desire for tranquillity in the area. Kissinger had already responded to the new songs of peace with several assurances made directly to Cairo.

Israel's leaders did not understand at that time why the encirclement of the Third Army was of such concern to Kissinger. Only later did they learn that in Moscow Kissinger had promised that the Third Army would not be encircled. Israel's refusal to collaborate in a promise it did not know of brought a furious message from Sadat. Kissinger then went to the White House and the result was a message from Nixon to Sadat containing a further promise that the United States would open the road to the Third Army for Egypt. In any event, the message said, the United States would not allow Israel to starve out the besieged Egyptian force.

Kissinger had also already let Sadat know that if territories were what the Egyptians wanted then only with the help of America, not the Soviet Union, would they be able to get them. It was not the first time that the Americans made such a promise to Cairo. It had been done in May 1970 when Joseph Sisco said to President Gamal Abdel Nasser: "You can get almost anything you want from the Soviet Union—but territories you can get only from us." With Nasser the United States ran into a stone wall. Sadat, however, was a good listener. As Kissinger had decided to invest in Sadat, so Sadat was now deciding to invest in Kissinger. After all, what did he have to lose? Moscow would always receive him back with open arms.

Thus, as reports on the slow bargaining at Kilometer 101 came in, Kissinger paced nervously around his office in the State Department. From time to time he would throw out remarks about generals who knew how to fight but didn't know how to talk. After he lost hope that Yariv would open the road to the Third Army, he called the Israeli general "arrogant and boastful." Nothing but more war, Kissinger decided, would come out of the tent at Kilometer 101 and so he waited impatiently for Golda Meir.

From the outbreak of the war Mrs. Meir had lived on too many cigarettes and too much black coffee with too few hours of sleep. When her plane landed in Washington on Wednesday night, October 31, in addition to general fatigue she was suffering from severe indigestion. As if things weren't bad enough for her, there were front-page pictures in the American press that day of President Nixon and Ismail Fahmy, Sadat's special envoy, embracing on the White House lawn.

Her turn at the White House came early the following morning. It began cordially enough with Nixon welcoming her as an old friend. He was full of words of solidarity and sympathy for her people's recent trials. He was also generous with praise for her own firm stand.

Then the two politicians got down to practicalities. Nixon put his hand on Mrs. Meir's arm to soften the impact of his words, and he repeated America's guarantee for the existence of Israel, but he made two jolting points: an appropriate foundation for peace in the Middle East had been created, but Israel would have to pay for it with territories; and the United States would not allow Israel to destroy the Third Army. Nixon added that he could not go through another dangerous exercise such as the one with the Russians on October 24. "I can't do it every day," he said.

Mrs. Meir understood clearly. The United States would not aid Israel if fighting were resumed as a result of the Third Army affair. In order to strengthen this point Nixon repeated, this time orally, the written warning he had cabled her a few days earlier: if a resolution was introduced at the Security Council calling for an Israeli retreat to the October 22 lines the United States would veto it only if Israel opened a supply corridor to the besieged army. This was not a theoretical possibility. Nixon told her that a proposal for UN action was in Ismail Fahmy's briefcase when he arrived in Washington, but the president and Kissinger convinced him to wait for the results of their conversations with the Israeli prime minister.

The president did not insist on an immediate reaction. He refrained from getting into a long argument with her. That job was left to Henry Kissinger, who so far had merely been staring at the walls and, from time to time, cleaning his glasses with extraordinary energy.

Kissinger got his opportunity with the prime minister later that day. He got to the point at once. He wanted a path to the Third Army, and not just a path, but a road under the control of Egypt or at least the UN. In any event, he hammered away incessantly, it had to be out of Israel's control. Anything less than that would be unacceptable to Sadat.

Before dealing with the corridor, Mrs. Meir insisted on going back to his meeting in Moscow. If Kissinger had consulted with her before agreeing to the cease-fire this whole messy affair could have been avoided, she said. Kissinger repeated the tale of "technical interference with the communications system." Mrs. Meir reacted with a facial grimace as if to say: "Who are you trying to sell this fantastic story to?" She implied that Kissinger's behavior in such an important matter gave Israel more than sufficient cause not to put its trust in him or the administration he represented.

That sent Kissinger up the wall. He lashed out, "If there is no understanding and mutual trust between us, we have nothing to talk about. Let Simcha [Dinitz] and Joe [Sisco] talk."

The meeting ended acrimoniously. That evening the prime minister held a press conference. Replying to a question on her meeting with Kissinger, she said with a straight face, "There was no discussion on the question of a corridor to the Third Army."

In the meantime, that day, there was a fourth meeting at Kilometer 101, with Yariv's place taken by Major General Israel Tal. The discussion was on how to implement the exchange of the wounded prisoners. Tal suggested that the Israeli wounded be transferred all in one group because of their small number while the Egyptians would be transferred in several groups. But Gamasy objected. He finally admitted that the reason was not because of lack of trust in Israel, as Tal thought. He explained that President Sadat could not allow it to appear to the Egyptian public that all the Israeli wounded had been released while all the Egyptian wounded were not yet back, even though the time difference was only a few hours.

Tal showed understanding for Gamasy's problem and suggested that they divide the Israeli wounded into two groups. The first group would leave Cairo at the same time the first Egyptian group left for Cairo. The second group of Israeli wounded would leave at the same time as the last group of Egyptian wounded.

Tal's formula was finally accepted.

As expected, Kissinger calmed down after his outburst and met with Golda Meir again later that night. He seems to function best at those late night meetings, often wearing down the opposition with his limitless energy. But in Mrs. Meir, indigestion and all, he had more than a worthy opponent.

She opened the meeting on the attack. Before she would let the Third Army go, she said, she wanted to see all the Israeli prisoners back home. It was not a favor she was asking but a right provided by the Geneva convention. How could she explain to her people giving supplies to the Egyptian army while Israeli soldiers were still in Egyptian captivity?

Kissinger assured her that as soon as the corridor was open there would be no problem agreeing to an exchange of prisoners. Mrs. Meir would not budge. Then, settling herself comfortably in her armchair, she began a lecture that had been heard by every statesman who ever met with her. It covered the history of Judaism, Zionism, and the state of Israel, starting with the exodus from Egypt, through the Maccabees and Bar Kokba to the Russian pogroms and the Holocaust. Kissinger, who had heard the lecture before, had to listen all over again. There was simply nothing to be done to stop the flow of words from the old lady.

When Mrs. Meir finished Kissinger launched into his own peroration. Vividly he described to the prime minister all the terrible dangers that Israel would be facing if Mrs. Meir would not give in. "I do not say you are not right but I describe the realities for you," he explained. "The whole world is against you. Europe, Japan, the oil boycott. If you do not give the Egyptians a corridor to the Third Army, the Russians will come and do it with their helicopters. What will you do? Will you shoot at them? And what do you think the United States will do?"

He went on: The United States could not allow a one-sided Soviet action. It would turn the Russians into the heroes of the Arab world. In order to prevent it the United States would have to send its own helicopters loaded with food to the Third Army. Kissinger made one final point that would become a refrain heard in all future meetings: "Even the administration in Washington is against you. I am your only friend. But you have to help me to help you."

The meeting ended inconclusively with the prime minister stubbornly insisting on the priority of a prisoner-of-war exchange. Mrs. Meir reported to Jerusalem. The cabinet convened for a discussion and unanimously voted full backing for her stand.

In the meantime Defense Secretary Schlesinger was bluntly telling the visiting Israeli delegation that the extent of military aid contemplated by the United States was directly linked to Israel's willingness to cooperate with the administration in the political developments to come in the Middle East.

Mrs. Meir saw Kissinger again on Saturday evening, November 3. First Kissinger put on a repeat performance about the horrors that would confront Israel if she did not relent. Then, referring to his coming visit to the Middle East, he complained, "You are not giving me anything to go to Cairo with. I have nothing to offer them." Her stubbornness, he stressed, would also hurt Israeli interests. He reminded her of his expertise on prisoners of war acquired in his negotiations with the North Vietnamese. If results were wanted she could not simply rely on what was written in the Geneva convention, which made no impression on anyone. He too had been forced to make concessions, and if Mrs. Meir wanted to see the Israeli prisoners she had to bend somewhat. Kissinger defined the problem very simply and clearly: "The question is whether you want justice, or you want the prisoners."

All of Mrs. Meir's instincts rebelled against Kissinger's linkage of the prisoners' fate with political questions. But for all her stubbornness Golda Meir was not an impractical woman. She had no basis for arguing with Kissinger's definition of reality. Also, her conscience had weighed heavily on her from the start of the war and she could not now bear the additional load of the prisoners.

So she relented, at least some of the way. She would allow a corridor to the Third Army, she finally said, but the corridor had to be completely controlled by Israel. A UN inspection post could be set up at its starting point.

Kissinger grabbed the concession and went for

more. He concealed his satisfaction and said that Egypt would not agree. (Kissinger had already promised President Sadat an Egyptian-controlled corridor—something Mrs. Meir did not know.)

At this point Yariv broke in, saying that Kissinger was incorrectly evaluating Egypt's bargaining power. Egypt would be willing to pay a very high price for the corridor. The moment Israel gave Egypt control of the corridor, both Israel and the United States would lose their main bargaining card. And what would they use in further negotiations? Therefore it was necessary, said Yariv, to distinguish between giving the Egyptians some access to their Third Army and giving them physical control of the corridor.

Kissinger was skeptical. But Yariv continued. He argued that the moment Egypt got control of the corridor you were in fact giving them more than a corridor. You would remove the siege of the Third Army and therefore there would be no pressure on Egypt to make concessions. Kissinger was not convinced. He refused to bother himself with hypothetical consequences. He had given Sadat a promise and he intended to try to deliver.

To strengthen Kissinger's leverage on Israel, Sadat was also stepping up the pressure. At the end of the week he summoned the leaders of Syria, Kuwait, Saudi Arabia, Iraq, and Algeria to an emergency meeting to create the impression of preparations for drastic action. The Arab media drummed up threats of renewed fighting. Without any apparent cause a blackout was declared in Cairo and nine other districts.

Egypt also refused to carry out the agreement worked out at Kilometer 101 on the exchange of wounded prisoners. Suddenly Israel was told this problem had become political and linked with "other matters"—meaning the results of Mrs. Meir's conversation in Washington. It was clear that Sadat had decided not to make any move until he knew what the United States was able to get out of Israel. Egypt also proposed that the next meeting at Kilometer 101 be delayed till November 6, or after the results of the conversations in Washington were known.

On Sunday, November 4, the prime minister was hoping to rest up at Blair House, the official residence for visiting heads of state. But the phone began ringing early in the morning. The first call was from presidential assistant Alexander Haig. His message could be summed up in one line: "The president is furious." Mrs. Meir had no doubt that Kissinger was behind the call. Later Kissinger's friend Nelson Rockefeller also called. "Please don't be stubborn," he pleaded. "The president and Henry want it for your own good. It's the only way."

The only words of encouragement for the visiting prime minister came from ex-Supreme Court Justice Arthur Goldberg and AFL-CIO President George Meany. They told her not to give in.

Golda Meir returned to Israel on November 5 without adding one bit to the concessions she had already made. Kissinger flew to Cairo a day later.

The mood of the secretary of state was pessimistic as he landed at Cairo Airport on November 6, 1973. He feared that when he explained the Israeli formula for supply to the Third Army, Sadat would blow up. Kissinger assumed he would then have to put more pressure on Israel.

On his first night in the Egyptian capital he had a short meeting in the Hilton Hotel with Fahmy, who had recently been appointed foreign minister. The next morning at the meeting with the president, in which the two were alone for three hours, Kissinger learned how wrong his evaluation of Sadat's eagerness to reach an agreement was.

Kissinger explained the Israeli refusal to give up control over the corridor. Sadat was disappointed and tried to get more. Kissinger then argued that Golda Meir's government was simply not in a position politically to give more at this time and stay in power. He could go to Israel and try for more but he doubted that he would be successful and it would take up valuable time. Egypt, he argued, should be realistic and take what it could get now. In any event, looming on the horizon was a disengagement of forces that would include a more substantial Israeli retreat.

To Kissinger's surprise Sadat agreed almost immediately. That afternoon State Department spokesman Robert McCloskey called in the reporters to tell them the two main results of the meeting:

• A renewal of diplomatic relations between the United States and Egypt (they had been broken following the Six-Day War) and an exchange of ambassadors within two weeks.

• Under Secretary Joseph Sisco and Harold Saunders, the Middle East expert of the National Security Council, were going to Israel immediately.

The journalists didn't need any more. It was clear to them that Kissinger had reached an agreement with Sadat on a formula that had a more than even chance of being accepted by Israel.

Sisco and Saunders flew to Tel Aviv via Cyprus and upon arrival drove straight to a meeting with Mrs. Meir, Dayan, Eban, Allon, Elazar, and Yariv. After the meeting, Golda Meir convened the cabinet about 11:00 P.M. to deal with the proposals brought by Sisco.

Though Sadat had agreed to Israeli control of the corridor, the proposal spoke of three UN inspection posts: one near Kilometer 101, another at the outskirts of the city of Suez, and the third at the waterline facing the Third Army. Mrs. Meir remembered well that in her conversations in Washington she had consented to only one inspection post for the UN.

The wording of the proposal did not ensure that the supplies to the city of Suez and the Third Army would contain no military equipment. There was a reference to the October 22 lines. The cabinet instructed Mrs. Meir to demand changes in line with these reservations.

Next morning, November 8, after visiting the Pyramids, Kissinger flew to Amman. The plan was for Sisco and Saunders to rejoin the American party in the Jordanian capital with Israel's consent to the proposal in hand. But when Sisco received news of the results of the previous evening's cabinet meeting he called Kissinger immediately. The secretary of state was boiling. He regarded the Israeli reservations as pointless quibbling that could turn his triumphant trip into a complete failure. He immediately sent off two messages. The one to Mrs. Meir said that if Israel did not accept the proposal, it would be responsible for sabotaging the whole agreement. The second went to President Nixon, asking him to intervene. The president lost no time and sent a message to the prime minister almost identical in contents to Kissinger's.

The presidential message carried a lot of weight, but the problem of inspection posts remained. At another meeting with Sisco that day it was discussed heatedly, with Sisco blaming Mrs. Meir for violating the understanding that had been reached in Washington. Mrs. Meir threw the same accusation at Kissinger. After tempers cooled down Sisco assured her that the inspection posts were aimed at examining the contents of the supplies and did not challenge Israeli sovereignty over the road itself. Israel would also be able to participate in examining the Egyptian supply convoys.

Kissinger concluded his visit to Amman, with King Hussein flying him to the airport in a helicopter. His next stop was Riyadh.

In the meantime the Israeli cabinet met again. As

on October 22 and other days to come, their sense of lack of choice finally pushed aside doubts and hesitations. There was still a need for arms, lots of arms, and there was still need for diplomatic support for a long time. Only Dayan expressed any reservations. The clauses of the agreement were too insufficiently detailed for his taste, especially on the subject of exchange of prisoners. He said that Israel should insist on a firm timetable. But Mrs. Meir and the other ministers accepted Kissinger's explanation that it was the very lack of specificity that allowed the coming together of Egypt and Israel. Every attempt to discuss details at this stage might run the delicate agreement aground. It was preferable that the details be worked out after the signing, Kissinger argued.

The government then officially consented to what soon became known as the six-point agreement:

1. Egypt and Israel agreed to observe scrupulously the cease-fire called for by the UN Security Council.

2. Both sides agreed that discussion between them would begin immediately to settle the question of the return to the October 22 positions in the framework of agreement on the disengagement and separation of forces under the auspices of the UN.

3. The town of Suez was to receive daily supplies of food, water, and medicine. All wounded civilians in the town of Suez were to be evacuated.

4. There would be no impediment to the movement of nonmilitary supplies to the east bank of the canal.

5. The Israeli checkpoints on the Cairo-Suez road would be replaced by UN checkpoints. At the Suez end of the road Israeli officers could participate with the UN to supervise the nonmilitary nature of the cargo at the bank of the canal.

6. As soon as the UN checkpoints were established on the Cairo-Suez road there would be an exchange of all prisoners of war, including the wounded.

Satisfied with his success Kissinger flew off to another arena of triumph—Peking. While heavily engaged in conversations with the Chinese leadership, a message arrived from Jerusalem: difficulties regarding the agreement. The Israeli government requires further clarification.

What happened was that in contacts with Egypt and the UN it was discovered that there was still disagreement about two points:

• Israel insisted, on the basis of Sisco's clarification, that the entire road would remain under its control and sovereignty. But the UN interpretation was that the road axis would be under its control.

• The Egyptians wanted a broad interpretation of "medical aid" to the city of Suez that would include, for example, medical personnel. Israel opposed this, saying that it would not be able to verify whether these were actually medical people.

Then there was another sticking point that did not appear in the agreement. In a special cabinet meeting on Saturday, November 10, Israel demanded that the Egyptian blockade of the straits of Bab el Mandeb (which cut off the sea route to Eilat) be lifted.

Kissinger met immediately with his aides and sent Jerusalem the required clarifications. The supply road would be under complete Israeli control. Medical supplies would not include medical personnel. The lifting of the blockade could not be included in the agreement but he was promised by President Sadat that it would in fact be lifted. Jerusalem was reassured. The last obstacle to the signing of the agreement had been removed.

There was no holiday spirit at the signing ceremony on Sunday, November 11, at Kilometer 101. The only indication of anything exceptional were the dozens of journalists who had breached the cordon around the main tent. The ceremony was marked by petty disagreements, for example, whether the flags of each country should be flown or only the UN flag.

Yariv was smiling and greeted the journalists, but Gamasy was demonstratively somber. Clearly he had instructions not to behave as if he applied any significance to the agreement beyond technical military arrangements in carrying out the cease-fire.

Inside the tent the atmosphere was practical and cool. As always the two delegations sat facing each other. Siilasvuo, the commander of the UN Emergency Force, was seated at the end of the table. His position was defined in an addendum to the agreement in which the sides agreed that they "would meet in the regular place at Kilometer 101 under the auspices of the commander of the UN Emergency Force to sign the agreement and to discuss its implementation."

Without saying anything, Siilasvuo gave the two delegations the copies of the agreement. Yariv, Gamasy, and Siilasvuo each signed three copies in silence. Siilasvuo then got the consent of Yariv and Gamasy to let the photographers in.

Disagreements over the implementation of the agreement began almost immediately after the signing. The UN role under the six-point agreement was viewed differently by Siilasvuo and Israel. Siilasvuo felt he was authorized to build, without any delay, the inspection posts on the Cairo-Suez road, and that movement of Israeli army vehicles on the road would be prohibited. Siilasvuo's interpretations stood in stark contradiction to the clarifications of Henry Kissinger. Yariv argued there was nothing said in the agreement about banning the movement of vehicles. Siilasvuo did not deny this but he felt it was consistent with the spirit of section 5. Yariv answered that as much as he tried he could not find that "spirit." Siilasvuo was forced to retreat. Probably he just wanted to make things easier for the UN forces by removing foreign vehicles from the road. But it was an unnecessary and futile attempt that merely resulted in spreading distrust.

As for building the inspection posts, Israel read sections 5 and 6 of the agreement together. There was no way to separate the two. The inspection posts should not be established before discussing arrangements for the exchange of prisoners. General Siilasvuo, completely disregarding section 6, interpreted his assignment to establish the checkpoints as unlinked to other clauses.

Mrs. Meir and Dayan were furious. They regarded Siilasvuo's behavior as an attempt to circumvent the agreement that had been achieved with so much effort. And there was something else. At the first meeting on implementation Siilasvuo had asked the sides to retire to their own tents so that he could conduct discussions with them separately. Israel had put much effort into getting the Arabs to recognize the principle of direct negotiations. It was the only positive element Israel saw in Resolution 338, and at the previous sessions at Kilometer 101 Israeli and Egyptian officers were in face-to-face discussions. Now a UN general suddenly disrupted this positive achievement. For agreeing to this procedure Yariv was severely reprimanded, with clear instructions not to let it happen again.

At the next meeting when Siilasvuo began his opening remarks, Yariv interrupted him and said he had come to talk to Gamasy, not to Siilasvuo. Siilasvuo stuttered that in the agreement the auspices were his. Yariv interrupted again: auspices yes, intermediary no. He would speak directly to Gamasy and that's it. From then on the Finnish general made do with the role of chairman.

But the implementation negotiations were dragging, and on Tuesday, November 13, the prime minister announced in the Knesset that as long as the prisoners were not returned from Egypt the UN checkpoints would not be put up and not one gram of food or water would be transferred to the Third Army.

The message got through to Cairo. There were also other messages coming through from the city of Suez: no food, no water, no medicines, not even matches. On Wednesday, November 14, therefore, Gamasy and Yariv were able to agree on the following points:

1. Egypt would immediately give Israel a list of all Israeli prisoners of war.

2. Exchange of all prisoners of war would begin one day later, at 8:00 A.M., and would conclude within six to eight days.

3. Supply to the city of Suez would be the sole responsibility of the UN. For that purpose a checkpoint would be established near the train station in Suez.

4. Supplies would also be transferred to the Third Army. The amount of supplies to the Third Army and Suez would be 250 tons, including water.

5. Israel would immediately evacuate the checkpoints and turn them over to the UN.

Yariv and Gamasy shook hands warmly. Then the Egyptian general handed over the list of prisoners. The two came out of the tent. Yariv tapped the shoulder of his Egyptian colleague, saying: "You must remember that I want to be your guest in Cairo." And he added, "You must be my guest in Israel." Gamasy answered with a wide smile: "I hope so."

At 11:33 A.M. Thursday, November 15, a DC-6 leased by the Red Cross landed at Lod Airport. It carried the first group of 26 wounded Israeli prisoners. They were welcomed by a huge banner draped across the airport building: "Welcome back, heroes of Israel." Six women soldiers approached the ramp holding 26 bouquets of flowers. The first to mount the ramp was Mrs. Nina Katzir, the wife of Israel's president, Ephraim Katzir. A short distance behind her were Dayan and the chief of staff.

Several minutes later the prisoners started coming down the ramp, some walking unaided, some on crutches or on stretchers. The large crowd cheered for a long time, and the whole country shared the moment of joy on the radio. There were still, of course, the prisoners in Syria, but no one wanted to think sad thoughts that day.

Eighteen meetings were held at Kilometer 101 before they folded up the tents. Aside from technical details arising from the six-point agreement, such as the problem of supplies and the names of some prisoners, the major discussion centered on proposals for a disengagement of forces. Yariv and Gamasy managed to narrow the gap between their positions.

Officially Israel still insisted that the two sides exchange banks of the Suez Canal and retreat to the pre-Yom Kippur War lines. The territories to be evacuated would be turned over to the UN. In other words Israel had agreed to give up most of the canal line but not to Egypt. Egypt's official position called for a general Israeli retreat to the El Arish-Ras Muhammed line—halfway across the Sinai.

But Gamasy and Yariv knew these official positions were nonstarters and they were given permission to put informal proposals on the table. Unofficially Yariv offered the following: Israel would retreat from the west bank of the canal to a depth of 10–12 kilometers in the Sinai in return for a meaningful thinning out of forces for 30 kilometers on each side of the canal. He also demanded as a quid pro quo an Egyptian commitment to open the canal with free navigation for Israeli ships and to rehabilitate the cities along the canal.

Gamasy offered the following: an Israeli retreat from the west bank of the canal to a depth of 35 kilometers in the Sinai; a 15-kilometer UN buffer zone between the forces; an area of thinned-out army forces for 10 kilometers on each side of the buffer; a detailed timetable for further Israeli retreat until the complete evacuation of the Sinai; opening of the canal and rehabilitation of the cities when the Israeli retreat reached a line 60 kilometers from the canal.

The differences between Yariv and Gamasy focused primarily on the depth of the Israeli retreat and the thinning out of the Egyptian forces. The gap was significant. Yet it should be noted that the parameters of the informal proposals were not far removed from the agreement that would be worked out through Kissinger's mediation months later. But while Yariv and Gamasy were working hard to find points of agreement and to reduce the gap, a new obstacle appeared on the scene. At Kissinger's urging, the Geneva conference was to open in December and continue after the Israeli elections. But continue with what? What would be discussed?

Kissinger's opinion was that jumping straight into peace negotiations could break up the conference very early. He looked for something less pretentious, something that had a chance of immediate success. A disengagement-of-forces agreement between Israel and Egypt seemed ideal. Therefore Kissinger lost interest in the success of the talks at Kilometer 101 and he relayed his thoughts to both governments. Kissinger even called Ambassador Dinitz to complain that Yariv was moving forward too quickly and too independently, "What is Yariv selling there? Tell him to stop," he said to Dinitz.

Two weeks after the talks at Kilometer 101 closed down, in a discussion with Israeli leaders in Jerusalem, Kissinger himself admitted how close the two sides had come to an agreement at the tent. He told the Israeli negotiating team that if he had known how far the negotiations between Yariv and Gamasy had gone, his tendency would have been to push for a quick agreement. Several of the ministers then retorted that it was he, Kissinger, who had in effect blocked the successful conclusion of the Yariv-Gamasy negotiations.

Kissinger claimed that he did not know of Yariv's progress and all that was happening at Kilometer 101, but Yariv interrupted to remind him that immediately after every meeting a detailed report was sent to the State Department.

It is true that Kissinger never told Israel explicitly not to sign an agreement at Kilometer 101. But he did let the Israelis know that he preferred that the negotiations be moved to Geneva. Kissinger's preferences carried great weight.

And so a chance that could have turned into a historic precedent was missed. After 25 years of war and hatred, two generals, an Israeli and an Egyptian, were calmly talking to each other, even developing a friendship. If they were given the chance, Yariv and Gamasy might well have been able to reach the same agreement, on their own, that Kissinger arranged with so much media fanfare months later.

But Kilometer 101 was not an entirely wasted event. Some difficult problems were solved there, such as the prisoners and the supplies. It proved the possibility of fruitful negotiations between Israeli and Egyptian officers. The warm personal relationships developed there were sincere.

The topic of visiting each other's countries has always been a source of wry humor in meetings between Israelis and Arabs. Kilometers 101 was no exception. Yariv offered personal guarantees for Gamasy's safety when he visited Israel. And Gamasy offered similar guarantees when Yariv came to tour the Pyramids, provided, of course, he didn't show up in uniform.

They even joked about which of the two of them,

Yariv or Gamasy, deserved to win the Nobel peace prize. They compromised by designating Siilasvuo. Another time the two jokingly hoped the talks might be transferred to the Hilton Hotel, only differing about whether it should be the Cairo Hilton or the Tel Aviv Hilton.

On Thursday, November 29, 1973, Yariv and Gamasy met for the last time. They reconciled themselves to the fact that they had reached a dead end. Gamasy did not hide his intense disappointment. He saw it almost as a personal failure, so much so that Yariv found it necessary to comfort him. When they shook hands and parted, Yariv said, "I do not say goodbye but only *au revoir*."

But for Yariv and Gamasy it was indeed goodbye. When the negotiations on separation of forces resumed it was under different auspices. The two generals were in other jobs and the center of the stage was taken over by Henry Kissinger and his flying shuttle.

IV
Interlude in Geneva

The basis for convening the Geneva conference was section 3 of UN Security Council Resolution 338:

> The Security Council decides that, immediately and concurrently with the cease-fire, negotiations start between the parties concerned under appropriate auspices aimed at establishing a just and durable peace in the Middle East.

Mrs. Meir had agreed that there would be a ceremonial opening at Geneva before the Israeli elections with the stipulation that there could be no substantive discussions. The question of "appropriate auspices" did not take up more than a few minutes when the conference was first broached during Kissinger's visit to Israel on October 22. Kissinger stated flatly it meant the two superpowers. He also said that while he was in Moscow he received Egypt's consent to this interpretation.

The details of the conference were first discussed at greater length during Eban's visit to Washington on November 20. Kissinger told Eban that since the cease-fire the Arabs, led by Egypt, had changed their minds about the auspices of the conference. They now wanted the UN. Eban said it was out of the question to grant the auspices to an organization in which the Arabs have an automatic majority on any subject. Kissinger said he also wasn't very happy about the Arab turnabout, and he tried to find a compromise formula. He asked whether Israel would accept Waldheim functioning solely as a host. As usual Kissinger wrapped his proposal attractively. The presence of the UN as host, he said, would neutralize the demands of African and European states to participate in the conference. Eban said he would bring the idea to his government.

Kissinger then proposed the following scenario for the conference. The first session would be held on December 11, consisting only of opening speeches by the foreign ministers defining the general policies of their governments. There would then be one working session of all the participants to determine procedures for the rest of the conference. Kissinger suggested that the working session concentrate on determining a format for the discussions of the disengagement of forces.

At that moment such discussions were still going on at Kilometer 101. Moving the talks from the tent to the conference, Kissinger explained to Eban, would bring to the conference continuity on an issue not burdened with disagreements in principle, and not linked to other sensitive issues such as the Jordanian-Palestinian question.

Eban returned to Israel on November 23, and obtained Mrs. Meir's approval. The proposals were then approved by the full cabinet on November 25. One thing the government did not approve of was the date of the conference opening. Mrs. Meir demanded December 18, and she was supported by the entire cabinet. The official reason for Israel's desire to postpone the conference for a week was that the shorter the period between the conference and the elections, the less pressure on Israel to discuss substantive questions. But there was another unstated reason: the heads of the Labor party now understood the tremendous propaganda value of the convening of the conference. The closer the opening session to election day, the greater impact it would have on the Israeli voter.

On December 13 Kissinger left on another trip to the Middle East, aimed at tying up the last loose ends in preparation for Geneva, and also to try to get the Arab oil embargo lifted. As it turned out, the loose ends were considerable. Four potential stumbling blocks remained:

• The question of auspices. The Arabs were still insisting on a conference under the auspices of the UN.

• Palestinian participation. Egypt demanded that the official invitations to the conference keep the door open for participation by the Palestinians.

• Who would send the invitations for the conference? There were three possibilities: the United States would invite Israel and the Soviet Union would invite the Arab states; the United States and the Soviet Union together would invite both sides; the secretary general of the UN would send all the invitations.

• The Israeli prisoners in Syria. This issue caused a grim mood in Israel. Persistent rumors coming out of Geneva (the Red Cross) put the number of Israeli prisoners left alive at 24 at the most. Yet Damascus refused even to turn over a list of names and allow visits from the Red Cross. Israel was not going to sit with Syria at a conference under such conditions.

Kissinger's trip started with a visit to President Boumediene of Algeria. As he would do later in Saudi Arabia, Kissinger linked progress on political moves to the lifting of the oil embargo to the United States. He used a sophisticated mix of caresses and warnings. The caress was that the United States was striving toward peace in the area—a peace that would include an Israeli retreat from most territories occupied in June

1967. Only the United States was capable of influencing Israel in that direction. But, and here came the warning, one could not expect Washington to invest so much effort in a matter so clearly in the Arab interest when the sword of oil was aimed at its neck.

Faisal and Boumediene could not disregard Kissinger's arguments. In any event they were not interested in stretching things to the danger point. But before they lifted the embargo, they said, the producing countries wanted to see some results.

This understanding with Faisal and Boumediene was an incentive to Kissinger to continue with his efforts to bring off the Geneva conference and to hurry up the disengagement of forces between Israel and Egypt. These would provide the first results the Arab countries were demanding.

On December 16 Kissinger arrived in Israel. Of the obstacles standing on the road to Geneva, he removed two relatively easily. In a private meeting with Mrs. Meir he implored her not to be stubborn regarding the role of the UN in the conference. "What do you care," he asked, "if Dr. Waldheim sits at the head of the table? It will make him happy and won't harm anyone. I promise you that his role will only be ceremonial. The United States and the Soviet Union will run the show."

Mrs. Meir was pacified. As for the invitations, Israel had wanted the Soviet Union to send it a letter, thus creating some official contact, however slight, between the two states—and perhaps the first step toward the renewal of diplomatic relations. But Mrs. Meir was made to understand that the Russians could not be forced and it was not worth torpedoing the conference over it.

The Palestinian issue was a lot more difficult. The Israeli government had taken a clear position that invitations to any other countries or groups could be sent only with the agreement of all the primary participants. In other words, Israel demanded the right to veto any invitation to the Palestine Liberation Organization. Prime Minister Meir also would not hear of any specific reference to the Palestinians in the invitations, as President Sadat had demanded.

Years of political experience taught Kissinger to distinguish between positions that could be compromised and those that couldn't. Israel's position on the Palestinians was in the second category. He telegraphed that conclusion from Jerusalem to Gromyko, who then contacted Cairo. Toward the end of the day Kissinger received the Egyptian president's reply. Sadat gave up reference to the Palestinians in the invitation, but refused to grant Israel the right to veto an invitation at a later stage. To settle the matter Kissinger called in President Nixon for help. The result arrived in Jerusalem in the form of another firm message from Nixon to Mrs. Meir: Dr. Kissinger's attempts to convene the Geneva conference are essential. Please do not sabotage them.

Equipped with Sadat's concession and Nixon's message, Kissinger proposed the following formula: "The sides agree that the question of participation of other factors in the Middle East will be discussed at the first stage of the conference." To this formula there was added a private American obligation to oppose, to the point of veto, any invitation to the PLO without Israel's consent. This obligation, put in a "memorandum of understanding," allowed Israel to accept Kissinger's formulation.

Most painful and difficult of all was the problem of the Israeli prisoners in Syria. The Israeli government itself was sharply divided on what to do. Dayan's position was that if Syria did not fulfill Israel's two minimal conditions regarding the prisoners (giving the lists and Red Cross visits), Israel should not even go to Geneva. The prime minister, however, argued that Israel should go to Geneva but not par-

ticipate in the opening session if Syria was present.
Mrs. Meir said the world, and especially the United
States, would accuse Israel of torpedoing the conference if it stayed away from Geneva over this issue.
On the other hand, there would be understanding
for Israel if it merely refused to sit in the same hall
with Syria as long as the elementary conditions were
not fulfilled. By a majority vote the cabinet accepted
Mrs. Meir's position, and this was the message conveyed to Kissinger.

The prisoner issue was an old account between
Kissinger and Golda Meir. Both during her visit in
Washington and during the negotiations on the six-
point agreement, she complained bitterly that he
had promised this matter would be taken care of without delay. Kissinger put the blame on the Russians.
He claimed that he had sent a message to Moscow
reminding the Russians that Ambassador Dobrynin
had given him his word of honor that the prisoners
would be released. He had added, he said, that at
this stage, before the beginning of the Geneva conference, Israel was only asking for a list of prisoners
held in Syria. If the Soviets are incapable of carrying
out such a minimal obligation, the message said, it
would have to influence U.S. trust in Soviet promises.
He also stressed to the Soviet Union that the United
States could not guarantee that Israel would remain
at the conference if this condition was not fulfilled and
that the United States would support Israel's position.

But although Kissinger supported the Israeli demand regarding the prisoners, he opposed the tactics of
tying together the question of the lists with the
continuation of political contacts. Syria at the time
wanted Israel to present it with a proposal for a disengagement of forces on the Golan Heights. Syrian
President Hafez al-Assad had been told of Yariv's
proposals at Kilometer 101 by Sadat. He felt insulted,

according to Kissinger, that though he had also participated in the war, he was not receiving anything, while Sadat was getting quite a bit.

Mrs. Meir disregarded this argument. Certainly, she said, Assad is not so unintelligent he doesn't understand the difference: Egypt released Israeli prisoners. Syria must at least hand over the lists according to the Geneva convention—unless, she said, the convention stipulates an exception for Assad. Kissinger replied that the Syrian president didn't give a penny for the Geneva convention. Even the Egyptian example cut no weight with him. His model was North Vietnam. Assad pointed out over and over again that the United States negotiated with the North Vietnamese for three years without receiving a list of prisoners.

Mrs. Meir and Dayan were against giving Assad any kind of proposal without the lists. Dayan said he did not believe that an Israeli proposal would soften the Syrians. He recalled that immediately after the war, Israel had offered to allow the return of 10,000 Syrian farmers to their villages on the Golan Heights, and offered to turn over to the UN two positions on Mount Hermon. Assad was not at all impressed by this proposal. Mrs. Meir added that the minute Israel offers something or accepts a proposal, Assad just ups his demands.

But Kissinger did not give up. He stressed again that if Israel wanted the prisoners and Syria's participation at the conference, it must act in a conciliatory manner. If Israel turned the whole affair into a moral question, then Assad would not feel he was under any pressure. Assad had told him that he wanted to give the lists only after the conclusion of the disengagement talks, and the prisoners themselves after the implementation of the disengagement agreement.

When Kissinger continued to press, Mrs. Meir glared at him with burning eyes:

There will be no disengagement talks before we receive the lists! There will be nothing. We will not be present in the same room with the Syrians who are torturing and slaughtering our men! It is elementary! Whether it is moral or not—it is elementary! And from a practical point of view, if Assad gets all that he wants—what would be left for negotiations?

Kissinger smiled. "Is that all that Assad wants?" he asked rhetorically. "He wants an Israeli retreat from the entire Golan Heights," Kissinger reminded everyone.

Mrs. Meir was not happy. She still felt deep bitterness, mainly toward the Soviet Union. She refused to believe, she said to Kissinger, that with all the arms that the Soviets had poured into Damascus, they could not influence Assad to hand over the lists.

Kissinger, however, was not surprised that Russia had no influence in Damascus despite its arms shipments. After several meetings with Assad he said he actually felt a certain sympathy for the Soviets. And a "senior official" in the American party described it the following way: "If there are strange creatures, they are the Syrians. I have never seen anything like it. Discussions with them are the worst diplomatic experiences I have ever known."

Kissinger continued to plead for some formula that would enable him to continue discussions with the Syrian president. Finally he was authorized to make a general declaration in Damascus to the effect that Israel was willing to enter negotiations for separation of forces with Syria, and that its position in the talks would be "logical."

One technical problem remained—the date of the opening. Sadat was ready to start immediately. Israel had no substantive reason to want a delay except for the general elections to the Israeli Knesset on December 31.

The 1973 election campaign was conducted in an atmosphere of public uncertainty unprecedented in Israel. The war had shaken the foundations of faith linking the citizens with the government. Doubts were expressed regarding the very meaning of the state and the fitness of the leadership.

This mood was also having its effects inside the party which had held power since the establishment of the state. The ruling Labor party's two most charismatic personalities, Golda Meir and Moshe Dayan, were regarded by the public as the main culprits responsible for the disaster. Now that their images were badly tarnished, rivals inside the party were emboldened to challenge their authority. The result was that as the elections approached, the party seemed to have lost its élan and was in a state of internal disarray.

Complicating the Labor party's electoral problems was the fact that it had to face a united opposition for the first time in the 25-year history of the state. Shortly before the war Major General Sharon, one of the country's most charismatic and controversial military leaders, had resigned from the army and gone into politics. Within a few months he had managed to pull together the traditionally splintered parties of the right into a new electoral bloc called the Likud. Then during the war Sharon had been called back into service and led the Israeli counterattack across the Suez Canal. The newly united party was therefore going to the polls led by the only genuine hero of the war, while the Labor party was being led by those the public regarded as responsible for the blunders of the war. The prognosis, to put it mildly, was not bright for the incumbents.

The Labor party had only one powerful issue going for it. If it could show the voter, despite its misdeeds during the war, that it provided the only chance for peace, it could hope to survive.

Kissinger, who needed the militant Likud in power

like he needed another headache, supplied the gimmick for the Labor party—the Geneva conference. If the Israeli foreign minister were seen shaking hands with Arab foreign ministers, it would not hurt Labor's electoral chances, as Kissinger had reminded Eban as early as October 22. The Likud party, of course, raised hell and demanded that the government not enter into any obligations or essential discussions before the voter had had his say.

The government had to agree to that demand of the opposition. (In fact it had already arranged with Kissinger and the Egyptians that all substantive discussions at Geneva would be put off at least until January 7.) But there was nothing to prevent Mrs. Meir from arranging that the ceremonial opening of the Geneva conference, with Israeli and Arab foreign ministers shaking hands before the TV cameras, be staged as close as possible to the Israeli elections on December 31.

A short time after the end of Kissinger's meetings in Jerusalem, the American ambassador in Beirut received a message with instructions to go to Damascus and relay Israel's message to President Assad. The ambassador did so and Assad responded as expected. On December 18, Syria officially announced that it would not participate in the conference.

That day, a letter of invitation to Geneva arrived in Jerusalem. In it, Waldheim called to Israel's attention a letter which he had received from Kissinger saying:

> The sides agreed that the conference would be under cosponsorship of the Soviet Union and the United States. The sides also agreed that the question of participation of other factors in the Middle East would be discussed in the first stage of the conference. Our hope is that you will find it possible to participate in the opening of the conference.

Waldheim's own contribution was short and modest: "I convene the conference on Friday, December 21, 1973, at 10:30 A.M., in the Palace of Nations in Geneva."

Together with the marble and the statues, many hopes had been invested in the Palace of Nations over the years. Only the physical grandeur was left. Those who had met in this majestic building had failed to prevent a cruel world war and other bloody and pointless local conflicts.

Understandably, then, there was much skepticism among the dozens of journalists from all over the world. Not many were willing to bet that the opening session of the conference would even take place. Despite the official announcement in Damascus, everyone was guessing about the Syrians' real intentions.

Plans regarding the Syrians were discussed by Eban with Kissinger and his party. Sisco proposed that Israel would sit at its table in the conference hall and would exit only if the Syrians showed up and entered. Eban would then explain the reason for his exit to the journalists waiting on the steps of the palace. The idea was promptly rejected. It was clear to the members of the Israeli delegation that such a step would be seen negatively by world public opinion. After all these years, representatives of the Arab states and the state of Israel are sitting at a peace conference —and the Israelis walk out for "some list of prisoners." The delegation would follow the instructions of the cabinet: if Syria came to Geneva, the Israeli delegation would not enter the conference hall. If Syria did not come there was no problem.

The problem of the tables also had to be taken care of before the opening. Waldheim had reported to Eban that the Egyptian delegation was opposed to having its table next to the Israelis' and had demanded that the empty Syrian table be placed between them. Eban would not hear of it. He said to Waldheim that he would not sit next to an empty table and thus emphasize the isolation of Israel. But when Eban entered the chamber on Friday morning, he found out that despite his clear instructions to Waldheim, the Israeli table was placed next to Syria's. He immediately about-faced and exited, leading his delegation back out to the corridors.

For the next 40 minutes Dr. Waldheim, pale and excited, was seen running from one delegation to the other, trailed by a retinue of aides and secretaries. It was Kissinger who finally managed to come up with the saving formula: Egypt and Israel would sit on either side of Waldheim. The Americans would sit to the right of the Egyptians and the Russians to the left of Israel. The empty table would be put to the left of the Russians, and next to it, completing the circle, the Jordanians.

At 11:10 A.M. the gold-plated doors of the hall opened wide and the delegations entered. When Eban passed near the Russian table he was not certain how to behave. Gromyko solved the problem. He got up and shook Eban's hand warmly.

Dr. Waldheim very ceremoniously gave the floor for the first statement to Gromyko. After the usual and expected accusations against Israel, Gromyko detailed the Russian principles for solution of the Israeli-Arab conflict:

• No territories to be annexed by war. Therefore Israel must retreat from all territories occupied in June 1967.

• Ensuring respect for and recognition of the sovereignty, territorial integrity, and political independence of all states in the Middle East, and of their right to live in peace. That applies to Israel too.

• Securing justice for the Palestinians. Their legitimate rights must be defended.

There was one surprise in the speech. It was the first time since June 1967 that Moscow spoke in public of the recognition of Israeli sovereignty within the borders of 1967.

Next to speak was Kissinger, who was very careful not to identify the United States with the positions of any of the states involved, including Israel. Like the previous speaker, he spoke of recognized borders, guarantees, security arrangements, and a search for a solution to the legitimate interests of the Palestinians. In one matter he left no room for doubts: the road to peace through Resolution 242 was long and one should move along it "step by step."

The plump Egyptian foreign minister, Ismail Fahmy, laid down Egypt's conditions for peace: an Israeli retreat from all territories, including Jerusalem; restoring the national rights of the Palestinians; political independence and territorial security for all states in the area; international guarantees by the powers or by the UN as additional security. Fahmy also hinted that if and when Jerusalem were given back, it would not be under Jordanian sovereignty—a clear gesture toward the Palestinians.

It was the prime minister and foreign minister of Jordan, Zaid al Rifai, who took the most extreme stance. He referred to Israel as a foreign body in the area of the Mediterranean, guilty of murder and tortures on the west bank of the Jordan. His demands, however, were the same as Fahmy's.

It was 12:25 P.M. when Rifai concluded his speech. Waldheim wanted to adjourn and start again the following morning. But Eban insisted that he speak that very day. Postponement of his speech, he felt, would make the first day of the conference look like "the day of the Arabs" in the world press. Waldheim consented, and it was decided to resume the meeting at 3:30 P.M.

Eban delivered a polished exposition of the Israeli position: a peace treaty in content and in spirit; a cessation of hostility in propaganda, education, and economic relations; opening of the Suez Canal for free navigation; determining defensible borders; international cooperation, including the oil countries, for solving the problem of the Palestinian refugees; no room for an additional Palestinian state in the area; Jerusalem is the unified capital of Israel, but Israel does not demand control over the holy places of other religions; a willingness for territorial compromise and a retreat to agreed-upon borders in partial or general agreements.

Throughout Eban's speech, Fahmy was seen taking notes very excitedly. Immediately after Eban concluded his remarks, Fahmy asked for permission to speak. His relative moderation of the morning disappeared. Israel was responsible for Deir Yassin, Karameh, the massacre of Beirut, and mass murders, he charged venomously. And he concluded, "We do not have elections in a few days and I am not obliged to speak for internal purposes."

Kissinger, who had been yawning a lot, began exchanging frantic whispers with Sisco as Fahmy spoke. Everyone feared an explosion was about to occur that would smash the delicate structure erected with so much effort. Waldheim asked if anyone else wanted to speak. All eyes, especially Kissinger's, turned nervously to Eban. When the Israeli foreign minister remained quiet, everyone breathed a sigh of relief. The secretary general quickly adjourned the meeting until the next day at 11:00 A.M.

Perhaps to try to reduce the tension, and perhaps because it was customary, Waldheim asked Fahmy's consent to hold a cocktail party for all the delegations. Fahmy not only would not consent but opposed it very firmly. He had nothing personal against Eban, he said, but this would be bad, very bad, from the internal Egyptian point of view. He told Waldheim that during the discussions at Kilometer 101 a picture of Gamasy and Yariv shaking hands appeared in the media and this caused Sadat much trouble with Arab extremists. But, insisted the secretary general, the United States and the Vietcong participated in a cocktail party while they were still fighting—so why not Israel and Egypt in a state of cease-fire? The Vietcong and the United States are not Israel and Egypt, Fahmy said emphatically. And that was the end of the cocktail party.

Eban had no intention of spending his free time in Geneva sailing on the lake. In preparatory discussions in the Foreign Ministry, it was agreed that this might be an appropriate place for opening contacts with the Soviet Union; Moscow might be more amenable now to the idea of a renewal of diplomatic relations. The logic was that the Soviet leadership understood they could not effectively carry out their role as cosponsors of the conference when they had no diplomatic relations with one of the sides. It would leave the area wide open for initiatives by the U.S. secretary of state.

At their first meeting in Geneva, Eban had asked Kissinger to sound out Gromyko on the possibility of a meeting. Gromyko's affirmative answer was personally relayed to Eban by Kissinger as the two were waiting to enter the hall for the opening session of the conference.

On the afternoon of December 22, 1973, Eban strode into the palatial residence of the Soviet delegation, sensing that a warm and friendly reception awaited him. Sitting down next to Gromyko and his assistants, Eban and his aides were showered with offerings of superb vodka and the finest Havana cigars. A beaming Gromyko opened the conversation by recalling the days when they represented their respective countries at the United Nations. He reminisced about the excellent New York restaurants, the good plays he had seen, and from time to time threw in some gossip about colleagues from other countries.

Gromyko easily moved from the personal touch to the political level. The last time they had met, he said to Eban, was in 1966. Since then many things had occurred. When he observed Eban and his colleagues at the Palace of Nations he had wondered—what are the Israelis thinking? He decided he would ask them, and so he was glad they were meeting.

Then Gromyko abruptly reminded Eban of the Soviet Union's support for the establishment of the state of Israel. Again he stressed that the Soviet Union regarded itself as the catalyst in the creation of the state and "it does not regret it." Furthermore, he declared ceremoniously, "Whoever acts against the existence and sovereignty of the state of Israel will find themselves in conflict with the Soviet Union."

The question, however, was how to see to the security of Israel. Gromyko did not think that the answer could be found in the method of territorial annexations. His formula to ensure Israel's security was in creating good relationships with the neighboring states, secured by international guarantees. In the light of the October war, hadn't Israel re-examined its theory of "secure borders"? asked Gromyko.

Eban was not persuaded. "After all," he replied, "you also made sure of secure borders in Finland, and yet borders are more essential to us."

Gromyko had no reaction to Eban's comment. Instead, in a seemingly friendly but cautious tone he brought up a new lament. At some point, he said, you will begin to wear thin on the United States. They cannot go on supporting you endlessly.

Most of the conversation was conducted in English, in which Gromyko is fluent. Only when he wished to state official Kremlin positions did Gromyko shift to Russian. He refrained from speaking in the first person or mentioning names, preferring to use the phrase "the Soviet leadership"—perhaps to stress the authority with which he spoke. Or perhaps it was to remind his guest that he was now a member of the Politburo, the supreme ruling body of the Soviet Union, an honor he could not claim during his previous contacts with Eban.

There were six others in the room—three aides on each side. At one point Gromyko breezily turned to Eban and said: "Look, something strange is occurring. Sitting here are six men" (with his finger he counted the assistants) "who are thinking the same thing: 'How can we leave our two ministers so that they can speak alone?'" Everyone in the room burst into laughter. The six assistants immediately got to their feet and exited, leaving the two foreign ministers for a private tête-à-tête.

Gromyko wanted the privacy to discuss the tricky question of renewal of diplomatic relations. There had been much talk about this, he said, and he wanted to clarify the situation.

Not wanting to leave any doubts about his own position, Eban emphasized that it was not he who brought up the subject. The Israeli foreign minister wanted it clearly understood that he was acting in accordance with the policy of his government that any initiative for renewing diplomatic relations had to come from the state that initiated the break.

Gromyko explained that public opinion in the Soviet Union would neither understand nor accept a renewal of relations with Israel unless there were some political event to justify such a step.

Eban wondered to himself: When had there ever been an independent "public opinion" in the Soviet Union? Moreover, since when has this factor been given any weight in the Kremlin's calculations? He concluded that when Gromyko spoke of public opinion, he actually meant the Arab states. But he wanted to know what Gromyko meant by a "political event."

Gromyko explained that he was thinking of "meaningful progress" in the negotiations with the Arab countries. And from there he went on to discuss the disengagement of forces and the Geneva conference—where the Soviet Union clearly had strong designs.

Before the conference it had been agreed with Kissinger that the discussion of disengagement of forces would be renewed in Geneva on January 7, 1974. To Gromyko this wasn't good enough. He wanted the discussions to begin immediately after the opening session of the conference. He explained that Egypt was in a difficult political situation and one could not send Fahmy back to Cairo empty-handed. Gromyko did not mince words; he was insistent, almost pleading.

Eban replied that Israel had decided not to renew the discussions before its national elections scheduled for December 31. He explained that public opinion in Israel would react negatively to such crucial negotiations by a government about to end its mandate. And what would happen if the present government were not re-elected, Eban wondered? Gromyko laughed loudly and reassured Eban that he expected to meet with him at least ten more times.

But Eban was not willing to make any such assumptions. He indicated that he would convey Gromyko's request to the Israeli government but insisted that even if the government agreed to renew discussions immediately after the opening session, it would be under the clear condition that no decisions would be made before the election.

The last subject that Gromyko indicated a strong interest in was maintaining the Geneva conference format. He conceded that the conference was not a forum that would prove substantive at all times, but despite it he implored Eban to maintain a permanent Israeli delegation in Geneva.

What would they do here, Eban wanted to know?

Gromyko countered that Geneva was a delightful city, with nightclubs and restaurants galore. As for himself, he intended to leave Vladimir Vinogradov in Geneva, "even if he had nothing to do and even if he were to climb Mont Blanc night and day."

The meeting ended in a friendly atmosphere with the two foreign ministers agreeing, on the initiative of Gromyko, to continue meeting at international gatherings at which they were both present.

A day later when Eban reported to Kissinger on the meeting, he asked his interpretation of the expression "meaningful progress," which Gromyko had laid down as a condition for renewal of diplomatic relations. Kissinger felt it referred to a disengagement-of-forces agreement. Eban was more pessimistic. He thought that it referred to an overall agreement, or at least a partial agreement which included a substantial Israeli retreat.

Eban had gone to the meeting thinking of renewal of relations but it was now clear that this was not high on the list of Gromyko's priorities. There is no doubt his primary concern was the disengagement-of-forces agreement and the continuity of the Geneva conference. The intensity of Gromyko's concern indicated that Egypt was in distress.

The last thing that Sadat wanted was a renewal of the war, his chances of winning being very small, and the possibility of losing all his advantages being very great. On the other hand, because of general Arab considerations he could not allow a political freeze, not even for the short period between the opening session of the conference and January 7. Gromyko came to the meeting with Eban primarily as a messenger from Sadat. He wanted to achieve an immediate continuation of the disengagement talks and pledges for the preservation of the Geneva conference.

Analyzing the conversation between the two foreign ministers, Jerusalem later reached the conclusion that all of Gromyko's talk of renewal of diplomatic relations was lip service aimed at softening up the Israeli government. Support for this evaluation was the manner in which the meeting was publicized in Russia. Only the Russian radio channel in Hebrew carried the report. A week later it was mentioned in *Pravda*, in an article speaking of "the fruitful activities of Comrade Gromyko in Geneva." The article merely said that he had met with all the foreign ministers, including Israel's.

Gromyko was not content with trying to persuade Eban; Kissinger was also told categorically that Brezhnev and Sadat could not wait until January 7. Kissinger then recommended that Israel reply favorably to the Soviet-Egyptian demand. It is not wise, he told Eban, to refuse a technical proposal and by so doing stir up Egyptian dissatisfaction. Working groups could meet and chat about anything under the sun besides substantive matters until after the Israeli elections. He would guarantee it. He had consent on that from both Gromyko and Fahmy. All they wanted was to be able to publicize in the Arab world that negotiations for a disengagement-of-forces agreement had begun.

Eban conveyed Kissinger's new request to Jerusalem. Mrs. Meir summoned the cabinet immediately. Unwillingly, but with little choice, the cabinet once again gave its consent. Disengagement talks between Israeli and Egyptian military delegations would begin in Geneva on December 26. Major General Mordechai (Motta) Gur would head the Israeli delegation, since Yariv had now left the army to run for the Knesset.

The talks that began on December 26 were no more than a lot of chattering—a playback of what had already been said at Kilometer 101. No one hoped or expected that any news would come out of Geneva. The focus of all political moves became Kissinger. All else simply froze. As for the fate of the plenary session—there was some talk of reconvening it at the foreign ministers' level in January but no one was sure what would happen.

While the generals were talking and enjoying the pleasures of Geneva, the Labor party suffered the worst blow in its history, with the right-wing bloc— the Likud—picking up a significant number of seats. Labor barely managed to keep the reins of power and was given the opportunity to form a new government. For Golda Meir and Dayan it was one last chance to recoup their damaged reputations by steering the country through the difficult negotiations to come.

V

The First Shuttle

Whatever else it might have accomplished, the Yom Kippur War at least shattered the illusions and misconceptions that had been one of the principal roadblocks to an agreement between Israel and Egypt. Regarding the nature of those illusions, there is on record a joint confession rare in its honesty. It occurred during a break in one of the meetings between Kissinger and the Israeli leaders when he and Golda Meir started reminiscing about the recent events they had been through.

Mrs. Meir was analyzing Egypt's president. "With all the reservations I feel toward Sadat, I have to admit that the preparations and the timing of the attack were perfect," she said sadly.

Kissinger was meditative. After a few seconds he said very quietly: "I do not want to blame anyone, but during the year of 1973 it was possible to prevent war if we had only seen what was coming."

The prime minister, never one to absorb criticism easily, asked incredulously, "What do you mean?"

Kissinger explained: "Do you remember what we all thought before the war?—that we never had it better, and therefore there was no hurry? We and you were both convinced that the Arabs had no military option which required serious diplomatic action. Instead of doing something we joked about the shoes the Egyptians left behind in 1967.

"Do you remember," he went on, "when I reported to you on my meeting with Hafez Ismail in Washington? What did I do in those conversations? I talked with him about the weather and every subject in the world just so we wouldn't get to the subject the minister thought most important. I played with him. I toyed with him. My aim was to gain time and postpone the serious stage for another month, another year."

Kissinger continued: "You know what? I remember now that Ismail told me several times that the present situation could not continue. He asked me whether the United States did not understand that if there weren't some agreement then there would be war. He expressed surprise that the United States didn't do something about it."

Kissinger sank into his armchair. "There wasn't even a slight smile on my face, but in my heart I laughed and laughed. A war? Egypt? I regarded it as empty talk, a boast empty of content. He invited me to come visit Egypt. Maybe because he read my thoughts and was hoping that in a meeting with Sadat I would understand the situation as it really was. But I did not dream of a trip to Cairo. Who is Sadat? We all thought he was a fool, a clown. A buffoon who goes on stage every other day to declare a war. We were convinced that he was a passing episode. That his days were few."

As Kissinger spoke Mrs. Meir stared at him as if she were having problems digesting it all. "But," she said finally, "we always asked for proximity talks with Egypt, and President Sadat wasn't excited by it."

With some impatience Kissinger replied: "Let's put a hand on the heart, Madam Prime Minister. Once again, I do not blame anyone, but to what extent did we really want the proximity talks? I would say that the effort we made was very slight. In effect we waved the proximity talks only to calm Sadat, in order to give him a reason to sit quietly."

This time Mrs. Meir did not argue. When she finally spoke, it was almost in a whisper: "But it didn't work. He refused to sit quietly."

The major reason that Mrs. Meir (and Kissinger too) thought that Sadat would have to sit quietly was the myth known as the Bar-Lev Line. The line was the basis for a whole set of military and political assumptions which shaped Israel's policy after the Six-Day War. The fortified line, the Golda Meir government thought, was strong enough to either throw back or hold up any Egyptian attack across the Suez Canal long enough for the rest of Israel's forces to move up and destroy the enemy. Furthermore, it was assumed that the Egyptians also knew this and would never dare to move. Since the Egyptians lacked a military option the Bar-Lev Line would ultimately force them to negotiate on Israel's terms.

That illusion came crashing down when the Egyptian army sliced through the Bar-Lev Line as if it were made of paper. Naturally after the Yom Kippur War the Israeli government was more amenable to the idea of giving up control of the canal line as part of an interim agreement with Egypt. It quickly gave Yariv authority to informally discuss a ten-kilometer retreat in his discussions with Gamasy at Kilometer 101. When the Kilometer 101 talks closed down and Henry Kissinger stepped into the picture as an active intermediary, one of his first moves was to invite Defense Minister Dayan to come to Washington to present the Israeli position on a disengagement of forces with Egypt.

The choice of Dayan was not coincidental. For six years the minister of defense had been the one person in the cabinet to argue consistently that Israel's presence on the canal line was less than ideal from the military and political point of view. Even in the middle of the Six-Day War, when Israeli units were rolling across the Sinai with minimal opposition, Dayan suggested to the cabinet that the army stop at the Mitla and Gidi passes, about 35 kilometers from the canal. His first argument was strategic: the Mitla and Gidi passes were much better defense lines than the canal. The second argument was psychological and practical: Egypt would never reconcile itself to Israel sitting on the bank of the canal. It would thus become the cause for incessant and needless tension that would impose on Israel, with its limited resources, a heavy security and economic burden.

Dayan's analysis was prescient. Yet in those days of military glory, cold logic had no resonance. The rest of the cabinet would not be content with one meter less than what could be achieved. The green light was given to the army commanders to move on to the canal. The photographs of happy Israeli soldiers bathing in the waterway gave the people of Israel satisfaction and pride. To Egypt, however, the photos were like salt in open wounds. As Dayan predicted, the canal was immediately closed to navigation. Afterward a long and costly war of attrition was fought along the waterway—and Israel's security expenses went sky-high.

On August 7, 1970, Israel and Egypt managed to reach agreement on a cease-fire for three months. Later on three more months were added and then one more month. From then till Yom Kippur 1973 the cease-fire was more or less observed from day to day by mutual consent.

Dayan began to think of a partial agreement immediately after the cease-fire went into effect. He was anguished about the possibility of a renewal of the war of attrition. He thought an Israeli retreat from the bank of the canal could prevent it. Furthermore,

Dayan believed that such a retreat could achieve a formal cease-fire for many years, perhaps even an end to belligerency.

In September 1970 reports started appearing in the press on proposals for a partial agreement, with attribution to sources "close to Dayan." The plan envisaged an Israeli retreat to a line close to the Mitla and Gidi passes and a token presence of Egyptian soldiers on the east bank of the canal.

Leading the opposition inside the government was Dayan's rival, Deputy Prime Minister Allon, who received support from the chief of staff, Major General Chaim Bar-Lev. Allon was against any retreat from the canal of more than ten kilometers and was opposed to even one Egyptian soldier on the east bank of the canal. Allon's reasoning was that Israel had to retain the option of a quick return to the canal if needed. Of course it was precisely the radical essence of Dayan's proposal to give up control of the canal. Dayan understood that only such a concession would be accepted by Sadat and gain Egyptian concessions in return that would bring peace for many years.

Prime Minister Golda Meir finally supported Allon's position, accepting the argument that control over the canal had to remain in Israel's hands as a constant threat to Egypt. With Mrs. Meir opposed, Dayan's proposal was dead.

On February 4, 1971, in a long speech to the nation, President Sadat dealt with the idea of a partial agreement (while describing the idea as an Egyptian initiative):

> We add now a new Egyptian initiative to all our attempts in the past to find a solution to the problem, and we see in it a true test of our willingness to implement Security Council Resolution 242. We demand that during the period of this cease-fire there will be a partial Israeli retreat from the east bank of the Suez Canal. If that is carried out, we will be

willing to clean up the canal immediately in preparation for reopening it to international navigation.

On February 9, 1971, Mrs. Meir responded to Sadat's proposal in a political speech to the Knesset. She did not even mention the possibility of retreat. Self-righteously and typical of those years, she said that as far as Israel was concerned Sadat could open the canal that very day.

Various efforts at mediation were made by U.S. Secretary of State William Rogers and by UN envoy Gunnar Jarring. There were many trips to the Middle East, but all foundered on the rigid Israeli insistence that there would be no more than a ten-kilometer retreat from the waterway and that no Egyptian soldiers could cross the canal. The last concrete proposal was brought to Israel in August 1971 by Joseph Sisco. If Israel would agree to retreat to a line close to the Mitla and Gidi passes and also allow a token presence of several hundred Egyptian soldiers on the east bank of the canal, along with reference in the agreement to Resolution 242, then, Sisco said, the Egyptians would be willing to agree to an end to the state of war.

Dayan was the only supporter of Sisco's proposal in the cabinet. All the rest, led by Mrs. Meir and Allon, opposed it sharply. And that brought to an end the affair of the partial agreement. Only another terrible war would resurrect it.

When Dayan arrived for talks with Kissinger on December 7, 1973, he carried the official Israeli position, which still spoke only of an exchange of banks of the canal. This time, however, it was obvious that Israel could not afford to stick rigidly to its position. In addition, Dayan was quite willing to let Kissinger know his private views. After some general discussion of the overall prospects for peace, and after stating

the official position, Dayan gave Kissinger a proposal
that was almost identical to the one he had floated
as a trial balloon back in 1970. He offered an Israeli
retreat to a line ten kilometers in front of the Gidi
and Mitla passes. In return, he wanted substantial
demilitarization in the forward areas, an Egyptian
obligation to open the Suez Canal, rehabilitation of
the canal cities, and lifting of the Egyptian blockade
of Bab el Mandeb. Kissinger was enthusiastic except
for the extent of demilitarization contemplated by
Dayan, which he felt would be difficult for the
Egyptians to accept.

Most importantly, however, Kissinger realized that
in the present circumstances Dayan's private position
could easily be turned into the official position of the
Israeli government. The day after his discussion with
Dayan, Kissinger left for his second trip to the Middle
East, the main purpose of which was to lay the ground-
work for the Geneva conference and try to get the
Arab oil boycott lifted. But Kissinger also intended
to begin the process of turning Dayan's private position into an official position in preparation for the
negotiations to come after January 1.

After stopovers in Brussels and Algeria, Kissinger
arrived in Cairo on December 14. Two days of meetings with Sadat made it clear that the Egyptian view
of a disengagement-of-forces agreement had also
moderated considerably since Kissinger's last visit on
November 6. Previously Sadat had insisted on an
Israeli retreat to the El Arish-Ras Muhammed line—
halfway across the Sinai. Now Sadat said he would be
satisfied with an Israeli retreat to east of the Gidi
and Mitla passes. There were other changes as well.
Sadat was now amenable to limited-forces zones and
significant restrictions of armaments. In November
he had opposed any restrictions.

Kissinger listened to all this with interest. He knew

that Sadat's proposals were not yet acceptable to Israel, but he also knew they were not his last word. In addition, Sadat offered a gesture on the Suez Canal, promising that if it were opened as a result of an agreement he would allow Israeli cargo through. The canal could be opened, he told Kissinger, in six months, and he said he would begin cleanup operations immediately after an agreement was signed.

After leaving Cairo Kissinger flew on to meetings with King Faisal in Riyadh and Syrian President Assad in Damascus. Then, on December 16, Kissinger's specially built Boeing 707 landed in a driving rainstorm at Ben-Gurion Airport near Tel Aviv. This time there were protest demonstrators at the airport instead of crowds welcoming the hero of the cease-fire. They carried placards which read: "Kissinger Deserted Formosa, Is Israel Next?" and "America: Et Tu Brute?" There were only a few dozen youngsters from the right-wing movements, but they reflected a growing public uneasiness about Kissinger's real intentions. It was no secret that Kissinger was beginning to pressure the government. Since 1967 the public had taken it almost as an axiom that the territories were Israel's best bargaining card, to be surrendered only for full peace. Now they were beginning to hear rumors of a one-sided Israeli retreat.

Still, at this early date Kissinger didn't have that much persuading to do. In a meeting with the Israeli negotiating team that evening the official position of an exchange of banks with the Egyptian forces was dropped fast. Instead, a ten-kilometer retreat from the canal was offered. And it was Allon, who in 1970 had opposed allowing any Egyptian troops on the east bank of the canal, who now told Kissinger that Israel would agree to some Egyptian forces on the east bank. It was clear that conditions had changed radically.

The Israeli ministers were only insistent on two

points: Israel would not retreat beyond the Mitla and Gidi passes, and the level Sadat was contemplating of Egyptian military forces on the east bank was not acceptable. The Israeli ministers also raised the question of an Egyptian agreement to an end to the state of belligerency. It was a gesture for the record—a reminder of what Israel was after.

The nervousness in that meeting came only when Kissinger, sounding a little like the Harvard professor of old, started lecturing the Israeli ministers on his general strategy. Kissinger explained that the aim of the disengagement talks was to circumvent the need to talk now about borders and final arrangements. The success of the talks would also lead to another achievement—the lifting of the oil embargo. This would also end Israel's isolation by easing the pressure put on her primarily by the Western European states and Japan. No one in Israel should have the slightest doubt, warned Kissinger, that the failure of the disengagement talks would break open the dam holding back the pressures on Israel, this time not for a partial retreat, but a complete retreat to the June 4, 1967, borders.

To strengthen his argument Kissinger told the Israelis he was amazed by Sadat's behavior. The Egyptian president was so far not using his full political power created by the new international situation in negotiating for an agreement. Indeed, Kissinger thought that Sadat could have used the international situation to achieve an overall agreement on his terms. At the most, said Kissinger, Sadat would have risked a new war, which the whole world would blame on Israel anyway.

Why, then, didn't Sadat use the situation to press for a total Israeli retreat? Because, Kissinger answered himself, Sadat had fallen victim to human weakness. It was the psychology of a politician who wanted to see himself—and quickly—riding triumphantly in an open car through the city of Suez with thousands of Egyptians cheering him.

In Kissinger's opinion, Sadat had two options: first, to try and achieve an agreement, through the aid of the United States, in a relaxed atmosphere. Second, to try and reach the same goal with the help of the British, the French, the Japanese, and the Soviets, but in a climate of international crisis with the United States being dragged along behind the other states. To take the second option Sadat did not even have to go to war. Several local incidents and a continuation of the oil embargo would be sufficient, Kissinger argued.

Given the situation he just described, Kissinger recommended that Israel be generous in contemplating a retreat from the canal. He always believed, he said, that Israel never knew when to give way. Since the conflict with Egypt was linked to the international situation, and since, in Kissinger's opinion, Israeli forces on the west bank of the canal were overextended anyway, he thought this was the right time to give way.

There was an additional consideration. In the State Department and the Pentagon dozens of officials were waiting for the opportunity to bring about a turn in American Middle East policy—from an Israeli orientation to an Arab orientation. Only the success of the disengagement talks could stop these men, Kissinger warned.

Mrs. Meir understood the picture that the secretary of state was drawing. She said it was all justification for a one-sided Israeli retreat, an agreement that was not based on mutuality. Of course, she said, Sadat would put in a lot of pretty words about sending home part of his army or opening the canal. Maybe he would do it and maybe not. Then, she said, it is true that one should also consider the views of Douglas-Home, the French, the Europeans, the Japanese. She knew, she said, that even if Sadat were to start a war no one would regard it as unjust, because justice in Europe is not worth much these days.

She continued excitedly:

> The world wants an Israeli retreat to the 1967 borders, or, more correctly, the world wants oil, believing that it will get it after Israel carries out a total retreat. It is very possible oil would actually start to flow after the signing of a disengagement agreement, but what happens afterward? The oil embargo could be renewed again, and this time with the aim of pressuring Israel to retreat to the 1967 lines. Since this is the case Israel has to determine for itself when to take on the big confrontation with the world—a confrontation that cannot be prevented. Right now Israel still has certain advantages. The Suez Canal is in its hands and its forces are encamped on the west bank 100 kilometers from Cairo. If Israel gives up these two advantages it would not have anything left as a bargaining card for the time when the world pressures it to return to the 1967 lines.

Mrs. Meir lit a cigarette with shaking hands and went on:

> The worst thing is that as far as the world is concerned it doesn't matter who is the aggressor. The aggressor and the victim are in the same boat. Not even in the same boat—because the aggressor has oil and therefore he is just and the blame falls on the other side. In this world, Israel cannot be just.

When she finished she half-turned her back on Kissinger, perhaps subconsciously, as if she were turning her back on the world he represented.

In responding, Kissinger made it clear that his view of international morality was just as cynical as hers. After all, he had had even more contacts with heads of state. He cited the Japanese as an example. At a recent meeting with Japanese Prime Minister Kakuei

Tanaka, the subject was the hostility that Japan showed Israel during the oil embargo. Tanaka explained that he was facing general elections, and that he had to prove to his people that he was defending their interests. The prime minister said that he did not have a Jewish population in Japan, so he didn't have to consider this point. According to Kissinger this was the most anti-Semitic remark he had ever heard, though it did not surprise him. In any event, he generally assumed the Japanese were unreliable, and that one could never know what treacherous acts they would commit behind one's back.

The point, said Kissinger, was to try to live with the world as it was. As for Israel, Kissinger thought it had to gain time, an expensive commodity that the disengagement agreement would purchase. Kissinger was more optimistic than Golda Meir regarding another oil embargo. Not that it was impossible, he said, but if the same weapon were used a second time the element of surprise would disappear. The West would be prepared next time.

The oil-producing countries would also be more hesitant, he said. It was one thing to impose an embargo during a war; it was a different matter to do so only because political talks were not progressing well. Algerian President Houari Boumediene well understood that the rich Western states could live without his oil a lot easier than he could live without their money. And even King Faisal was aware that another embargo could have implications for his internal political situation.

When the question of opening the Suez Canal and rehabilitating its towns was discussed, the Israelis raised the idea of involving the Soviets in putting pressure on the Egyptians. Kissinger opposed this strategy firmly. The disengagement agreement with all its components, he argued, had to have the appearance of being achieved through Sadat's moderation and the efforts of the United States—all with complete disregard for the Soviets.

Lurking behind all the general talk, as always, was the very practical question of U.S. arms aid to Israel. The Pentagon is to blame for everything, Kissinger said. Schlesinger had clear instructions to give equipment to Israel—but he was disregarding the instructions. The Pentagon was arguing, of course, that he, Kissinger, had held back the airlift during the Yom Kippur War. But he swore it was not so. It is not important what Schlesinger told you, Kissinger said, looking toward Dayan. The facts speak for themselves, he said. Then came the practical point. Kissinger made it clear that he would be able to overcome the Pentagon's obstructionism only if and when he brought home a political achievement in the form of a disengagement agreement between Israel and Egypt.

Despite the emotional arguments with Mrs. Meir, the full day of meetings had convinced Kissinger that a first-step disengagement was clearly within reach. (Indeed, it was the Israelis who had to remind him of how close they had come to an agreement at Kilometer 101.) The only question was where and how. As he left Israel for Washington on December 17, Kissinger was still inclined to see the agreement coming out of Geneva after the Israeli elections on December 31, with him playing the crucial role of middleman.

Three days after the election, Dayan was dispatched to Washington. He met with Kissinger on January 3 and 4, and it soon became clear that Israel wanted an agreement, and quickly. Dayan invited Kissinger to come back to the Middle East immediately to get the disengagement talks rolling again. Dayan was convinced that Geneva was not an effective forum, that only Kissinger could move things along. In addition, Dayan whetted Kissinger's appetite by once again giving him his "private" opinion in favor of an Israeli retreat to the area of the Mitla and Gidi passes—in return, of course, for political concessions. Dayan stressed that his opinion was still not shared by most of the members of the cabinet—but a push from Kissinger could convince them.

Kissinger checked with Sadat and found out that the Egyptian president was just as interested in another visit as Dayan. Still, when Kissinger left on Thursday, January 10, he was thinking only of narrowing the gap. He assumed that the discussions in Geneva would continue until the end of January, and planned, therefore, to make only a quick visit— one stop in Egypt and one in Israel.

The Boeing 707 touched down at a small military airport at the holiday city of Aswan, on the banks of the Nile, where President Sadat was recuperating from a case of bronchitis. Kissinger toured the famous dam and the surrounding historic sights between long conversations with the Egyptian president. As Kissinger later described it, Sadat's main problem was his perception of Israel's negotiating position. He had been informed of hard-line proposals for disengagement that had appeared in the Israeli press. Kissinger had to explain to Sadat that the Israeli government is combined of various parties and that no plans became final until ratified by the Israeli Knesset. He also let Sadat in on Dayan's "private" ideas, which made Sadat much more optimistic.

Toward the end of the discussions Sadat stated firmly that something had to occur very soon because he was under attack by Arab extremists. He was also under severe pressure from the Soviets to make them part of the negotiating process. Then, as if by chance, Sadat asked Kissinger the specific objective of his visit. Kissinger replied that he hoped to promote an Israeli proposal that could create the basis for the continuation of negotiations in Geneva.

Wouldn't it be better if Kissinger stayed in the area so they could finish the affair quickly? asked Sadat. Instead of Geneva? asked an amazed Kissinger. Absolutely, replied the Egyptian president.

And so the first of Henry Kissinger's Middle East shuttles began that day.

In Israel, the 707 landed at 6:10 P.M., Saturday, January 12, 1974. American security men quickly jumped out and surrounded the ramp on both sides. Kissinger walked down the ramp with a big smile on his face. After touching Ambassador Keating's shoulder he warmly shook hands with Eban. To the press he declared: "I am glad to be here. I expect friendly and useful talks. Thank you."

If the Israeli public were beginning to be somewhat suspicious of the shuttling secretary of state, they were nonetheless dazzled by him. He was now a full-fledged international superstar and his comings and goings were turning into showy media rituals.

On the first shuttle there was a helicopter flight up to Jerusalem, then a motorcycle convoy to the cordoned-off King David Hotel. Inside the lobby of the hotel dozens of American Jewish tourists waited, singing *"Ave'nnu Sholem Aleichem"* (We Bring Peace to You). An old lady screamed, "Henry! Henry!" and Henry stopped dutifully nearby and gave her a big smile and a wave.

While Kissinger checked into his room for a short rest and a change of clothes, the journalists from his plane mingled in the lobby with the resident foreign correspondents and Israeli journalists. Each group pumped the other for information. The Kissinger entourage wanted to know what the Israeli cabinet ministers were leaking, and the Israeli journalists wanted to know what Kissinger, in the guise of "a senior official," had told the journalists on the plane.

Kissinger first went to pay a courtesy visit to Mrs.

Meir, who was in bed with a case of the shingles. The first meeting with the Israeli negotiating team started at 9:30 P.M. in the Olive Room, in the basement of the King David Hotel. Present on the Israeli side were Dayan, Eban, Allon, and several lesser officials, including Ambassador Dinitz.

The first item on the agenda was the line of retreat, which all agreed would be the key to success or failure. Sadat's starting position was anything but good news. He was insisting on an Israeli retreat beyond the Gidi and Mitla passes. The Israeli team of ministers told Kissinger this was out of the question. The passes were first-rate bargaining cards which Israel was reserving for negotiations on a final agreement.* A proposal that Israel should move back to the peak of the passes was also rejected out of hand by the ministers.

Kissinger warned that the negotiations could fail on this point and Israel would then have to consider the alternatives. But Kissinger started thinking out loud: Perhaps Sadat would be conciliatory after all. Kissinger remembered that during Mrs. Meir's visit to Washington in October 1973 she presented demands on Sadat that Kissinger considered impudent—yet Sadat had accepted them. Was it, as Allon now suggested, that she had correctly assessed Sadat's distress? Kissinger's ego refused to accept such an evaluation. He argued that Sadat had agreed to Mrs. Meir's demands because they were presented as American proposals at a time when Sadat badly needed to improve his relations with the United States.

Tactically the immediate question was whether to present Sadat with an Israeli map showing a final line of retreat or one that would be the basis for more bargaining. Kissinger advised the Israelis to go ahead

---

* The passes were given up in the next interim agreement, in September 1975.

and present a final map. In explaining why, he made a comparison between Sadat and Assad, the president of Syria. You had to make an evaluation of who you were negotiating with, Kissinger said. You could never present a final position to the Syrian president because he would always bargain for more. Sadat, however, was capable of accepting certain positions as final and reconciling himself to them, according to Kissinger.

And so for his trip back to Aswan, Kissinger was given an Israeli map which showed a final retreat line some 20 kilometers east of the canal. Sadat at first refused to accept it and the reactions of Egyptian Chief of Staff Gamasy and Foreign Minister Fahmy were even more extreme. In a meeting with Kissinger they started shouting and denouncing the Israeli proposals so heatedly that Sadat had to ask the two senior officials to leave the room. Apologizing about the incident, Sadat said that Gamasy and Fahmy were good men but did not understand that an exaggerated emphasis on the technical points of the Israeli proposals could distract from the points of the agreement in principle. With Fahmy and Gamasy out of the room they made some progress. Kissinger explained to Sadat that there was no chance Israel would move even one meter further back on the eastern line, in the direction of the passes, and that the agreement could fail on this point. Sadat, apparently ready to compromise from the beginning on the eastern line, seemed reconciled. On the other hand, he stubbornly refused to accept the proposed southern terminus of the line, which, he argued, was too close to the canal and gave Israel control over the Gulf of Suez. Egypt could not live with it, he said.

On his return to Jerusalem, Kissinger vividly described to the team of negotiators the arguments between Sadat and his advisers. It is hard to believe that Kissinger did not realize that these arguments had been mostly a show put on for his benefit. Nevertheless, he used the incident to try to convince the Israelis that Sadat was a moderate who should not be pushed too far because of his internal opposition.

Kissinger's tactics helped, however, and the affair of the southern line was solved with a typical initiative by Dayan during a garden party in Kissinger's honor at Dayan's house in Zahala, a suburb of Tel Aviv. In the middle of the party, Dayan, Kissinger, Sisco, and Elazar retired to Dayan's bedroom. A big map was spread out on the double bed. Kissinger started explaining why Sadat was objecting to the southern line. Dayan cut the explanation short and said: "If I were Sadat, I too would not have agreed to a line so close to the Gulf of Suez." Right there Dayan took out a pencil and drew in a new Israeli line farther back from the Gulf of Suez.

The concession satisfied Sadat on the substantive issue, but he still had a psychological problem accepting an official Israeli proposal. Kissinger solved the problem by presenting the map as an American proposal.

Israel had its own psychological problem when it came time to translate the proposal into the dry language of an official agreement. Sadat wanted the document to read that Israel was "retreating" to the agreed-upon line. The Israeli team of ministers refused to accept the term "retreat." Once again the impasse was bridged by a delicate verbal formula devised by Kissinger. In the final official agreement, the clause on the new line read as follows:

[B]
The military forces of Egypt and Israel will be separated in accordance with the following principles:

1. All Egyptian forces on the east side of the canal will be deployed west of the line designated as line A on the attached map. All Israeli forces including those

west of the Suez Canal on the Bitter Lakes will be deployed east of the line designated as line B on the attached map.

2. The area between the Egyptian and Israeli lines will be a zone of disengagement in which the United Nations Emergency Force will be stationed. The U.N.E.F. will continue to consist of units from countries that are not permanent members of the Security Council.

3. The area between the Egyptian line and the Suez Canal will be limited in armament and forces.

4. The area between the Israeli line, line B on the attached map, and the line designated as line C on the attached map, which runs along the western base of the mountains where the Gidi and Mitla passes are located, will be limited in armament and forces.

5. The limitations referred to in paragraphs 3 and 4 will be inspected by U.N.E.F. Existing procedures of the U.N.E.F., including the attaching of Egyptian and Israeli liaison officers to U.N.E.F., will be continued.

The deep-seated suspicion generated by the 25-year-old conflict manifested itself most strongly in the bargaining over the restrictions on forces in the forward disengagement zones. Each side was concerned with the possibility of another war and haggled over every soldier and piece of equipment.

Egypt's initial position was that it should be allowed to maintain one and one-half divisions in the forward zones. Israel's counterproposal was for no more than two or three battalions. When Sadat was informed of the Israeli position he burst out: "With such a force I could not pretend that it was in my power to protect the canal."

It was Gamasy who had put forward the Egyptian proposal in terms of divisions. Dayan understood the purpose immediately. Divisions come with extra supporting forces such as artillery and engineering units. Battalions do not.

Finally Sadat abandoned Gamasy's approach with the comment that he was an excellent general but not a statesman; he agreed to deal in terms of battalions. He offered a figure of ten battalions. Israel countered with eight. With characteristic humor Kissinger prevailed on the Israelis to give in. He said that he had no objection to going back to Aswan over two battalions, but the Israelis knew that it would end up with nine. So why bother the American secretary of state over one battalion?

Israel had orginally wanted to keep the forward zone free of tanks. Sadat, however, wanted 200 tanks. He explained that the topography of the area required that many for adequate defense, but, more importantly, the tanks were necessary for the morale of his troops. After a round trip between Aswan and Jerusalem Kissinger got Sadat to accept 100 tanks. One more trip back and forth and Sadat came down to 30—which Israel accepted.

As for artillery, Sadat agreed to an Israeli formula whereby the range of fire of each side should not reach the front lines of the other side. But a particularly complex problem arose over the placement of the SAM antiaircraft missiles. The SAMs had enabled the Egyptians to cross the canal in October and the memories of the early reversals were still painful for the Israelis. Israel therefore wanted the missiles as far back as possible, to protect Israeli airspace. Since Israel estimated the range of the missiles to be 40 kilometers, it wanted the SAMs that far back from Israeli forward lines—or 20 kilometers west of the canal.

Sadat rejected the Israeli position. First, he argued that the maximum forward range of the missiles was only 35 kilometers. Second, he said that if he had to move the missiles back 20 kilometers from the canal the topography would not be suitable for their emplacement.

The Israelis refused to compromise. Five kilometers, Kissinger was told, made the difference between a secure airspace and one under constant threat. Kissinger became angry and argued that Israel was playing into the hands of those opposing an agreement in Cairo, namely Fahmy and Gamasy. When this argument did not make the required impression Kissinger lost his control and screamed that it was Egypt and not Israel that was making all the big concessions in the negotiations. One of the ministers replied that it was Israel which was being asked to make a one-sided retreat. Kissinger dismissed the Israeli argument. Retreating from the canal wasn't really a concession, he said. Israel could not afford to stay on the west bank of the canal anyway, because it would be forced to keep its reserves mobilized. Israel, he thus concluded, was in a poor situation and Sadat, through his concessions, was actually helping out.

Kissinger's outburst did not help him much. Dayan finally said that if Kissinger put himself in Sadat's shoes he would see that the Egyptians had civilian population centers near the canal while Israel had only army units. Therefore it was in Egypt's interest that Israel's artillery be out of range of its civilian population. In order to achieve this Sadat would have to move his SAM missiles back to the line Israel was demanding.

Kissinger flew back to Aswan again and discovered that Dayan was right. Sadat accepted the Israeli demand that the missiles be moved back the full 20 kilometers from the canal.

Once the details were agreed on, the peculiarities of Middle East political psychology emerged again. Sadat was opposed to having a clause in the agreement in principle that would put limitations on his military forces in an area that was sovereign Egyptian land. He told Kissinger that extreme Arab leaders were already saying he wanted a disengagement zone and a thinning out of his forces as an alibi not to have to go to war.

Sadat therefore proposed that the details of the thinning out of forces and arms restrictions be spelled out in identical private letters sent by President Nixon to him and to Prime Minister Meir, which both heads of state would sign. In consulting with his aides Kissinger expressed amazement over this unprecedented proposal. It meant that the two chiefs of staff would sign the agreement in principle while the heads of the two states would only sign an addendum. But Kissinger did not state any objection to Sadat and the unprecedented procedure was carried out.

Israel's bitter past experiences colored all the discussions on the role of UN forces in the buffer zone. Particularly remembered was the sudden evacuation of the UN Emergency Force on Nasser's demand in June 1967. In order to keep this from happening again, Israel started out by demanding that the UN force this time be permanent. Alternatively, Israel suggested that only the Security Council should decide on the force's removal, and it wanted a U.S. commitment to veto any proposal opposed by Israel.

Kissinger dismissed both Israeli requests. He argued that from the perspective of world public opinion it mattered little if Sadat decided to go to war by ordering out the UN forces or crossing the UN zone with his own troops. In either case public opinion, particularly in the United States, would put the blame on Egypt as it did in 1967 when Nasser ordered the UN troops out of the Sinai.

However, as Allon reminded Kissinger in a private conversation, this did not prevent war in 1967. Kissinger answered Allon with a look of disdain of the kind a teacher reserves for a slow student. "But Yigal," he said, "if one of the sides wants war, there will be war—with or without the UN force. The most that you can get out of the UN force is public opinion and an early and precise warning of aggressive intentions."

But since Israel was more interested in preventing a war than in a victory in the arena of American public opinion, one of the ministers tried another tack. He proposed a joint American-Soviet force as a substitute for the UN force. The new suggestion only sent Kissinger's blood pressure up. He described the proposal as a "strategic disaster," arguing that any presence of Soviet military forces in the Middle East was extremely dangerous. Second, he said, the reaction in the American Congress to such a proposal, coming after the affair in Vietnam, would be very harmful for Israel.

Behind the arguments, of course, was a deep gap between Kissinger and the Israelis on the whole subject of dealing with violations of agreements. To Kissinger each violation was evaluated individually in terms of what actual gains and losses might accrue. The Israelis regarded each agreement as a moral test of the trustworthiness of their Arab protagonists. That at least is how Golda Meir saw the matter as she brought up Egyptian violations of the 1970 cease-fire agreements when President Nasser moved his SAM missiles up to the canal. Mrs. Meir reminded Kissinger that for three weeks the United States had refused to acknowledge that there were any violations of the agreement. Kissinger's characteristic response was that Israel had actually benefited from the whole affair. As a result of the Egyptian violations, he said, Israel had received massive new quantities of arms from the United States. In addition, the pressure of world opinion on Israel for an overall agreement softened. Mrs. Meir would not relent, however. She pointed out that the price paid for the arms was very high: Israel had to reconcile itself to the SAM missiles remaining on the canal. There was a silence in the room as everyone understood the conclusion she was driving at: three years later those missiles had allowed the Egyptians to cross the canal.

All this was good enough reason for Israel to demand a strong and permanent UN force as insurance against violations of the agreement. But it did not get a permanent UN force and finally accepted Sadat's argument that such a force would be an admission on his part that the disengagement agreement resembled a final arrangement granting Israel sovereignty in Sinai.

Israel's only achievement was in arranging that states with which it did not have diplomatic relations would not participate in the UN force. Kissinger had assured the ministers that there would be no problem fixing it with Secretary General Waldheim. Kissinger believed that he could get Waldheim to do anything for him by flattering him till he was "breathless." (Waldheim himself had once told a senior diplomat at the UN that he knew of no man who admired him more than Dr. Kissinger. A "senior American official," however, told the Israelis that he knew of such a man—Dr. Waldheim himself.)

Kissinger finally ended the argument over the UN with some humorous bantering with the Israelis. He told them that at least the two sides could get out of the range of fire, but the UN force would be trapped in the buffer zone. Dayan smiled and replied that the sides would shoot at each other over the heads of the UN soldiers. Kissinger countered that the sides would probably be shooting at the UN more often than they shot at each other. "Not often, just sometimes," concluded Dayan.

The final formulation of the clause in the agreement concerning the UN force was essentially Kissinger's. Nothing specific was said about countries that did not have diplomatic relations with Israel—but in excluding permanent members of the Security Council he took care of the Soviet Union. As for the other states that did not have relations with Israel, Kissinger had arranged it all with Waldheim as promised.

In return for its one-sided retreat Israel had asked for some political steps that could mean progress toward peace—or at least the elimination of hostile acts. Kissinger immediately dismissed the specific Israeli request for an "end to belligerency." It was unachievable, he said, and in any event it was a worthless formula. As an historian, he learned that all wars in history broke out between countries which were in a state of peace. The strange situation in the Middle East, he concluded ironically, was that hostilities broke out between countries who were in a state of war. All that Sadat was willing to grant was a general reference in the agreement to "maintaining the cease-fire."

As for other possible political steps, Dayan focused on the Suez Canal. He assumed that if Egypt opened the canal for navigation and rehabilitated its cities, this would reduce the risk of another war. Another step that might prevent war was getting the Egyptians to allow Israeli shipping through the canal.

Sadat's response was that the opening of the canal was in Egypt's interest. If Israel wanted a commitment on that it was okay with him but he could not put it in the official agreement and thus give the appearance that it had been an Israeli-initiated demand. Kissinger came up with a formula that became a precedent for future negotiations: Egypt would give a commitment to the United States. Then the United States would give a similar commitment to Israel.

However, Sadat would not hear of allowing Israeli ships through the canal until a final peace agreement was signed. He would consent only to the passage of Israeli cargo on ships not carrying the Israeli flag. Israel accepted Sadat's offer but in turn insisted that all the Egyptian commitments—the opening of the canal, the rehabilitation of the cities, and the passage of Israeli cargo—would have to be fully implemented before any new agreements could be negotiated.

Kissinger assured the Israelis that Sadat had consented to their conditions and that it was incorporated in a separate memorandum of understanding between the United States and Israel. As it turned out, though, Kissinger was being less than candid with Israel. Egypt had made a general commitment about opening the canal and allowing the passage of Israeli cargo, but would not be pinned down to a date, not even that it must occur before further negotiations. Therefore, Kissinger's written guarantees to Israel were worthless. (He would come to the area in the spring of 1975 to try to wrest another agreement out of Israel before the canal was even opened.)

One last obstacle was taken care of in characteristic fashion by Dayan. Sadat had presented a demand that the road to the city of Suez be turned over to Egypt 48 hours after the signing of the agreement. Kissinger could not understand Sadat's haste and he called it the Egyptian president's "strange complex." Dayan, however, said that he understood the Egyptian sensitivity in this matter. Suez, Dayan explained, was to Sadat what the city of Port Said had been to President Nasser during the 1956 war. Port Said had been attacked by the British forces. It had almost surrendered but held out heroically and became an important national symbol for the Egyptians. As with Port Said, Dayan concluded, the city of Suez also was on the verge of being occupied by the Israelis during the Yom Kippur War, but managed to hold out and thus became another symbol of Egyptian national pride.

Chief of Staff Elazar had been opposed to the immediate opening of the road to Suez. But Dayan, without consulting his colleagues, turned to Kissinger and said: "Do you want the road to Suez to be opened 48 hours after the signing? Forty-eight hours it will be."

The major subject under discussion at the last meeting in Jerusalem was the date of the signing ceremony. Kissinger wanted to finish the whole affair by January 19, 1974, when he was supposed to return to the United States. For Israel the agreement required ratification by the full cabinet and the Knesset. The new Knesset, which had been elected on December 31, was to gather for its first session on January 31, but everyone agreed that the signing of the agreement should not be delayed that long. It would be explained to the Egyptians that a formal ratification by the Knesset was necessary but that the Israeli government (which had a safe majority in the new Knesset) had no doubt that the Knesset would ratify the agreement.

Getting the approval of the full cabinet was a problem of a different sort. It had to be reported to daily, and Kissinger was concerned about premature leaks coming from the cabinet about the details of the agreement. Someone on the Israeli negotiating team suggested to Kissinger that leaks were also coming from other sources, namely, high officials in his own party. Kissinger rejected the allegation. The kind of control he exercised in the State Department, he said, prevented unintentional leaks.

That touched off a barbed exchange between Kissinger and Allon, with the Israeli deputy prime minister saying that the Israeli cabinet ministers certainly knew how to keep their mouths shut when it was necessary. Kissinger replied that he had never seen any evidence of it. That was especially the case, he reminded Allon, about the airlift and the cease-fire controversy during the war. He said angrily that when the Israelis caused political damage with their leaks he could correct it, but when through the leaks they started questioning his honesty, it was something he could not accept.

Dayan dismissed the whole argument about the leaks with great disdain. Whether there was a cabinet meeting or not, he said, all the ministers would read about today's discussions in the morning papers anyway. Dayan did not believe that early publication could prevent an agreement that both sides really wanted. And so finally they all agreed that the government meeting would take place the next day as scheduled. The agreement was duly ratified.

On Friday, January 18, close to noon, there was another meeting at Kilometer 101. This time across the table from Lieutenant General Gamasy was Lieutenant General Elazar. The two chiefs of staff quickly signed the first disengagement-of-forces agreement between Egypt and Israel.

Not for a moment was there any doubt who was in control of the negotiations. Kissinger kept things moving at his desired pace by using all his charms and diplomatic skills. He was alternately flattering, angry, understanding, stubborn, forgiving—all according to the needs of the moment and the person he was negotiating with. He treated Mrs. Meir with great respect. He could deal matter-of-factly with Dayan. He patronized Allon (the only minister he called by his first name). He treated Dinitz like one of his students. He was diplomatically correct with Eban.

No doubt Kissinger turned on his charm in Aswan, but in Sadat he found a worthy match. The Egyptian president never tired of waving the flag of peace for Kissinger, knowing well that he would pass along his impressions to the Israelis. Sadat emphasized over and over his desire to develop the Egyptian economy, how he wanted to widen the canal, perhaps even build another canal—all as intimations of his constructive intentions. On the other hand, he never mentioned touchy subjects such as Jerusalem and the Palestinians, which might have raised the political temperature in Israel.

In Aswan it was Kissinger who was truly charmed, so much so that he refused to see or hear anything that would disrupt his vision of Sadat as a moderate. As one example, he refused to take seriously the fact that the Egyptians continuously shelled the Israeli army positions as a means of keeping up the pressure all during the resolutions. All the Israeli negotiating team's approaches over this were rejected by Kissinger with the comment that only a successful conclusion of the negotiations would take care of the shooting.

In the meantime Israeli soldiers were being killed daily. At one point, trying to demonstrate how much encouragement the Egyptians were getting from Kissinger's indifference, Dayan recounted a report made by one of the field commanders of the UN Emergency Force. The commander stated that one day he had been asked by the Egyptian commander in his sector to move his men a few kilometers. "What for?" asked the UN officer. "We are about to start shelling," replied the Egyptian officer honestly. The UN commander refused to move his men, so the Egyptians moved over a little and started shelling the Israelis right in front of the UN force.

If Dayan thought this story would have any effect on Kissinger he was wrong. Kissinger found the story amusing but did not change his views on the seriousness of the Egyptian shelling.

Kissinger, of course, viewed all of the problems concerning the disengagement of forces in a global context. For him disengagement was one more link in the policy of détente. But Senator Jackson's opposition to détente was becoming even stronger and Kissinger raised complaints in this regard with the Israelis in the midst of the negotiations. The price he eventually intended to extract from the Soviets for the trade agreement, Kissinger told the Israelis, was Soviet moderation at Geneva, and Israel should support him on this. Emigration of Jews from the Soviet Union was an important issue but not important enough to disrupt the policy of détente, he argued. If Israel could persuade its friends in Congress and elsewhere to remove their support for Senator Jackson's amendment, Kissinger argued, the path would be cleared for a policy he considered beneficial for Israel in the long run.

All that had to be done to gain the cooperation of the Soviets was to satisfy their appetites—to "wave a seed of grain in front of their eyes," as he put it to the Israeli ministers. He was disappointed, he said, that Israel was not cooperating with him in this matter. When Ambassador Dinitz reminded him that Israel was not supporting Senator Jackson, Kissinger replied that it was not enough for Israel not to actively support the Jackson amendment. He expected it to be active in opposition to Jackson. He could not understand what he saw as Israel's political blindness. "You only see what is under your nose," he kept saying over and over. "You don't see the global picture." He refused to consider the fact that Israel did see the global picture but drew different conclusions for its own policy.

To try to convince the Israelis that they should follow his lead, Kissinger was not above boasting about how easily he could handle the Soviets, and how inept they were. One of the most fantastic stories he told the Israeli ministers was his description of the SALT talks held in Moscow in 1973. At the first session held in the Kremlin, he recounted, the Russians seemed to have gone wild. They slammed the table and accused Nixon of being a war criminal in Vietnam, among other epithets. It was a diatribe, said Kissinger, that in the nineteenth century would have been sufficient cause for a declaration of war. Of course nothing of the sort happened. Nixon sat calmly and even seemed amused by the commotion. He knew it was all just a show intended for the protocol to be sent to Hanoi, to prove that Moscow was not indifferent to North Vietnam's struggle. And indeed, close to midnight, the Soviets reached the conclusion that they had said enough for the protocol. The smiles returned to their faces and Brezhnev jovially and generously invited all to a dinner, during which many glasses were raised in toasts to President Nixon and to friendship and brotherhood between the two nations. The dinner concluded at 1:00 A.M. Then Brezhnev, filled with the good cheer of many glasses of champagne, proposed that the SALT talks begin on the spot.

The two delegations moved to a separate room to continue the discussions while Nixon and Brezhnev went to bed. Joining the Soviet delegation at this time was Deputy Premier Leonid Smirnov, the man responsible for Soviet military production.

Kissinger began the discussion by describing the points that concerned Washington about Soviet missile strength. In doing so he detailed the performance qualities of Russian missiles. Smirnov's face turned red and he started shouting in Russian. Kissinger didn't understand what he was saying or the reason for the outburst. Nor could the Russians calm him down. It was necessary to take Smirnov out of the room. During the break Kosygin explained to Kissinger that Smirnov found it hard to digest the fact that a foreigner, moreover an American, was so thoroughly knowledgeable about Soviet armaments. Twice more Smirnov had to be taken out of the room to calm him down before the Soviet official finally accepted the bitter fact. And then when he started to speak, through a translator, he turned out to be a first-rate expert and a brilliant man, and it was through this conversation that Smirnov became one of the two

Soviet personalities Kissinger said he admired. (The other was Marshal Andrei Grechko.)

Kissinger's unique advantage during the shuttle was that he was the only one who knew what both sides were saying and thinking all the time. To each of the sides he was able to relay only the items that served his own aims—an advantage he used both in Jerusalem and Aswan. In Jerusalem he was helped by the fact that the Israelis had no clear maximum and minimum negotiating plan. Kissinger warned the Israelis about this more than once and even implored them to formulate such a plan. But at the same time he used its absence to his gain.

On at least one issue Israel paid dearly for allowing itself to be dragged along by Kissinger. At the beginning of the negotiations the Israelis were firm in their insistence that the UN force be permanent or at least be given a long mandate. But the mere declaration by Kissinger that such a demand was viewed by Sadat as tantamount to a final agreement was enough for Israel to give it up—though there was little basis for Kissinger's evaluation. The result was a procedure that required the extension of the UN mandate every six months. This was then used by Egypt (and Syria too) for periodic political pressure on Israel. Thus, instead of the stability that the disengagement agreement was supposed to bring to the southern and northern fronts, the period close to the renewal of each mandate turned into days of tension and saber rattling.

Israel's confusion was most apparent on an issue that was at the heart of the matter—the "end of belligerency." Israel's opportunity here was a rare one. Sadat's desire to get rid of the Israeli army on the west bank of the canal was so great that a firm Israeli stand on this point might have been successful, or at least partly so. But after brief lip service to the notion at the beginning of the negotiations, the Israelis just dropped the subject, which perhaps provides us with an explanation for Sadat's concessions in the area of restriction of forces and armaments. It is probable that Sadat feared an Israeli demand for an end to belligerency more than anything else and when this was removed from the agenda he was willing to make far-reaching concessions just so the Israelis would not wake from their sleep.

Kissinger later described his own approach to the Middle East negotiations as modeled after the Vietnam negotiations. This is the way he made the connection to his aides:

> The similarity between the negotiations in Vietnam and the Middle East is that the United States then, just as Israel at the end of 1973, was in an inferior position. Everything was against the administration in Washington—public opinion and both houses of Congress. It was clear that sooner or later America would have to get out of Vietnam. The problem was to gain time. So we had to wear down the other side and get a better agreement. The strategy was simple: always be one proposal ahead of your rival and for each counterproposal reply with a new proposal. In this way you could always ensure that your own proposal would be discussed. Parallel to that, Hanoi played into Washington's hands when it opened an offensive that enabled the United States to renew the heavy bombing of the north and thus wear down Hanoi even more.

By his own testimony Kissinger conducted himself most cleverly in the negotiations with North Vietnam. But several months later, when South Vietnam fell into the hands of the North without anyone lifting a finger, officials in Jerusalem recalled the analogy with great concern.

Most extraordinary and unprecedented of Kissinger's techniques were the triangular and secret agreements. Kissinger was thus able to solve issues that Egypt was willing to agree to but not in a written

public agreement with Israel. The issue of the opening of the canal and the rehabilitation of its cities is
the outstanding example—but not a very successful
one. Even before the ink was dry on the agreement
Sadat's announcements began. On January 18, the
date of the signing of the agreement, he said in Aswan:
"The opening of the Suez Canal is conditioned on
an Egyptian decision because it is a sovereign Egyptian matter. When the disengagement takes place we
shall see what our decision will be." Four days later
in Algiers, Sadat said: "There is no connection between the opening of the canal and the last military
agreement regarding the disengagement of forces. The
question of the canal concerns Egypt only."

From Israel there was silence. Everyone believed
or wanted to believe that Sadat's declarations were
for internal purposes only. But Sadat, in fact, was
waiting for another of Kissinger's missions so that Israel
would have to pay twice for the privilege of having
the canal opened. Only after the Kissinger mission
failed in March 1975 did Sadat decide not to wait
any longer. The canal was opened for navigation on
June 5, 1975, the eighth anniversary of the start of the
Six-Day War.

Why did Kissinger do it? Why did he take it upon
himself to fly back and forth for the long and tiring
talks over all the little details? Politically there were
three objectives that Kissinger was after:

• In the White House there was a president who
desperately needed a political victory that Kissinger
could bring from the Middle East and which, he
thought, could blunt the mounting attacks over the
Watergate affair.

• Also desirable was a renewed penetration of the
Arab world by the United States, at the same time
pushing the Soviet Union, which had seemed so
immovable till the Yom Kippur War, out of the area.

• Last was the lifting of the Arab oil embargo against the United States. The embargo was eased at the beginning of the negotiations and lifted a short time thereafter.

But all these important political factors do not fully explain Kissinger's fanatical devotion to his objective. There was also a good deal of personal incentive. He enjoyed every minute of the shuttling. He drew great pleasure from the international attention focused on him, from the expectations that he was a magician who could pull rabbits out of his hat. He enjoyed the tumult and excitement that accompanied him wherever he went. Around him now was fashioned the image of an omnipotent diplomat and political magician, which was like the elixir of life in his veins.

On Thursday evening, January 17, 1974, after the official announcement of the agreement was made in Washington, Jerusalem, and Cairo, Prime Minister Golda Meir hosted a dinner for all the participants in the negotiations. On this occasion, for the first time, Kissinger allowed himself a statement with a Jewish reference. To the guests he said: "The Jewish people, who have suffered so much in the last generation, deserve to live in peace and tranquillity." It was a routine remark, the likes of which had been made by many non-Jewish statesmen. But coming from the son of Jewish immigrants it was possible to understand that Kissinger felt his standing with the Arabs was now so firm that such a remark could no longer hurt him.

Conscious of this triumph and of the momentum it carried, Kissinger left the next day for Damascus to lay the basis for the disengagement agreement between Israel and Syria.

VI

The Damascus Shuttle

By direct flight it is less than 200 miles from Jerusalem to Damascus, but it must have seemed to Henry Kissinger as if he were travelling between separate planets. The aftermath of the Yom Kippur War had left Israel and Egypt more inclined to strike a deal, but it had only widened the gap between Israel and Syria.

For Israel the stumbling block was Syria's treatment of its prisoners of war. No one knew the precise number—not how many had been taken alive by the Syrians or how many had survived the brutal treatment that was standard operating procedure for Damascus. Only rumors flourished. Optimists spoke of 100 prisoners left; pessimists of very few. From Syria there was no word, not even a hint. It was a closely kept secret because Syria appreciated the value of the card it was holding. By attempting to exploit Israel's special sensitivity, however, it was hardening attitudes in Israel.

For the Syrians the burning emotional issue was the Golan Heights. The Israeli attitude on the former Syrian territory was, if anything, more determined than before the war. The Heights overlooked Israel's lush Galilee. The people of that area could still vividly remember the days before the 1967 war when they were forced almost daily into shelters because of incessant Syrian artillery bombardment from the Heights.

Long before the war the government determined that the Golan Heights would not be returned. In order to strengthen their resolve, perhaps to inoculate themselves against external pressures, a network of new settlements was established on the Heights. One of the sacred principles of Zionism had been never to desert settlements—for any price. Thus, new facts were created, making negotiations with the Syrians virtually impossible.

Complicating everything, after the war, was the fact that Syria had nothing to sell, with no military achievements to show. Indeed it was the Israeli army which advanced 30 kilometers into Syrian territory and was 50 kilometers from Damascus. By purely military considerations, the last thing Israel should have been interested in was retreating from its new line.

After the cease-fire Israel presented two conditions for either sitting with Syria in Geneva or entering into a disengagement-of-forces negotiation. Syria must turn over the lists of prisoners and allow visits to them by Red Cross representatives. President Assad wanted the negotiations, or, more correctly, he wanted Israel out of the area it had conquered in the Yom Kippur War and which had put it dangerously close to Damascus. But he feared that the moment he gave up the only card in his hands Israel would avoid negotiations with him. And so a dialogue of the deaf began. Israel demanded lists and Syria wanted to negotiate for a disengagement of forces. Each side was ready to fulfill the others' demands only after its own demands were carried out.

Here was an impasse to truly tax Kissinger's diplomatic talents, and his endurance. While he was finishing up the negotiations with the Egyptians he had explained to the Israelis that the Syrian question could be approached through two possible negotiating routes. One was to go back to Geneva and hope the Syrians would come; the other was to continue the step-by-step approach with him. Kissinger argued that going back to Geneva now would open up a Pandora's box of explosive issues, such as the west bank of the Jordan, the borders of '67, and the PLO.

Of course, Geneva also no longer fit in with the American interest. As long as Kissinger continued to orchestrate the step-by-step negotiations, he did so as a soloist. A comprehensive negotiation at Geneva would have demoted him to merely one of the players. It was as a soloist in the Aswan-Jerusalem shuttle that he had opened a wedge to the Arab world for the United States; now he wanted to open it a lot wider through a shuttle to Damascus. The Israeli government, fearful of Geneva and with nothing much to lose, gave him the go-ahead.

Flushed with his success on the southern front, Kissinger arrived in Damascus on Sunday morning, January 20. After only a few hours in the Syrian capital he sent a message to Jerusalem that he was returning to Washington but that his plane would land at Ben-Gurion airport for a short stopover at 4:00 P.M. He asked Israeli ministers to meet him there. At the scheduled time Defense Minister Dayan and Eban were waiting. But the talks in Damascus lingered and Kissinger's plane was late. At 5:30 Allon showed up at the VIP lounge where Dayan and Eban were waiting. Five minutes later Dayan got up and asked Eban to express his regrets to Kissinger; he could not wait any longer, he said, because he was scheduled to give a lecture to the Young Guard of the Labor party at 6:00 P.M. Lecture or not, it was undoubtedly Allon's appearance which unnerved Dayan. He believed his old rival, the minister of education and culture, should have nothing to say in these initial political contacts.

Close to 6:00 P.M. Kissinger landed and Eban and Allon entered the plane. When Kissinger saw them he seemed piqued and asked for Dayan. Eban relayed Dayan's apologies, but it soon became clear that Dayan had not missed anything. Kissinger told Eban and Allon that Assad was extreme and irrational. He was demanding half of the Golan Heights in return for his consent to a disengagement-of-forces agreement. Kissinger said he did not expect the Israelis to give Assad's proposal serious consideration. Yet he was convinced that it was not the last word from Damascus. Basically, he said, Assad is interested in negotiating a disengagement of forces, but it will be a long and arduous process. In order not to allow a vacuum to develop, Kissinger had prevailed upon Assad to send a ranking delegation to Washington. He asked Israel to do the same. The whole conversation lasted only a few minutes and then Kissinger's plane took off.

From Washington, Kissinger focused on finding a formula through which Israel's initial conditions regarding the prisoners could be met while at the same time reassuring Syria about Israel's intentions on a disengagement agreement.

On Sunday, February 3, Jerusalem received a message from Kissinger saying that an understanding had been reached with the Syrians on the following procedure: Syria would give Kissinger the list of prisoners; Kissinger would turn the list over to Israel and would receive for transmittal to Syria a proposal for a disengagement of forces on the Golan front; Syria would then allow Red Cross visits to the prisoners. Kissinger said it could all take place within a few days.

Mrs. Meir instructed Cabinet Secretary Michael Arnon to conduct a telephone poll on Kissinger's proposal. This was an exceptional procedure, but she knew that bringing Kissinger's compromise proposal to the cabinet would cause a sharp argument, with uncertain results. A vote over the phone, on the other hand, did not permit debate or argument, and the government quickly gave its approval by a majority vote. Kissinger received the green light to come to the area to carry out the three-sided exercise.

On Wednesday, February 27, the Boeing 707 landed again at Ben-Gurion Airport. Kissinger came down the ramp and announced that he had brought Israel good news. There was no need to say any more; everyone knew what he meant. Quicker than ever Kissinger was hustled into a helicopter for the ride to Jerusalem and went straight to the prime minister's office. Mrs. Meir was waiting for him. They shook hands and he gave her a sheet of paper. The prime minister sat down and looked at the names of the Israeli prisoners. Slowly tears started pouring down her wrinkled, tired face. She called in Chief of Staff Elazar, a man who had known years of war and suffering, and he too looked at the list and brushed away tears.

All that night the lights remained on in dozens of apartments throughout the country. Sitting and silently waiting for a message were parents, brothers, sisters, friends, and lovers. Of the more than 100 waiting families, the hopes of only 70 were fulfilled as special messengers came with the good news that their sons or husbands were on the list.

The next day Kissinger was back in Damascus. He gave Assad Israel's proposal for a disengagement of forces that would take place within the bulge conquered by Israel during the Yom Kippur War. Assad presented a map of his own in which he demanded half of the Golan Heights. The formal gestures had been made. Further explorations would take place in Washington. Kissinger left Damascus, and then Red Cross representatives started visiting the Israeli prisoners.

Eban was in Washington on March 11. But in a meeting with Kissinger he had little new to offer. Golda Meir was insisting that the separation of forces take place within the Israeli-held bulge, and Israel would not retreat past the pre-Yom Kippur War lines. Kissinger did not give up. He told Eban that he expected a more conciliatory position when Dayan came. (It had already been reported that Dayan was in favor of a retreat from the city of El Quneitra, which was on the Israeli side of the pre-Yom Kippur War lines.)

When Eban returned to Israel he told Dayan what Kissinger had said. Dayan replied that he was trying to persuade the cabinet to make a more generous proposal. He asked if perhaps Eban could help. He also expressed doubt about the usefulness of his own trip to Washington since he did not think he could say anything new yet to Kissinger.

And, in fact, when Dayan got to Washington he could only repeat Eban's earlier words. Kissinger tried to bring El Quneitra into the conversation, but Dayan had to stick to the official position of the government. In the meantime there had been absolutely no give in the official Syrian position. Kissinger decided it was time for another trip to the Middle East to do some on-the-spot persuading.

One of the reasons that Kissinger wasn't getting much movement out of the Israeli government was that in the period since his last visit the political leadership had been going through a period of turmoil unprecedented in the history of the country. A wave of public protest continued to mount against the old guard. Soldiers recently demobilized after the Egyptian disengagement agreement were going into the streets in massive public demonstrations, the main target of which was Dayan. The major responsibility for the

Yom Kippur War blunders was pinned on him, and his resignation was demanded.

Outwardly it looked as if Dayan was managing to hold firm against the pressure, but slowly the public attacks on him began to nibble away at his usual confidence. Then there was an incident that pushed him over the edge. At a funeral ceremony for fallen soldiers, bereaved parents spat on his car while he was sitting in it. Two days later, on February 25, he made a dramatic announcement that he would not serve in Mrs. Meir's new government, which she was about to present to the Knesset.

At first Mrs. Meir tried to dissuade Dayan, appealing to his sense of national responsibility. But Dayan insisted that in the conditions that had been created, he could not function effectively. Reluctantly she reconciled herself to the loss of her political ally.

On Sunday March 3, 1974, Golda Meir appeared in front of the Labor coalition (the Labor party plus the Mapam party) in the Knesset to present her proposed new government—a list on which Rabin's name had replaced Dayan's as minister of defense. After she finished reading the list, a discussion ensued in which severe criticism was heard over the fact that younger and newer faces were not included. It was of course legitimate criticism. But with the kind of control that had been customary in the Israeli Labor party, the words sounded like heresy to the old leader. She realized that with Dayan gone she too was vulnerable, and she decided to preempt.

Mrs. Meir's answer to her critics came in a low, muffled voice, but it jolted her audience of party officials out of their seats. "Even before the war I begged not to head the government again," she said. "Finally I agreed because I did not have enough backbone to insist on my own wishes. If I had insisted I would have left my post in a much better personal condition. How did I come to such a punishment? But it is my fault, not yours. With no hesitation I would say that it is not the desire to rule but the will to serve the people that has directed my life." There was a pause, and a sigh, and she reached the climax. "All is well that ends well. I thank my friends who spoke open-heartedly and those who did not speak. I beg your pardon. This evening I will inform the president of the state that I have ended my service. I hope that you will find a way to inform the president who is your new candidate."

Her decision to leave was probably totally spontaneous, but it was a brilliant political stroke. Within hours a steady parade of frightened leaders came to her house begging her to come back. If the party had received an early warning of what was coming it might have managed somehow to do without her. But now it suddenly found itself faced with the prospect of a bitter struggle for choosing a successor, a struggle that could tear the party apart. The alternative, the lesser of the two evils, was to beg Mrs. Meir to come back on almost any conditions.

She received the delegations with one aim only— to bring the party to its knees. Only after the parade of delegations had ended, and only after all the factions expressed their loyalty, did she agree to change her decision. The party apparatus breathed a sigh of relief while the whole country watched with amazement at this demonstration of self-abasement in front of a tired 75-year-old woman.

No one was calling for Dayan to come back, but with Mrs. Meir seemingly in firm control of the party once again, the defense minister thought he saw an opening to reassert himself. He told Mrs. Meir that he would rejoin her new government and she enthusiastically agreed. Dayan needed some way of explaining his personal zigzag without further damaging the little credibility he had left. Fortunately, that night a military report was relayed to the government on an increase of tension on the northern front. In an unprecedented step, Mrs. Meir allowed Dayan to release the military report for publication. He cited it as the reason for his return. But the public was not deceived. The press severely criticized the use of military matters for political and personal advantage. And so, in fact, Dayan's public image only suffered more. The demands for his resignation mounted to an even greater pitch.

This time she had identified herself too closely with Dayan and the attacks on him began to undercut her own position more clearly. Almost as soon as her new government was sworn in it was in crisis. On Wednesday, April 10, 1974, the prime minister appeared in front of the Labor alliance in the Knesset. For days she had once again been under heavy pressure by the heads of her own party to fire Dayan. Similar approaches were directed at Dayan but he stubbornly rejected them. There was an almost mutinous atmosphere in the party branches. She understood that this time she was confronted with the alternative of either firing Dayan or quitting herself. Tired and exasperated, she chose the second course. "I can no longer carry this burden," she told the Labor party and this time it did not get on its knees. There were no pleas and no delegations. On Thursday, April 11, 1974, she announced her resignation formally in the Knesset. The resignation of the prime minister being equivalent to the resignation of the whole government, her action meant the fall of Moshe Dayan as well.

Until the party could choose a new candidate for prime minister, and until the candidate could organize a new government and present it to the Knesset for approval, Mrs. Meir's outgoing cabinet would continue to serve, as prescribed by law, as an interim government. It was generally understood that the interim government would serve through the end of the negotiations with Syria.

As Henry Kissinger arrived in Israel on Wednesday, May 2, to begin round two of shuttle diplomacy he faced a more purposeful Israeli negotiating team. The political crisis had been solved by Mrs. Meir's resignation. She and Dayan, who would lead the team of ministers, were now able to concentrate all their energies for the task at hand. The negotiations were their last hurrah and they were determined to go out with the right agreement.

There were also some new faces on the negotiating team. In addition to Mrs. Meir, Dayan, Eban, and Allon, the prime minister had co-opted Rabin and Peres to the group. Rabin had just been nominated by the Labor party to head the next government and Peres was the likely next minister of defense. Also sitting in on the talks was the new chief of staff, Major General Gur. (Elazar had just been forced to resign as chief of staff as a result of an investigating committee report holding him mainly responsible for the failures in the war.)

There was also a new face in the Kissinger party—39-year-old Nancy Maginnes, who had become Mrs. Kissinger at the end of March, and was now his constant shuttle companion. At the welcoming ceremony at the airport Eban said: "We have come to Lod to welcome Mrs. Kissinger who is on her first visit to Israel. To our pleasant surprise we found out that accompanying her is the secretary of state of the United States and we welcome him too."

Kissinger's timetable had him returning to Washington no later than Thursday, May 9. Thinking perhaps of the one-week shuttle with Egypt, he assumed that if the negotiations could not be concluded by that date it would be better to postpone them and resume in another forum. But Kissinger never kept his own deadline or the new ones he set for himself. It turned into an exhausting and tension-filled 32-day odyssey accompanied by the thunder of guns.

On the northern front the Syrians had opened a war of attrition and intended to negotiate while keeping Israel under the pressure of daily casualties. Kissinger made a perfunctory effort to get Assad to agree to a cease-fire, but he gave up quickly. To the Israeli complaints Kissinger replied that the shooting would stop only when the agreement was signed. Israel for its part did not make the cease-fire a condition for participation in the negotiations, though such a demand certainly would have been accepted by Israeli public opinion and even by the world.

Israel needed the agreement, needed it badly, to heal its severe war wounds in the conditions of a cease-fire. The Syrians knew it and Kissinger knew it. The American secretary of state, who had conducted the Vietnam negotiations under the pressure of heavy American bombing raids, was not that unhappy about the shooting. He understood that the key to an agreement was in Israel's hands. Israel had territory to give up. The thunder of guns, he believed, could lower Israel's resistance while he talked.

At the first meeting with Kissinger the Israeli negotiating team stuck stubbornly to their position that the disengagement of forces should take place within the 30-kilometer bulge inside Syria conquered by Israel during the war. Israel's first map resembled, in form, the agreement with Egypt. There was a buffer zone in the middle, and on either side limited-forces zones. The width of each of the zones would be ten kilometers.

Kissinger no longer tried to maintain the pretense of being a neutral mediator who was merely facilitating the exchange of proposals between two sides. He immediately tried to undercut the opening negotiating stance of the Israelis. The Syrians, he warned, would reject this proposal out of hand and the results would be terrible: a war of attrition, an increase in the tension, finally a general war that Egypt would have to join. Israel's international situation was awful, he kept reminding the ministers. The nations of the world were waiting for the opportunity to push Israel to the '67 borders. All the hard-won political achievements of the United States in the Middle East would go down the drain, and the Soviets would be in the streets of Cairo again. The only way to prevent it, to keep the Arabs on the side of the Western world, said Kissinger, was by providing proof that relying on the United States pays.

Trying to disabuse his listeners of their illusions, Kissinger painted a dark picture of Israel's situation:

> Israel does not have a choice between a good alternative and a bad one, but between two bad ones. The first is to remain stubborn, allowing the negotiations to fail with all the consequences for relations with the United States. The second alternative—territorial concessions with a security risk. What is preferable? This, unfortunately, can be known only after the fact. If a war does not break out for several years then the territorial concession will seem justified. If it does break out then the concession is unjustified. It is also not clear if there will be an agreement even if Israel makes concessions, because it is hard to know anything with President Assad. He thinks and acts differently from the way a man of Western civilization does.

Specifically, Kissinger wanted Israel to offer a retreat beyond the "purple line" (the pre-Yom Kippur War cease-fire line). From the beginning Kissinger pressed the Israelis to offer a line that not only might be acceptable to Damascus but that, were it rejected, would do the least political damage to the United States and would leave a loophole for possibly renewing negotiations at a later date. In Kissinger's view the operative principle had to be a proposal as close as possible to the final agreement with Egypt. Assad, he thought, would have difficulty refusing conditions Egypt had already consented to. In other words, Israel had to offer Assad some land which he had not held before Yom Kippur because Sadat had come away with a piece of land on the east bank of the Suez Canal.

But the Israeli negotiators stuck to their guns. Kissinger flew off to Damascus on May 3 with an Israeli disengagement plan entirely on the Syrian side of the pre-Yom Kippur War lines. When presented with the Israeli map Assad turned almost violent. As reported by the Americans, he spoke of the proposal as a personal insult, aimed at adding yet another humiliation to the humiliations that were imposed on Syria so far. It was proof, he said, that Israel had not abandoned the road of conquest. Syria wanted no less than Sadat got.

Another subject that fell on deaf ears in Syria was Israel's request for an exchange of wounded prisoners. The entire prisoner issue would only be solved in the final agreement, Assad insisted. He feared that consenting to an exchange now would be interpreted in his country as a surrender to Israeli demands. The fact that the matter involved 12 Israeli wounded in return for 25 wounded Syrian soldiers did not affect that evaluation.

That first shuttle trip to Syria was an experience in itself for the American party. It was remembered by the proverbial "senior American official" like this:

> When we got into the conference room with Assad and his men, the room was locked and it was almost completely dark. We did not know why and we didn't ask. Every time we had to go out to the bathroom we had to announce it so that someone would open the door. When we reached our rooms in the hotel we

could not fall asleep. The lights in the corridors were brightly lit, and since the doors of the rooms were made of glass the light glared in our eyes and prevented us from sleeping. Very tired, we dragged ourselves to the plane only to find out that in addition to the sleeplessness we had all picked up some *turista*.

For the rest of the shuttle the American party arranged to spend their nights anywhere but Damascus.

From Damascus the Americans went on to Cairo to seek some moral support from President Sadat. Sadat, however, was in a dilemma. On the one hand, he explained to Kissinger, he very much wanted the success of the negotiations, to take him out of isolation as the only Arab leader to sign an agreement with Israel after the October war. But he could not allow himself to be accused of overlooking Syrian interests. Therefore, he said, he must support the negative position of Syria regarding the map that Israel offered. Nevertheless, in order to speed the negotiations, Sadat sent an urgent messenger to King Faisal of Saudi Arabia and Algeria's President Boumediene to report developments to them and to persuade them to use their moderating influence on the Syrian president.

While Kissinger was away, Mrs. Meir and Dayan held a private meeting in which they discussed the necessity of making a concession on the line of retreat. Dayan said that if they had to give in it should be in the El Quneitra area. He argued that the city itself was not that strategically essential for Israel. On the other hand, in the past it had been a bustling city, the pearl of the Golan for the Syrians. Giving the city to Assad, even though it was completely destroyed in the wars, would satisfy his need for prestige. They then agreed that Dayan would privately offer Kissinger an "unofficial" proposal that Israel would be willing to part with the eastern part of the city.

When he got back to Israel on May 5, however, Kissinger was already insisting that Israel had to give up all of El Quneitra and the three strategic hills to the west of the city. When the group of ministers emphasized the importance of the hills, Kissinger became visibly annoyed. He viewed their arguments as a transparent attempt to conceal the true Israeli interest—the civilian settlements. The United States, he said, like most other countries, never supported the establishment of the settlements on the Golan Heights in the first place, and it had no intention of changing its position now. Building the settlements was a grave error that reduced the room for territorial compromise in these negotiations, and in the negotiations to come.

When Mrs. Meir heard him lecture Israel she jumped out of her seat and confronted Kissinger:

> What does that mean? What moral justification does Assad have altogether to demand even one meter beyond the purple line? After all, it was Syria together with Egypt that started the war. It is not possible to start a war and then complain of an insult when the war is lost. And the same goes for the war of 1967. If the Syrians hadn't started a war then all the territories they want today would have been in their hands. In the meantime there have been two wars; many were killed and severely wounded. Now Syria just wants to turn the wheel back. Does Israel have to pay the price of Assad's defeats?

There is no doubt that the war had deeply affected the old leader. Even before the October war she was not an optimist regarding Arab intentions. The war apparently ate away her last bit of trust. There is no doubt that she was repenting for the sin of complacency in the days before the war. And the memory of the first days of the war, when the Syrian army was at the foot of the Golan Heights, haunted her like a nightmare. The only thing Kissinger could say after her outburst was that is was he and not she who had to confront Assad the next day. "Believe me," he said, "that is not at all a pleasant mission."

The next day, on Monday, May 6, the Israeli proposal for a retreat from the eastern part of El Quneitra became an official government position. The details of the proposal were that the ghost city in the north would be divided into three zones. In the center would be a civilian administration run jointly by Israel and the UN; on the east, a joint Syrian-UN civilian administration. The western section would remain under exclusive Israeli sovereignty. North of the city of El Quneitra there would be an Israeli retreat from the purple line of 1 to 1½ kilometers. Parallel to that the Syrians would retreat a similar distance on their side of the line. This combination of two to three kilometers would constitute the UN buffer zone. Israel would also retreat from the area of Rafid in the central sector of the '67 cease-fire lines to straighten out the line, and this area would be turned over to the UN.

Kissinger was off in Amman that day, mostly to soothe the Jordanian king by letting him know that America was not forgetting him in the crescendo of political negotiations all around him.

When Kissinger returned to Jerusalem he was hardly overjoyed by the Israeli proposal. All this talk about a third of the city that is not even a city, he said, was petty quibling. Assad wanted the whole city, including the hills around it, and Kissinger bluntly informed the Israeli negotiators that he supported Assad's position. In his opinion Israel was exaggerating the importance of the hills. Several times he referred to them contemptuously as the "Himalayas of General Gur." He was convinced that Israel could and must find a defense substitute for the hills. As for the city, anything less than the whole of El

Quneitra wasn't even worth speaking about. And he was convinced that President Assad would not be content with less than an Israeli retreat all along the purple line.

The arguments over a few hundred meters here and there were beginning to exasperate the secretary of state. At one point he burst out:

> Such bargaining is not dignified for an American secretary of state. I am wandering around here like a rug merchant in order to bargain over 100 to 200 meters! Like a peddler in the market! I'm trying to save you, and you think you are doing me a favor when you are kind enough to give me a few more meters. As if I were a citizen of El Quneitra. As if I planned to build my house there!

But it was not just cheap haggling. The strategic problem was El Quneitra's proximity to Kibbutz Merom Golan, one of the new settlements. To defend the Kibbutz, Israel wanted to keep it as far as possible from the Syrian lines. Having already said he was against the establishment of the settlements in the first place, Kissinger did not think that Assad would be impressed by the Israeli argument. He preferred to leave the settlements out of the discussion altogether, as if they weren't there. But this was something the Israeli negotiators couldn't afford to do.

In the middle of his arguments with the Israelis about El Quneitra Kissinger had to fly off to Cyprus for a little diplomatic sideshow with Gromyko. The Soviet foreign minister had shown up in Damascus to try to get some Soviet input into the negotiations, but the Syrians were not giving him much to do. They had even let Kissinger know ahead of time that he was coming, offering to cancel the visit if Kissinger thought it would upset the negotiations. Kissinger did not object but let Gromyko know he would not be able to meet with him in Damascus where the Russian was publicly declaring that Israel had to withdraw from all the Arab lands taken in the 1967 war. Instead, a meeting was scheduled for Cyprus.

So, on Tuesday, May 7, the two foreign ministers met for five hours in a room put at their disposal by President Makarios. Kissinger gave Gromyko a guarded report on the progress of the negotiations, hoping to pacify him so that he didn't feel it necessary to come to Damascus again. When Gromyko argued forcefully that Israel had to be forced to retreat from half of the Golan Heights, as the Syrians were demanding, Kissinger replied that he didn't mind if Gromyko flew to Tel Aviv the next day to try to persuade the Israelis. Gromyko declined the offer and flew back to Moscow instead. He was not heard from again during the negotiations.

On Wednesday morning, May 8, Kissinger returned to Damascus. Assad still insisted on an Israeli retreat all along the purple line, including all of El Quneitra and the hills. A partition of El Quneitra was out of the question. How could he repopulate the city if there was a military line crossing its center? the Syrian president wanted to know.

Yet there was some progress. First of all, Assad accepted the Israeli map as a basis for further discussions and gave up his demand for half the Golan Heights. In addition, he hinted that for an additional Israeli concession regarding the line he would reply with a concession of his own.

Kissinger kept flying. On Thursday morning, May 9, he was in Riyadh. That afternoon he was in Alexandria with vacationing President Sadat. In neither city did Kissinger receive much support on the Israeli map, which was described by President Sadat as a "scandal."

While Kissinger was traveling, the Israeli proposal

in full detail was published in the Israeli press. On returning to Israel Kissinger was furious. "What are you doing to me?" he shouted at the Israeli negotiators. "I come to Sadat in order to report to him on the negotiations and he shows me *Haaretz*."

Allon thought the leaks had come from the Security and Foreign Affairs Committee of the Knesset, to which the government had to report regularly. Kissinger wanted to know why the government couldn't censor the items out of the press.

Mrs. Meir turned to Chief of Staff Gur, who replied that he had consulted with the chief military censor and it seemed that there was nothing to be done. It would be political censorship, and illegal, said Gur.

Kissinger continued to press. Couldn't the negotiators report less to the committee and to the entire government?

Dayan replied that this was out of the question. There was a procedure that had to be followed, a certain law and order.

"What law and order?" shouted Kissinger. "You won't get far with this kind of law and order."

At this stage Ambassador Dinitz delicately commented that many leaks apparently were coming from the American delegation. Kissinger went wild. "You blame the Americans?" he asked incredulously. The journalists who accompanied him, he said, knew nothing except what he told them. And he only told them what served the negotiations. But, he said, every time he left Israel he saw Marilyn Berger (of the *Washington Post*) bursting into the plane and running amok with a pile of papers. Where did she get them? he wanted to know.

Allon concluded this episode by reminding Kissinger that the Israeli government was composed of various parties that did not always cooperate. That was the price that had to be paid for democracy, said

Allon. The Arab states would have to learn to live with the fact that their neighbor was a democratic country.

Kissinger's next visit to Damascus was even more exasperating—and there Kissinger couldn't vent his anger so openly. The Syrians suddenly started upping their demands. Kissinger was learning that in negotiations with Damascus anything was possible. Not only did Assad want El Quneitra and the hills, and an Israeli retreat all along the '67 cease-fire line, but he now demanded the deserted villages of Achmadia, Botmia, and Assha in the south of the Golan, and the Druze village of Majd El Shams in the north. The demands were presented as an ultimatum with total refusal to discuss other elements of the disengagement until they were met.

An atmosphere of emergency suddenly enveloped the discussions. Kissinger informed Israel and Syria that if an agreement were not achieved by Tuesday, May 14, then on Wednesday he would return to Washington. He pressed Israel to consent to the new Syrian demands and this led to another harsh exchange of words between himself and Golda Meir, who told him that she would report to the government that whenever she claimed that a certain area is of strategic importance to Israel he rejected it, but when the Syrians wanted two more destroyed villages it became important, absolutely essential.

Kissinger was stunned. He wasn't ready for such an accusation. If she reported that to the full government, he told her, then everything was lost. He had never said anything of the sort, he claimed.

Mrs. Meir did not give way. Of course he did not say it explicitly, she told him, but that is the way he had been behaving.

Kissinger turned to the members of his party, searching for support. Is that what he had been saying? he asked. Naturally all the members of the American delegation shook their heads. But the expression on Mrs. Meir's face remained angry and Kissinger went over to the counterattack:

> I am very sorry that matters have reached this point, but you cannot expect me to say amen to every position of yours. I have the right to doubt the political conceptions of Israel without being accused right away of indifference to your security.

The full cabinet convened in an atmosphere of crisis for a long, difficult meeting at the end of which Kissinger was told that there would be no retreat all along the line. However, Israel agreed to give up one of the abandoned villages and made its big concession on El Quneitra, offering to evacuate the whole city on condition that the Syrians would agree to the line proposed by Israel, would abandon their demand for an Israeli retreat from the other villages, and would consent to a buffer zone with a substantial thinning out of their forces.

At a meeting with the negotiating team Kissinger indicated he was still unsatisfied with the new Israeli proposal. The Israeli front line would pass practically on the outskirts of El Quneitra. The Syrians would not consent to it, he said. He wanted Israel to retreat a certain distance away from the city.

There then developed one of the angriest exchanges of the negotiations. Kissinger proposed a way out of what he expected would be an impasse with Assad. He would entice Assad by showing him a map on which only the military line was drawn and not the sovereign political line. The difference was that the sovereign line passed through the outskirts of El Quneitra but the line where the forward Israeli army units would be stationed was several hundred meters back from the city.

Kissinger suddenly heard Dayan interrupt, saying he could not allow Kissinger to do that.

Amazed, Kissinger asked why not. Dayan replied that it would be improper procedure to show Assad a line which the government had not approved. With his awkward English, Dayan said it would not be "constitutional."

At this point Kissinger blew up. From the "constitutional" point of view? he shouted. Was Dayan willing to go and persuade Assad with the Israeli constitution? he asked mockingly.

Dayan shook his head stubbornly.

Okay, Kissinger continued to shout. He was willing to return to Washington and explain to the Foreign Affairs Committee that the negotiations failed because Dayan insisted on installing his barbed wire on the outskirts of El Quneitra. How would Israel look then?

But Dayan insisted. He didn't know how Israel would look and Kissinger could do as he wished, he said, but he could not authorize Kissinger to show only the military line.

Kissinger lost his control completely and started shouting and waving his hands:

> One cannot cooperate with you in any matter. After all, it is I that would have to speak to Assad tomorrow and not you. What will I tell him? That I do not support your position? Because, sir, I really don't support it! Absolutely not! Maybe you would like to add something more to the map? Maybe you would like to write on the El Quneitra area that it is demilitarized?

Dayan kept his cool. Absolutely, he said.

Kissinger sunk deep into his armchair. He mopped his brow, not believing what he was hearing. He told Dayan to take the map, and threw it across the table at the defense minister. He kept shouting:

> Write on the map whatever you want. I no longer care. From my personal point of view the best thing that could happen is that this negotiation will fail.

No one would count it in my favor if the agreement succeeds anyway. But everyone will attack me if, after the agreement, there are problems. So please write. Why don't you write?

There was complete silence. Dayan did not touch the map lying in the middle of the table. He only looked straight ahead with his one penetrating eye. Kissinger was breathing heavily, trying to gain control of his nerves.

Just then an American security man entered the room with Kissinger's glasses, which he had left behind at the hotel. He marched directly to Kissinger and handed them over. The American secretary left the security man's hand hanging in the air. He froze him with a stare and asked if the young man didn't know there was a certain hierarchy. The security man was confused and did not know what to do. Ambassador Keating, who was sitting at the end of the table, finally came to his aid by signaling him over. The glasses were given to Keating, then to Sisco, who finally gave them to Kissinger. Protocol had been preserved. The Israelis exchanged shocked glances.

But Kissinger's outburst apparently had some effect. A day later, in order to prove its goodwill, Israel consented to give up one of the three hills to the west of El Quneitra.

Kissinger took the new Israeli concessions to Damascus, but they didn't work. There were additional demands, this time for the return of the village of Kushniye and several small villages nearby; also the straightening of the line from Rafid to El Quneitra.

At this point Kissinger started speaking openly of the end of the talks, and his aides began preparing an announcement. The guidelines for the announcement included words of praise from the Syrian president for the positive role played by the United States in the negotiations. That was necessary in order to lessen the impact of the failure on the U.S. drive to return to the Arab world. A second guideline was that the announcement should leave an opening for the renewal of the talks at a later date.

Still, when he met with the Israeli negotiating team Kissinger showed he had not lost his sense of humor. He opened the meeting with a mock announcement that the American delegation had decided to give commendations to the Israeli negotiators. Rabin, he said, was commended for eating the most salted almonds during the talks; Eban was the champion eater of sweet almonds. Allon had consumed the greatest number of both. Dayan was commended for his surgical skills in peeling oranges and apples and Peres for courteously passing the refreshments from one end of the table to the other. And then Mrs. Meir interrupted and said: "What about me? You did not dare mention me."

Kissinger continued the joking by telling how he had found his way to Assad's heart:

> In one of the meetings I told Assad that one day I arrived at my office in the State Department and found Sisco in there measuring the rugs and the curtains. Immediately I understood that Sisco was planning a coup against me. Assad burst out laughing and said he would arrest Sisco in Syria. I replied that would not be necessary since a threat is enough to weaken Sisco's resolve. From then on every meeting in Damascus started with Assad's question: "How is Sisco's coup progressing?"

There was another blow to the negotiations the next day, Wednesday, May 15, when a group of Palestinian terrorists seized a schoolhouse and over 100 Israeli schoolchildren as hostages in the town of Maalot. Their purpose was clearly to disrupt the negotiations. A legacy of blood was left before the horrible day was over: 24 Israeli civilians and 1 soldier dead, 3 dead terrorists and 63 students wounded.

Kissinger spent the tragic day waiting at his hotel. As he later told the ministers, he received a lesson in Israeli thinking from a waiter at the hotel. The dialogue went like this:

> Kissinger: What do you think of my role in the area?
> Waiter: There has to be peace. I admire your efforts.
> Kissinger: What are you willing to give up?
> Waiter: Nothing.
> Kissinger: Then should I stop the negotiations?
> Waiter: Absolutely not. I am willing to give ten years of my life for peace.

At that point Kissinger turned to the laughing Israeli ministers and said: "You see. Ten years of his life he's willing to give, but a few kilometers absolutely not."

Kissinger and the ministers decided not to allow the murders in Maalot to affect them. Despite their exhaustion they convened at 10:00 P.M. to continue the discussions.

The meeting did not bring any essential change in the Israeli position, except for an offer that there would be no Israeli military presence on the outskirts of El Quneitra and the peaks of the hills.

When Kissinger left the next day for Damascus, he was not excluding the possibility that this would be his last trip to the Syrian capital. While there, he made a proposal of his own that Israel would retreat another several hundred meters from El Quneitra. He did this without any assurance that Israel would agree to it. In any event, the Syrians were still insisting on all three hills. UN soldiers or Australians or even American soldiers could sit on the peaks, Assad said, just so the Israelis would not sit there looking down on El Quneitra.

It seemed that all was lost and that nothing was left but to draft the joint announcement on the suspension of the talks. But it was difficult for Assad to accept the fact that Egypt, which he despised and did not trust, would emerge from the war with territorial gains while he was left with the Israeli bulge stuck like a bone in his throat. He also raised with Kissinger his suspicion that if he left the circle of agreements in the Middle East, Sadat might make a quick separate peace agreement with Israel. So at the last moment, the Syrian president implored Kissinger to make another attempt.

In a gloomy mood Kissinger arrived back in Israel, where he got an additional Israeli retreat of 150 meters outside of El Quneitra. He had no assurance that this would make much difference with Assad, but he left for another round in Damascus on Saturday, May 18. This is absolutely the last attempt, he said to the Israeli team of ministers. Another three or four days of merchandising rugs and he would lose his sanity, he said.

Suddenly, 15 days after Kissinger started the shuttle, Assad pulled him back from defeat by giving up his demand for the remaining two hills. This was on condition that Syria would reecive an American commitment—which Kissinger gladly gave him—that there would be no heavy weapons on the hills that could inflict damage on the city of El Quneitra.

Kissinger did not quite know what to make of this achievement. On the one hand, he was glad that the ice was broken. On the other hand, he expressed the fear, half seriously, half humorously, that from now on the Israelis would believe in his power to wrest concessions from the Syrians and this would toughen their position.

Assad's modus operandi was obvious. He would not give up one meter or one hill until he had brought the talks to the verge of crisis. But he was always careful not to go over the edge. He was just stubborn enough to keep Kissinger running back to pressure the Israelis for another hundred meters or another village or hill. Only when he was convinced that Kissinger had squeezed as much out of the Israelis as possible and was about to go home did he finally relent on the line of retreat.

Now that the retreat line was finally settled—or so everyone thought—they could turn their attention to defining the buffer zone, the limitations of armaments, the UN force, and other subsidiary issues. A joint Israeli-American working group was formed to start shaping a draft agreement. They still did not understand the amazing Syrians.

The Israeli draft contemplated a buffer zone occupied by the UN just as in the Egyptian agreement. But this time each country would have two limited-forces zones on its side of the buffer zone. Israel proposed that in the first zone (i.e., bordering on the buffer zone) each side would be limited to 2 battalions of infantry comprising no more than 2,000 soldiers; 36 120-millimeter mortars; 12 armored troop carriers; 6 80-millimeter mortars; 4 batteries of antitank missiles; and 2 tank battalions with a total of 60 tanks. The total number of troops in the first area on each side would be no more than 3,000.

Each side would have no more than 10,000 troops in the second zone, with no more than 140 tanks and one short-range artillery battalion.

Israel wanted an immediate exchange of prisoners as soon as the agreement was signed by the two sides.

Kissinger took the Israeli proposal with him to Damascus on Monday, May 20. What he heard there almost floored the secretary of state. Assad came back to the Israeli line of retreat again, demanding an old and almost completely destroyed building several hundred meters from El Quneitra that had once served as the Syrian command post for the Golan Heights, and another small village near which there was an Israeli post.

Kissinger, who thought he had heard everything, now had to return with the new Syrian demands. Once more Kissinger asked Israel to make a little concession on the line of retreat so that they could go on to discuss the limited forces zones.

Golda Meir was furious. It is not possible, she said, that in every round Assad brings up more territorial demands. For some reason Kissinger's anger was directed at Jerusalem. He complained bitterly that it wasn't respectable for the U.S. secretary of state to fly back and forth from Damascus to Jerusalem over every hundred meters. If there were no more movement he would return to the United States, he told Mrs. Meir. Was she willing to give him something to bring to Damascus? he asked her. Not even an old Syrian command post?

Mrs. Meir's reply was almost contemptuous:

> Why should you bring them something? You did so every time until today. If you get them used to the fact that on every visit you bring them another piece of land then they will never stop making demands.

In fact, she was right. Israel refused, and the Syrians this time did not insist. They had made an effort, and when it didn't work they dropped it.

So it was back to the thinning out of forces and the size of the zones. Syria insisted that the width of the thinned-out zone—only one, not two—should not exceed six kilometers. In it they wanted 9,000 soldiers, 54 artillery pieces, and 100 tanks. Syria refused the principle of limiting the range of artillery.

Syria also refused any reference to prohibition of paramilitary action in the agreement. On the matter of the prisoners it proposed an exchange of the wounded prisoners within 24 hours after the signing of the agreement and the exchange of all the prisoners within 24 hours of the signing of an implementation agreement.

The disappointment in Israel was intense. The meaning of the Syrian position, Mrs. Meir said, was that Israel would carry out a one-sided retreat getting nothing in return—no thinning out, no commitment to prevent paramilitary activities—nothing meaningful. Israeli forces would still be under the threat of Syrian artillery fire and so would the Israeli settlements. Mrs. Meir said flatly that she could not accept this.

Kissinger rejected Mrs. Meir's argument. Disengagement agreements are not military but political acts, he said. The political effects of the agreements, from the global point of view, are much more important than any military or territorial advantage. Kissinger warned the ministers again that if the negotiations were to fail now after an agreement on the line had been achieved, the accusatory finger of the whole world, including the United States, would be pointed at Israel.

When Kissinger finished speaking he was shocked to hear oppositon from within his own delegation. Braving a reprimanding look from his boss, Sisco said that in his opinion Assad's refusal did not stem from internal political difficulties but from the hope that his artillery could be a means of pressure against Israel in the future. Kissinger looked at Sisco and said no more.

Once more there seemed no way out but to start thinking of drafting an announcement of the end of the talks. But Kissinger, who had started smelling success, made another trip to Damascus on Thursday, May 23. And there the bargaining started again.

As Kissinger traveled back and forth almost daily, the two countries slowly traded soldiers for guns, the size of the thinned-out zones for the number of UN troops. After a while Syria finally accepted the two thinned-out zones and Israel allowed more troops and tanks. They compromised on the size of the UN force in the buffer zones, with Syria insisting on calling them observers rather than troops.

When all the details were almost wrapped up, one last crisis almost exploded the whole package deal.

Israel demanded that Syria's commitment to a cease-fire would also include terrorist activities. Israel feared that Syria would restrain its army but would send terrorist units—or at least look the other way when they infiltrated across the borders to attack the settlements on the Golan Heights. Israel would then be in a difficult situation. Retaliatory action against the terrorists in the buffer zone or in Syria would be a violation of the cease-fire by Israel.

But Assad said to Kissinger that he could not make any such declaration publicly. The Israeli government made it clear that this matter was a life-and-death issue. So there was a need for another saving formula: the United States made a commitment to Israel that in case of penetration of terrorists from Syrian territory Israel would be able to retaliate in Syrian territory as well. The United States, it would say in the commitment, would not regard this as an act violating the disengagement agreement and would veto any proposal in the UN Security Council directed against Israel over this matter. Mrs. Meir approved the arrangement and the long, wearying negotiations were over.

On Wednesday, May 29, 1974, the prime minister held a reception for the Americans and Israelis who had taken part in the negotiations. Mrs. Meir, who knew that this would be her last official appearance as prime minister, was emotional:

Today all our efforts that seemed impossible are crowned with success. From this day I hope that quiet will now prevail on the northern borders, a day when mothers and children, both in Syria and Israel, will be able to go to sleep quietly.

Kissinger, happy and smiling, kissed her on both cheeks. She was amazed: "What, you kiss women as well?" Kissinger burst out laughing.

Later, more seriously, he said, "We did not always agree with our Israeli colleagues, but we felt that the hope for peace exists in Israel and in this people who have suffered so much and who so much deserve a long and lasting peace."

Mrs. Meir then commemorated Kissinger's prodigious labors: "Except for the chief of staff," she said, "there is possibly no other man who knows every hill and every mountain near El Quneitra as Kissinger does."

Certainly from the point of view of sheer effort and the talents he exhibited (few of which had been needed with Egypt), Kissinger deserved the compliments that the prime minister bestowed on him. He shuttled back and forth dozens of times, covered thousands of miles, and never seemed to tire of endlessly going over the same arguments. He exhibited all the facets of his personality. He joked, was furious, told stories, pressured, threatened, soothed, and philosophically explained. He rarely lost his cool. Even on those occasions when he genuinely lost his temper he was back to business very quickly.

It is doubtful, though, that Mrs. Meir of all people was all that taken with his diplomatic achievement. Kissinger was never willing to get into Israel's shoes, to try to see the dangers from its national perspective. Israel's "unique situation" of being surrounded by enemies who want to destroy it—he himself had described it that way to the journalists on his plane— this understanding was of a philosophical nature with Kissinger. It did not come into play in his practical decisions. He shut his ears to arguments regarding the strategic importance of the lines or the hills. He insisted on regarding the Israeli position as petty bargaining, and used every means of pressure in his attempts to move Israel from its position. Kissinger simply was convinced that Israel had to sign an agreement, any agreement, even if it had to be in the spirit of the Syrian demands.

Kissinger's approach could have been understood if he believed the agreement would open an era of peace, or at least would bring calm to the area. But he did not believe that about the Middle East, certainly not Syria, any more than he believed in it for any other sensitive area in the world. He remains a pessimist, believing that fundamental problems cannot be solved. At the most one can soften the damage and put out fires. In his view, agreements such as the one with the Syrians buy time, that is all.

Gaining time could be a legitimate goal. The question Israel was confronted with was how much it had to pay for this time—not more than several years of time at any rate. Israel had to consider what would be its strategic situation when the time ran out. Seeing things this way, one could not simply disregard Israeli sensitivity regarding the hills and the line. Kissinger, no doubt, understood it, but he refused to pay attention to the ultimate consequences.

Unfortunately, Israel was conducting negotiations not only with Syria but also, perhaps primarily, with the United States. If an agreement was not achieved with Syria, it was essential to Israel that Kissinger leave the area without holding Israel to account for the failure—which could have had severe implications in the field of military and political aid. It made concessions not mainly to Syria, but to Kissinger.

Considering these objective handicaps, the Israeli team this time were a lot tougher than during the negotiations with Egypt. This time they had done their homework. They prepared a list of targets that they wanted to achieve and targets they *had* to achieve. And they knew how far they were willing to retreat. The affair of the city of El Quneitra is illustrative. The decision to give it up, all of it, had already been taken by Mrs. Meir and Dayan early in the negotiations. But it was decided to surrender it street by street—a strategy that proved its efficacy. For every street in El Quneitra, Assad was forced to pay something. There can be no doubt that if from the beginning Israel had been openly willing to give up all of El Quneitra, it would have been forced to give up all the surrounding hills too. Golda Meir and Dayan knew they would have to have an agreement, but from the beginning they followed a policy calculated to minimize the damage.

On Friday, May 31, 1974, close to 12:00 noon, the Palace of Nations in Geneva was once more a meeting place for Arabs and Jews. Two military delegations entered the conference hall with frozen expressions on their faces. Also on hand were delegations of the United States and the Soviet Union, and the chairman, Major General Siilasvuo. Since Syria had not participated in the Geneva conference, its delegation was titled a "joint Egyptian-Syrian work team" and an Egyptian officer accompanied the Syrian officer as an observer. There were no smiles, no handshakes between the two delegations. Following the demand of the Syrian delegation there also was no press. Thirty minutes after they entered the hall the delegations left it. The agreement, which for a month had seemed to be hanging by the thinnest thread, was signed.

About 1:00 P.M. the shooting ended on the Golan Heights front for the first time since the war broke out on October 6, 1973. On Saturday, June 1, 1974, the 12 wounded Israeli prisoners landed at Ben-Gurion Airport. Israel that day returned 25 wounded prisoners to Syria.

For the two Israeli architects of the disengagement agreement the signing in Geneva meant the end of the road. On Monday, June 3, 1974, Mrs. Meir and Dayan sat in the Knesset chamber and, together with 59 other members, raised their hands to vote for Rabin's new government in which Peres was the minister of defense.

The two leaders who nine months ago had been walking legends were responsible politically for the results of the Yom Kippur War. But they subsequently made every effort possible to reduce the damage. In the Syrian negotiations Mrs. Meir was the rock of the Israeli team. Only she was able to stand up to Kissinger, even rebuke him, when she thought he was taking a negative and unjustified approach to Israel.

Dayan contributed the ideas, the conceptual approach. In both disengagement agreements it was Dayan who showed Kissinger the opening. With the Syrians it was Dayan who understood that the key to the disengagement agreement was El Quneitra. Kissinger, who understood Dayan's role well, regretted his departure very much.

But Golda Meir and Dayan had to go. It was time for them to pay the full personal price for the blunders of the Yom Kippur War.

The era of the legendary leaders of Israel was over. But Kissinger's step-by-step diplomacy still had some distance to run. Soon there would be a new team of Israeli negotiators to test their wits and endurance against his.

VII
The Battle for the Passes:
The Last Step

In Israel the torch passed to someone younger and more pragmatic. Indeed, many commentators in Israel saw Prime Minister Rabin's ascendance as somewhat like the coming of Camelot. He was Israel's first sabra prime minister, and as he was sworn into office on June 3, 1974, three days after the agreement with Syria was signed, he seemed to bring a breath of fresh air with him. Having been chief of staff during the Six-Day War, he was one of the few genuine heroes left. In his early fifties, plain-spoken, with boyish good looks, he had hardly a blemish on his meteoric military and political career. (There had been a public accusation that he had suffered a 48-hour anxiety attack on the eve of the Six-Day War, but most people tended to ignore this as malicious gossip.)

When Mrs. Meir decided to step down Rabin was one of the few people available untarnished by the recent military and political disasters. In the years preceding the Yom Kippur War he was away in Washington serving effectively as Israeli ambassador to the United States. On the second day of the war Mrs. Meir kicked him out of the war room and appointed him chairman of the fund-raising effort in Israel—a demeaning position for an ex-chief of staff.

For Rabin it all turned out well. When Pinchas Sapir, the boss of the Labor party, looked around for a new face, there was Rabin, clean and unmarked. Despite Sapir's support in the Labor party's central committee, it was surprisingly close as Rabin defeated Peres by a vote of 298 to 254. The vote was also a great boost for Peres, who had been a close ally of Dayan. As a result, Peres was given the Defense portfolio. Rabin then dumped Eban and the foreign affairs portfolio was given to Allon. Each of the three top ministers now represented a different faction of the party.

The new triumvirate did not have much time to break in. Within two weeks of the swearing in of Rabin's government, Kissinger was back in the area, and this time he brought along his president. Richard Nixon's Middle East trip was, of course, a desperate and transparent attempt to divert attention from the Watergate scandal that was closing in on his administration. But both the Rabin government and President Sadat were more than willing to go along with the charade. Rabin called the visit an "important political event."

Sadat went much further. He turned out three million Egyptians to line the streets of Cairo in a Roman-style victory parade for the man with only one foot left in the White House door. In return Nixon came bearing an expensive gift for Sadat. The United States committed itself to build a nuclear reactor for Egypt.

Though the Americans stressed that the reactor would be for peaceful purposes only, the very thought of a nuclear installation in the hands of the Arabs was enough to give the Israeli leadership palpitations. Specialists knew that it was possible to convert such a reactor to military uses. The most disturbing thing was that the Israelis only learned about it by reading the newspapers.

Kissinger immediately sent a soothing message to

Jerusalem. Egypt, he explained, needs the reactor for domestic uses. If it didn't get it from the United States it would certainly approach Moscow. The American interest, which is also clearly the Israeli interest, said Kissinger, dictates that Egypt should depend on the United States, not Moscow, for the reactor.

This explanation was finally accepted by Rabin, Peres, and Allon. But they didn't have much choice. The question that continued to nag the Israeli leaders, as one of them put it, was "Why the devil did we have to learn about it from the media?" Israel had just signed two disengagement-of-forces agreements that to a large extent were based on trust in Washington's friendship and military support. This was hardly an auspicious beginning for the relationship. Furthermore, there was a disturbing history to the business of the nuclear reactor. Israel had been suspicious that Kissinger had made secret commitments to Sadat during the disengagement talks. Mrs. Meir had asked him about it many times—but the reply was always that Egypt had not asked for or received anything.

About three months after the agreement with Egypt was signed, an Egyptian delegation involved in building electric power stations visited America. An item in the Egyptian newspaper *Al Ahbar* reported that the delegation was conducting talks about a nuclear reactor. Mrs. Meir exploded when she heard of the news item, and she instructed Ambassador Dinitz to ask what was going on. Dinitz met with Kissinger and was told it was all nonsense. There was no nuclear reactor; it was merely technical aid.

Then why did an Egyptian paper publish such "nonsense"? Dinitz asked. The American secretary of state smiled contemptuously and gave Dinitz a classic Kissinger answer: it was all for internal needs. President Sadat had to convince his own people and the

Arab states of his achievements—and this was his way of doing it.

Dinitz forwarded Kissinger's explanation to Jerusalem where it was looked upon with suspicion but finally accepted with resignation.

President Nixon, who arrived in Israel on Sunday, June 17, was not asked about the nuclear plant. But it was one of the first questions put to Kissinger. He apologized profusely. At the beginning, he said, they had spoken only of helping with an electric power station, but the Egyptians kept up their pressure, and it developed into a nuclear reactor.

But why wasn't it possible to report to Israel ahead of time? Kissinger was asked. He dismissed the question with a wave of his arm and said it had merely been inadvertent forgetfulness.

The Israelis had another question. How would it be possible to verify that the reactor was not ultimately used for military purposes? Kissinger took off his glasses and, while calmly cleaning them, said he really didn't know. What did the Israelis suggest?

Kissinger seemed to be waiting for the Israeli answer, which was "American supervision." Kissinger then smugly replied that it wasn't a bad idea but that it would mean American supervision of the Israeli nuclear facilities as well.

The Israeli reaction was obvious. The whole matter was taken off the agenda. The Israeli leadership went out of its way to calm the Israeli public about the Egyptian nuclear reactor, arguing that after all it was better that the reactor should come from the United States than the Soviet Union.

The affair of the reactor was an ominous portent that Kissinger was not going to rest on the laurels of the two disengagement agreements. The United States could not afford a freeze. It needed more diplomatic momentum to expand its initial bridgehead in the Arab world. President Nixon didn't go into details—

which as usual were left to Kissinger—but he emphatically pointed out the general principles and the direction of the new moves. All roads now led to Jordan. Egypt and Syria would get their turn again, but right now King Hussein had to be given something.

Kissinger presented the American argument in detail. The choice Israel is confronted with, Kissinger told the ministers, is not simply whether to negotiate with King Hussein. It is whether to negotiate with Hussein now or be forced to negotiate with Yasir Arafat of the PLO later. Each day without an agreement with the Jordanian king strengthens the position of the Palestinian organizations in the Arab world. Kissinger warned the Israelis to be under no illusions about where this was leading. President Sadat had just made it clear to Nixon that continued procrastination by Israel would lead to all-out recognition of the PLO's claims to represent the Palestinians on the west bank of the Jordan River.

To Israel this was the most sensitive of all the territorial issues. Many Israelis, for religious and other reasons, were opposed to any retreat from what they called Judaea and Samaria, and considered the territories integral parts of the land of Israel. Because of this Golda Meir had publicly committed herself to going to general elections and putting the issue to the people if negotiations required any retreat from the west bank of the Jordan. There was a political reason too. The Labor party was in a government coalition with the National Religious party, whose party platform prohibited any retreat from the Jordan's west bank.

For the new government, too, the Jordanian issue opened up a Pandora's box of complicated political and ideological conflicts. Of the triumvirate, Allon was the man most willing to compromise. He was the author of a plan bearing his name which contemplated a substantial Israeli retreat from the west bank of the

Jordan in a negotiated peace agreement with Hussein. At the other extreme stood Peres, who had been opposed, along with his mentor Dayan, to any Israeli military retreat from the west bank of the Jordan, though he was willing to turn over civil authority to Hussein.

The prime minister had not yet been forced to take a position. He had no special attachments to Judaea and Samaria and had already said once that he wouldn't mind visiting the Jewish settlements there on a tourist visa. Furthermore, Rabin did not have the National Religious party in his government at this time. He thus seemed in an ideal position to dampen the ideological fervor over the issue and to move pragmatically.

But almost immediately Rabin made the same pledge as Mrs. Meir had done—to hold a national election over any retreat from the west bank of the Jordan. Perhaps it was his lack of experience, perhaps his sense of insecurity, perhaps it was just an inexplicable impulse. But his declaration severely restricted both Israel's and Kissinger's room to finesse an interim agreement with Jordan.

Nixon and Kissinger left Israel without having obtained any commitment from the Israeli troika on a next move with Jordan; but as they arrived in Amman, Kissinger did not seem disturbed. He had a basically cheerful message for Hussein, telling the impatient king that his turn had come. The United States would put its considerable weight behind a next move with Jordan, and there would be an interim agreement in the not-too-distant future.

But Kissinger had not reckoned with the Byzantine intricacies of Israeli internal politics. Rabin had trapped himself with his pledge of general elections over any movement on the west bank of the Jordan. Now, as he considered Kissinger's requests, he was afraid that any move with Jordan would result in a premature election in which he would be yanked out of the prime minister's chair he had just begun to warm up. To forestall the Jordanian option he started maneuvering almost obsessively for another step with Egypt. Peres, who was opposed in principle to any movement from the west bank of the Jordan, was content to let the prime minister carry the ball for him; and Peres was not displeased at how Rabin was tripping all over himself in his public statements over the Jordanian and Egyptian negotiating options. It was both ideological and political capital for a man who had his eyes set on being prime minister.

As Kissinger heard of Rabin's pronouncements he decided to send the Israelis a message. He dispatched Joseph Sisco to the House Foreign Affairs Committee, where the under secretary stated that Arafat had abandoned the road of terrorism for diplomacy and there was a chance that he would agree to take part in the Geneva conference.

Naturally Sisco's testimony quickly reached the government of Israel, and as Kissinger had assumed, it touched off a storm. Not that the Israelis took seriously the possibility of Arafat showing up in Geneva. What Jerusalem was upset about was that a high U.S. official had contemplated the possibility of negotiations between Israel and the PLO. Kissinger was in effect signaling Rabin that the Palestinian option existed for the United States if the prime minister continued to be stubborn about Jordan.

Of course, the State Department sent an "explanation" of Sisco's remarks to Rabin: the United States had not changed its position with regard to the PLO. But the clarification implied it was not inconceivable that the United States would shift in the future if Israel persisted in its refusal to negotiate an interim agreement with Jordan.

But that was not the last of the "messages." Kissinger called the Pentagon and issued instructions that

arms deliveries to Israel were to be slowed down—
not enough to hurt, but enough to be felt. A high
Pentagon official took down the message and promised
to forward it. Soon a return call came from the
official, who told Kissinger: "Schlesinger wants the
order in writing." Kissinger was angry, but went ahead
and put the order on paper. He knew as well as anyone that Schlesinger's demand to have it in writing
stemmed from the controversy over the airlift during
the Yom Kippur War.

Soon very familiar cables started coming into Jerusalem from the Washington embassy speaking of
unaccountable foul-ups and delays in arms deliveries
to Israel. The cables also said that when inquiries
were made the Americans denied there was any political reason behind it all—just technical and bureaucratic problems. Again, Israel got Kissinger's message
loud and clear.

It was in this atmosphere that the cabinet set a full
discussion of the Jordan issue for July 21, 1974, one
week before a scheduled visit by Foreign Minister
Allon to Washington. The day before the meeting
items appeared in the press indicating that Allon
would demand the authority to discuss with Kissinger
a partial agreement with Jordan before any further
moves with Egypt.

But at the last moment Allon stepped back from
an open conflict with the prime minister, and Rabin
came out of the meeting with a resolution to his
liking. The official government statement said that
Israel "would act for negotiations for a peace agreement with Jordan." The "peace agreement" referred
to was a not very probable final accord. It was clear
that the interim Jordanian option desired by Kissinger
was officially off the agenda of the Israeli government.

Kissinger was annoyed but decided to wait for
Allon. Kissinger invited his ex-student from Harvard
to Camp David for the weekend to work on him one

to one. Walking in the compound's magnificent gardens, Kissinger and Allon began by evaluating the overall political situation. Kissinger indicated that soon there would be no way out of prompt renewal of the Geneva conference "because the Soviets are pressing and there is a limit to how long they can be put off." Allon did not discount Geneva but found it necessary to tell Kissinger that Israel would not go if the arms shipments continued to be held up. Kissinger replied somewhat testily that Geneva was in Israel's interest and it was not doing the United States a favor by going. As for the arms shipments, Kissinger seemed insulted. He said he was tired of all this non-sensical talk of "pressures." Every time a screw in a machine broke he was suspected of holding back arms. How many times would he have to repeat that there never was and never would be any connection between political moves and fulfillment of the American commitments on arms supplies.

As Kissinger spoke, Allon had difficulty controlling himself, but decided not to press the issue. The two turned to the question of where the next political move should be made. Kissinger told Allon that the recent decision of the Israeli government was sheer folly. Rabin was blind, Kissinger said, if he could not see that he was achieving the exact opposite of what he wanted. Soon Rabin would not be able to speak to Hussein even if he wanted to.

Allon was in a dilemma. He happened to agree with every word just spoken by Kissinger, but he carried the millstone of the government decision. He told Kissinger of Rabin's fears. Any movement with Jordan would necessitate a national election, and it wasn't clear that the present government would come out on top. Did Kissinger want to see the extremist Likud in power?

Kissinger agreed there was a problem here, but, he wondered, why the devil did Rabin commit himself to having an election in the first place? Couldn't this stupid commitment be canceled? Kissinger asked. Allon said it was impossible. Kissinger then wanted to know about the Jericho plan. (There had been some discussion in Israel of offering King Hussein civil administration over the city of Jericho, on the west bank of the Jordan, without an Israeli military retreat from the area. It was thought this wouldn't necessitate a general election.) Kissinger then suggested a variation on the plan. Israel could retreat militarily but the city would be turned over not to Hussein but to the UN. Allon replied that this proposal could be considered.

The two foreign ministers went on to discuss possible next moves with Egypt. Kissinger wanted to know what Israel would give in a further interim agreement with Egypt. Allon said it depended on what Egypt gave in return, but two general principles applied: Israel wanted a public Egyptian commitment to nonbelligerency and demilitarization of all territories evacuated by Israel.

Kissinger smiled ironically. Israel might as well ask for the moon, he told Allon, because Sadat just could not do it. And furthermore, Kissinger wondered, what was all this continued fuss over "nonbelligerency?" It was a word empty of content, he said. If the Israelis listened to his advice they would ask instead for concrete things, such as an end to hostile propaganda and economic warfare.

Allon refused to be specific about a possible Israeli line of retreat. Kissinger kept badgering him, saying it would be only Allon's private opinion and "off the record." Allon refused the bait. He kept repeating the standard Israeli formula: "The depth of the retreat depends on the size of the compensation." Seeing that Allon would not budge, Kissinger volunteered his own view: "Without Abu Rodeis and the Mith and Gidi passes I do not think it will work."

After the Camp David discussions Allon returned to Washington to call· Rabin. Told about Kissinger's "Jericho plan," Rabin became very nervous. He consulted with some advisers who agreed that even this would require a general election. So he sent Allon an urgent message to inform Kissinger that his Jericho plan was out of the question.

Allon was shocked by Rabin's decision. His own view was that Rabin was wrong about the plan requiring a general election. More important, he viewed Rabin's impetuous intervention as a tactical blunder. It would have been possible to get Kissinger's Jericho plan off the agenda slowly, without a direct confrontation. Nevertheless, Allon carried out Rabin's instructions and told Kissinger. The secretary of state's outburst was expected. Tell Rabin that he will regret it, came the reply.

Allon did bring back two positive agreements with Kissinger. First, there would be a visit to Washington by the prime minister at the beginning of September. Second, the United States agreed not to come to any final conclusion on the Jordanian question without further consultations with Israel.

Before Rabin's visit, the long-simmering political earthquake erupted in America. Israel's "best friend in the White House" went into exile at San Clemente. With Nixon, Israel at least knew where it stood, and usually it had stood very well. Gerald Ford's pro-Israel record as a representative was well known, but in Jerusalem they understood this did not necessarily indicate how he would behave as a president. The general attitude was one of wait and see.

Israel did not have to wait long. King Hussein was in Washington the third week in August. On August 18, Allon was awakened after midnight by a phone call from the Foreign Office. A cable had just arrived from Dinitz carrying the joint declaration soon to be issued by Ford and Hussein. One line in the declaration almost jolted Allon out of bed: "It was agreed that consultations between the United States and Jordan will continue, in order to take up at an early and convenient date problems that are of special concern to Jordan, including an Israeli-Jordanian agreement for a disengagement of forces."

Allon called Rabin immediately. How long before the statement would be issued? the prime minister wanted to know. Allon replied that Dinitz had said five hours. The two ministers then decided to ask Kissinger to change the wording of the statement, to at least omit the expression "disengagement of forces." Allon sent a cable indicating his dissatisfaction and gently reminded Kissinger that he had broken his word.

Kissinger took the Israeli reaction straight to Ford. What did Kissinger think? wondered the inexperienced president. Kissinger's recommendation was not to change a comma of the declaration. He would handle the Israelis, he promised.

Within a few hours the joint statement, without any changes, was released to the press. Simultaneously a cable arrived in Jerusalem from Kissinger. What was all the noise about? he wanted to know. The joint statement merely spoke of continuation of "consultations." Kissinger reminded the Israelis he had only agreed not to arrive at any "conclusions" without consulting Israel.

Rabin was steaming with anger when the cable from Kissinger was put on the table in front of him. Since he and Allon knew that Kissinger wasn't as stupid as he pretended, they concluded that the secretary of state obviously took the Israelis for complete fools. Even a child would understand that when the United States declares that it will continue to "consult" for a disengagement of forces agreement it means that it is in favor of such an agreement.

A breach, however small, had now been opened in U.S.-Israeli relations. In the weeks before his trip to the United States, Rabin was to widen the gap with his frequent public statements on negotiations with Jordan. Trying to cover up the domestic political considerations that made him afraid of the negotiations, he openly scoffed at the argument that a freeze with Jordan would lead to the strengthening of the PLO. "King Hussein is not going to run away," he kept telling the public. Of course he deliberately ignored the approaching Arab summit meeting at Rabat and the warning that developments there would be very bad for both Israel and the king.

In the beginning of September Rabin arrived in Washington for the first time as Israel's prime minister. His initial meeting with Ford was not exactly a striking diplomatic success. As is customary at such meetings, the sides had already arrived at several arrangements, worked out by lower officials. The two heads of state were expected to offer the proposals to each other without acknowledging that lower officials had already come to an agreement.

Kissinger had instructed Ford to mention the arms shipments to be sent to Israel and link them to political progress in the area. Ford started telling Rabin of the arms that he had agreed to send to Israel. When he got to the tanks, Rabin suddenly interrupted. "What's the big deal?" he asked. "You agreed to that before." There was total silence in the room. Ford looked embarrassed. Sisco's eyes wandered to the ceiling. Dinitz rubbed his hands nervously. Only Kissinger saw the humor in the situation and after a moment commented, "Mr. President, I suggest that we go back to the Jordanian matter."

This episode would not be worth mentioning if it was not symptomatic of the way Rabin conducted the negotiations despite his five years' experience in Washington. As one of his Washington colleagues put it, "Diplomatically, Rabin is like a bull in a china shop."

On the Jordanian issue it was a dialogue of the

deaf. Rabin insisted on speaking of a "peace agreement" with Jordan, since he knew there was no chance for anything so grandiose to get off the ground. Kissinger wasn't interested. It would only fail and lead to a war, Kissinger insisted. Partial agreements were the only possibility now, he said, so it was pointless to waste time with empty talk of final peace agreements.

No practical conclusions were reached during Rabin's visit. But it was agreed that Kissinger would make another visit to the Middle East in the beginning of October to see what could be done, especially with Jordan.

The Kissinger visit was basically unproductive. He threw around a lot of ideas—a horizontal retreat, a vertical retreat, symbolic moves, etc. He even suggested that he mediate between Jordan and the PLO. Kissinger finally understood that he could not make a breakthrough on the eastern front. One evening in Jerusalem, after a tiring talk with the Israeli triumvirate, he said to two of his aides, "This team is incapable of doing anything. We are racking our brains to find some formula, and there sits a prime minister shivering in fear every time I mention the word 'Jordan.' It is a lost cause."

The Egyptian option didn't look any better. Israel was insisting on nonbelligerency though Kissinger said Sadat wouldn't hear of it. Kissinger was telling the Israelis that if they wanted an agreement with Egypt they would have to give up the passes and the Abu Rodeis oil fields.

Kissinger left Israel with nothing more than an Israeli promise to continue consultations on the Jordanian question. It was decided to send Allon on another trip to Washington in December.

Before Allon got to Washington, King Hussein had disappeared from the diplomatic map. On October 26, 1974, the Arab summit was convened in Rabat and stripped King Hussein of his right to negotiate for the Arabs of the west bank of the Jordan. In the king's place they installed Arafat, whose political platform openly called for the destruction of Israel.

All of Rabin's arguments came tumbling down on the rock of the Rabat summit. Though he had succeeded in avoiding the much feared general election, the price of Rabin's political victory was enormous. His policy had paved the road for Arafat directly to the speaker's rostrum at the General Assembly and to other international platforms.

Not that anyone can be certain that an agreement with Hussein was attainable. On the contrary, the chances were slight. But just the attempt would have given the appearance of movement on the eastern front and undercut the opposition to Hussein in the Arab world. That is what Henry Kissinger had in mind, and he was undoubtedly right.

After Rabat, Kissinger and Ford met to decide on a next move. They agreed that Jordan was a lost cause for the time being. At Kissinger's urging, they decided to push forward on the Egyptian option. Having previously warned Israel of the collapse of the Jordanian option, they could now use Rabat as leverage with Israel for an agreement with Egypt.

The plan was Kissinger's, but Ford would play the leading role. Several days after Rabat, Ford held a press conference. Replying to a question, he said, "There should be a continuation of talks between Israel and Egypt, and between Israel and Jordan or the PLO."

Israel got the message and was properly shocked. It was the first time that any American official, let alone a president, had expressed himself in favor of negotiations between Israel and the PLO.

It was not by chance that Kissinger was away in Japan when Ford made the statement. It allowed him to do the explaining to Israel. He responded to Israel's demand for clarification by saying that Ford's remarks were just a slip of the tongue. There was no change in the policy of the United States regarding negotiations between Israel and the PLO, he said.

Rabin, Allon, and Peres convened to analyze the Ford statement and Kissinger's clarification. They concluded that Kissinger himself had carefully worded Ford's statement before he left for Japan. The aim was clearly to express U.S. displeasure at the hesitancy and lack of activity of the Rabin government on the Jordanian issue while at the same time hinting that if Israel continued to procrastinate it would not be able to rely forever on Washington freezing out Arafat. The major aim, it soon became clear, was to soften up Israel for the Egyptian option.

Before Allon's departure for Washington the Israeli government began to reexamine the question of trying for a declaration of nonbelligerency from the Egyptians in an interim agreement. A committee was set up to look into the question, consisting of three top legal advisers—Minister of Justice Chaim Zadok, Attorney General Meir Shamgar, and the Foreign Office's legal adviser, Meir Rosenne. The three came back with the unanimous opinion that nonbelligerency has no meaning in international law. It was only the formulation "ending the state of war" that had a precise legal meaning, and that was the equivalent of a final peace. It was obvious that Egypt could not accept "ending the state of war" in the context of a disengagement agreement.

Despite the legal opinion, the negotiating team decided to make the end of belligerency an initial condition of the agreement with Egypt. The consideration was that even if "nonbelligerency" was an empty term, they could use it as leverage to obtain some practical political components, such as an end to economic warfare—just as Henry Kissinger had advised Allon in Washington.

A few days before Allon's departure for Washington, on December 3, 1974, an interview with Prime Minister Rabin appeared in the Hebrew daily *Haaretz* which created shock waves in Jerusalem, Washington, and the Arab capitals. Rabin performed an extraordinary political striptease. He wasn't satisfied with giving away Israel's negotiating position but revealed to the whole world his aims and motivations in negotiations with Egypt. He said Israel would try to separate Egypt from Syria, and would try to delay the negotiations until the U.S. elections in 1976, among other pearls.

As if that wasn't bad enough, Rabin also stated that the demand for a statement of nonbelligerency from Egypt was unrealistic.

When Kissinger was shown a transcript of the interview he could not believe what he was reading. "Why did he do it?" he muttered, shaking his head. "Has Rabin gone mad?" For all his anger Kissinger was at least pleased by Rabin's statement about nonbelligerency. He thought the Israelis had finally learned the lesson he was trying to teach them.

But Allon was in a frenzy. The interview had placed him in an absurd position. He was about to leave for Washington with a negotiating position that included a demand for nonbelligerency—a position that had been certified by the triumvirate led by Rabin—but in the meantime Rabin had declared publicly that the demand was unrealistic.

Sure that Rabin had torpedoed his mission, Allon left for Washington where he handed President Ford and Kissinger the Israeli proposal. It began with ten conditions:

1. Israel and Egypt would commit themselves publicly to ending the state of belligerency.
2. The territories that Israel evacuated would be demilitarized.

3. Egypt would commit itself to stopping propaganda and economic warfare against Israel.

4. The agreement to be signed would be called an "agreement" and not an "interim agreement."

5. Egypt would commit itself not to assist guerrilla activities against Israel.

6. The agreement would include a clause saying that it was part of a peace agreement to follow.

7. Egypt would commit itself not to join in any war started against Israel by any other country in the area.

8. The duration of the agreement would be 12 years.

9. Egypt would commit itself to implement the disengagement of forces before the implementation of the rest of the agreement.

10. Means for efficient supervision of the demilitarized areas would be determined.

In return for all of this, said Allon, Israel would retreat from 30 to 50 kilometers in accordance with the conditions and topography of the area. When Kissinger asked what this area included, Allon clarified that it did not include the Abu Rodeis oil fields and the Mitla and Gidi passes.

Allon got short shrift from Ford and Kissinger. Ford said the terms could not be achieved. Both of them said repeatedly that without a retreat from the passes and Abu Rodeis there would be no agreement.

Kissinger was amazed by the inclusion of the demand for nonbelligerency in the official proposal. He said to Allon that he had read Rabin's interview and thought Israel had abandoned the business of nonbelligerency. Allon stuttered something about the prime minister not being quoted correctly. Really? Kissinger wondered; he did not recall seeing a denial.

As for the proposal, Allon hinted to Kissinger that it was merely a bargaining position, the maximum that Israel hoped to get. He started giving clarifications, one of them being that though the formal demand was for a 12-year agreement, Israel would be satisfied with 5 years. If the proposal was forwarded to Egypt, Allon said, it should be sent with the clarifications he was now giving, and it should be considered only as a basis for negotiations. Kissinger promised that he would do this.

But again Kissinger did not keep his promise. His aim, as he explained it to one of his senior aides, was to make it clear to Israel that its proposals were out of line. He could do this best by getting a total Egyptian refusal to negotiate on the proposal. So Kissinger forwarded Allon's proposals to Egypt without any clarifications and without telling the Egyptians that it was just a basis for further negotiation. Of course Sadat rejected the proposal out of hand. Kissinger forwarded Sadat's answer directly to Jerusalem—and the only comment Kissinger appended was that Israel now had to come up with new proposals that could create the basis for further talks.

A whole month dragged by without any change in the official Israeli position. Now, at the beginning of 1975, the Israeli negotiating team had a ticklish problem. The leaders of the United Jewish Appeal in America wanted a top Israeli minister to come and help kick off the new fund-raising campaign. It was decided to send Foreign Minister Allon. But it became apparent that if Allon was in the States he could not avoid going to Washington and paying his respects to Henry Kissinger. The trouble was that Allon had nothing new to say to Kissinger about the Egyptian negotiations. Allon, feeling that nothing good could come of such a meeting, was of a mind to simply cancel the UJA appearance.

Rabin, however, convinced Allon to go ahead with the trip, arguing that it wouldn't do any harm. To give Allon something to say to Kissinger, the cabinet authorized him to invite Kissinger to the area for an "exploratory trip." The government wanted to convince the United States that it wasn't trying to delay the negotiations despite Rabin's words to the contrary in *Haaretz*.

On the eve of Allon's trip some cabinet members were nervous. Knowing Allon's more moderate views on the negotiations, they were afraid that once in Washington he would commit them to more concessions. It was the prime minister who calmed them. "Yigal Allon does not have a mandate to change the proposals that were decided upon," he said.

And indeed Allon didn't deviate from the official government guidelines. He told Kissinger that Israel was waiting for proposals from Egypt and had no new proposals of its own. Kissinger's trip to the area was set for the second week of February.

But while Allon stuck to the government line the indefatigable prime minister was at it again. With one swipe of the tongue he turned the whole government negotiating strategy upside down. Once more it was done in an interview with a journalist, and this time the lucky recipient of the scoop was John Lindsay, ex-mayor of New York and now a correspondent for ABC News.

Lindsay had come to Israel for an exclusive interview with Rabin. When it was broadcast on February 7, 1975, the whole world could hear the prime minister saying plainly and clearly that "in exchange for an Egyptian commitment not to go to war, not to depend on threats of use of force, and an effort to reach true peace, the Egyptians could get even the passes and the oil fields."

In Jerusalem Israeli officials were pulling at their hair, asking when the prime minister would overcome his impulse to shoot off his mouth. It was clearly the worst Israeli error during the whole lengthy negotiations. Before they had even gotten under way, the highest authority in Israel had told the Egyptians that they could get the passes and the oil fields. The business about a commitment not to go to war was understood by Egypt to be lip service. Hadn't Rabin in another interview already said it was "unrealistic"?

At a small, closed meeting Rabin tried to explain to some of his colleagues why he had done it. He said that if the negotiations with Egypt failed it was important for the world to know it was not because Israel was reluctant to give back territories, but because of Egypt's unwillingness to end the state of belligerency.

Time would tell how wrong Rabin's evaluation was. In the meantime Kissinger, who might have been happy with the concession under different circumstances, was again dumbfounded and furious. "That man is destroying the negotiations even before they start," he shouted. He could not understand what Rabin was after, and he called it "lunacy." Kissinger understood very well that having made the big concession up front, Israel would have a difficult time wresting a quid pro quo from Egypt. Then this might cause total failure of the negotiations.

The worst aspect of the whole affair was that it was prompted by personal rivalries and political intrigues inside the cabinet. At the time Rabin made his statement he was worried by his showings in the public opinion polls, as compared with his major rival, Minister of Defense Peres. Peres had managed to create an image for himself as the tough realist in the cabinet, defending Israel's interests by arguing that the passes must not be given up except for ending the state of belligerency. Peres was able to get this message across without saying it officially, by cleverly planted leaks and attributions to unnamed sources. He let it be known through those "sources" that if the government gave up the passes for anything less than an end of belligerency he would resign from the government.

Rabin's statement on the ABC interview was motivated primarily by political considerations—to try to match Peres's image of toughness and realism. His mistake was in saying openly what Peres could get across without having to take responsibility.

Confronted with an Israeli cabinet racked by internal political feuding, a diplomatically inept prime minister, and an Egyptian position that was hardening, Kissinger decided on another shuttle in March 1975. His first objective was to try to convince Israel to give up the demand for ending the state of belligerency and to retreat from the passes and the oil fields.

The Israeli negotiating position was still officially the same as it had been when Allon first presented it in Washington in December. Kissinger, of course, quickly reminded the Israeli negotiators of Rabin's new statement on ABC-TV. Peres, in turn, reminded Kissinger about the other part of the prime minister's statement—the part about ending the state of belligerency.

That provoked one of Kissinger's famous lectures. Hadn't he told the Israelis dozens of times that the business of ending belligerency was a lot of nonsense? He then gave his favorite example of why this was so:

> Take India and Pakistan. Between those two countries there is a state of peace that even you don't dream of, with open borders, full diplomatic relations, and exchange of ambassadors. Did that prevent a war? Sirs, your enthusiasm for words and formulas amazes me. I propose that instead you concentrate on the practical matters and on the examination of the alternatives.

After a bitter debate the cabinet came up with a few concessions, mainly to try to pacify the Americans. Instead of ending the state of belligerency, they would make do with an Egyptian statement pledging "nonuse of force." For that they would retreat to the center of the Mitla and Gidi passes. They still insisted, however, on retaining an electronic warning station located at Umm Hashiba, at the peak of the passes, even though technically this would be in the UN buffer zone.

But the Egyptians weren't giving an inch. As Kissinger suspected, they now knew they would eventually get all of the passes, so they were holding tight. Even Kissinger didn't try to deny to the Israelis that Sadat was being very hard and not offering much in the way of political concessions. He said he sympathized with Israel's predicament but that it should consider the alternatives realistically.

Kissinger tried to manipulate the Israelis into responding. On one of his flights from Cairo to Jerusalem he told the reporters in his entourage that he was carrying "new Egyptian proposals." The revelations of the "senior official" made immediate headlines all around the world, of course.

When Kissinger arrived in Jerusalem and reported to Rabin, Allon, and Peres, eyebrows were raised. Where were the new Egyptian proposals they had read about in the press? All they could see was a hardening of Egypt's position. Kissinger's purpose, naturally, was to create an impression of Egyptian moderation to make it harder for the Israelis to reject the Egyptian terms.

That evening a spokesman for the prime minister called a press conference and announced that Israel would reject the Egyptian proposals. This was before the full cabinet had even met to discuss the subject. One of the American reporters rushed to Kissinger's room in the King David hotel to give him the news. An angry Kissinger immediately called Rabin, who seemed to be expecting the call.

Kissinger said that it seemed to him he was wasting his time. If Rabin already knew Israel was rejecting the proposals, what was the purpose of them sitting together to discuss them?

Rabin's typically blunt answer shocked Kissinger. "I don't know. The decision whether to continue the negotiations is yours."

Kissinger swallowed hard. What does that mean? he asked. Had Rabin decided he didn't want an agreement?

Rabin answered that of course he wanted an agreement but not at any price. Israel wasn't willing to be continuously confronted with Kissinger's *faits accomplis*. He asked Kissinger what new proposals he brought from Egypt.

With feigned innocence Kissinger answered that he never said he brought new proposals. But the journalists said it, Rabin reminded him. Kissinger wanted to know if he was responsible for what the journalists wrote. Yes, retorted Rabin, in most cases he was responsible.

Kissinger knew there was no way to finesse the bull-like prime minister. There was a misunderstanding here, he finally said, but they mustn't let incidents like this distract them from the main purpose.

The discussions went on, but there was no way out of the impasse. The crucial moment came on Friday afternoon, March 19, 1975, as Kissinger arrived once more from Cairo empty-handed. Egypt was holding fast to its demand for a total retreat from the passes, it wasn't going to allow the Israelis to keep the electronic warning station on the peak, and it wouldn't offer an agreement of long duration.

Kissinger told the Israeli ministers not to be under any illusions that even if they signed the agreement they would get much respite. Within three months of the signing, Kissinger said, they would have to make further proposals to Syria and Egypt.

It was at that moment, already depressing enough

for the Israeli negotiating triumvirate, that a personal message came for Rabin from President Ford. The message was tough, even brutal. It asked Rabin to consent to Egypt's conditions and ominously warned of damaging relations between Israel and the United States.

The telegram from Ford arrived just before Kissinger sat down with the Israeli negotiating team, and it turned the meeting into an icy confrontation. Rabin told Kissinger that Israel would not accept dictation. He said that Kissinger knew well that up to that time Israel had made all the concessions while Egypt only hardened its position. He accused Kissinger of bringing in the president to pressure Israel.

Kissinger claimed he had nothing to do with the presidential message. He said the Israelis seemed to think that the president was a puppet whose strings were held by Kissinger. He said in disgust that if it were up to him he would have given up.

Rabin lit another cigarette, looked straight at Kissinger, and said, "I do not believe you." He accused Kissinger directly of not only asking for the message from Ford but of wording it.

On that note the meeting broke up. Kissinger returned to his hotel while Rabin convened the government for a final consideration of the Egyptian demands and the Ford telegram. Though the sabbath had started, even the religious ministers came for the deliberations.

At the King David Hotel Kissinger closeted himself with his aides and fumed at Rabin. Never, never had he been spoken to at a diplomatic meeting in such insulting terms, he said. When he calmed down he realized the telegram from Ford, or at least its timing, had been a tactical mistake. If Mrs. Meir had still been in charge, he thought, she would have reacted strongly to the telegram but then gotten on with the negotiations. But Kissinger was afraid that Rabin, conscious of his weakness and worried about his cabinet rivals, would put on an exaggerated show of toughness.

So Kissinger instructed one of his aides to call the prime minister's office and get hold of Ambassador Dinitz, even if he had to be pulled out of the cabinet meeting. Several minutes later Dinitz was on the line. Kissinger said he didn't think it would be such a good idea to read Ford's message to the whole government and wanted Dinitz to pass that thought along to the prime minister. Dinitz said he fully agreed with Kissinger, but it was too late. The telegram had just been read out.

Kissinger sat down in an armchair near the window and looked gloomy. "It's hopeless," he whispered to no one in particular. Kissinger and his aides continued their vigil. Close to midnight a call came in saying the meeting was over. Kissinger and several aides drove to the prime minister's office to hear his report on the government's decision. It was not unexpected—an almost total rejection of the Egyptian demands. The government was only willing to make a slight concession of a few more kilometers in the Abu Rodeis area and in the north.

Kissinger dismissed the Israeli gesture as meaningless. Looking, as one of the participants remembered it, "like a beaten man," he spoke very quietly.

> I am sorry to tell you that you will regret it. Your decision plays into the hands of your enemies in Europe and the whole world. I know quite a few people in Washington who will not regret the failure of the negotiations and not out of love for you. But I cannot tell you what to do.

Rabin nervously crushed his cigarette in the ashtray and told Kissinger he did not know whether they would regret it or not, but that he was sure, without any reservations, that they had done everything possible. They had gone to the limit of possible concessions, even though Kissinger wasn't able to bring any from Egypt.

Kissinger interrupted. Egypt did make concessions, he insisted. It had agreed to a mandate for the UN force of one year instead of six months, and then had agreed to a second one-year extension.

Rabin only replied that this wasn't enough. What Israel wanted, he said, was meaningful steps toward peace. There wasn't a trace of them in the Egyptian position, Rabin concluded.

Kissinger ended the discussion.

> As you wish. The decision is in your hands. I do not intend to fly to Egypt with these proposals, but I'll transfer them over the phone and wait for an answer—even though it is clear what the answer will be. We shall meet again tomorrow after I receive the answer.

On Saturday morning Kissinger toured the archaeological site at Masada, the mountaintop fortress where the Jews had made a last stand against the Romans two thousand years ago. While Kissinger was away his aides gave the reporters an account of the breakdown of the talks that was eventually published in the world press.

In this version Kissinger is supposed to have called Cairo Friday night and given the Egyptians the Israeli proposals. After a short interval the uncompromising answer of Egyptian Foreign Minister Fahmy came back to Kissinger's hotel room: "If this is all they have to offer, there is no reason for you to come back to Egypt."

What actually happened was entirely different. When Kissinger arrived at his hotel room on Friday night he called Cairo, as he had promised Rabin. But contrary to what was agreed, he did not report the new Israeli concessions to Sadat and Fahmy. Instead he told them there was no movement in the Israeli position.

Then, Sadat asked, in Kissinger's opinion it was hopeless?

So it seems, Kissinger replied.

At which point both of them decided that it would be better if Kissinger remained in Israel and announced the end of the negotiations there.

When the official announcement was made in Jerusalem the following night it clearly carried the implication that Israeli stubbornness had been the main obstacle. The newspaper accounts were full of gloomy predictions that the failure of the talks raised the danger of war within months, if not weeks. There was no doubt it was the Kissinger party that was the inspiration for these evaluations.

In his last conversation with the Israeli negotiating team Kissinger seemed to be trying to avoid recriminations. He said it would not be helpful if an argument now developed between the United States and Israel over who was to blame for the breakdown of negotiations. He asked the ministers to wait a few hours after the official announcement of the end of the talks before they issued their account to the press. The ministers agreed and quickly regretted it. Simultaneously with the official announcement of the end of the talks Sadat was holding a press conference in Cairo in which he blamed Israel. Egypt's version of the affair was soon being carried by world media; it took Israel hours to respond, and thus it lost the first round in the battle for world public opinion.

On Sunday morning on the way to the airport Kissinger stopped for a brief courtesy call on Golda Meir. He repeated his gloomy prophesies on the consequences of the breakdown of the talks. But Mrs. Meir stressed her full support for the position of the Rabin government.

One sentence from that conversation still remains

firmly in her memory. "I do not agree with you," Kissinger told her, "but despite it I won't say anything against Israel."

At the airport ceremony the reporters saw an entirely different Kissinger—subdued and somber. Tears filled his eyes, and his voice cracked as he spoke warmly of the prime minister and regretted the failure of his mission without blaming anyone. Then he walked briskly up the steps to the Boeing 707.

The plane had hardly taken off when Kissinger began his campaign against the Israeli government. To the assembled reporters he referred to Rabin as "a small man, whose only concern was what Peres might say of him." Allon was described as lacking strength and imagination and as someone who said one thing in Washington and something completely different in Israel in front of his colleagues. Peres was a "pseudo hawk" who lived under the shadow of Dayan but nevertheless spread terror among the other members of the cabinet. Israel needed a strong leader in this period, like David Ben-Gurion or Golda Meir, Kissinger complained. Instead it was stuck with three men concerned about their petty personal rivalries.

Back in Washington, Dinitz, the only live symbol of the Israeli government, suffered all of Kissinger's wrath. The ambassador was accused of not having accurately transferred Kissinger's thoughts to Jerusalem before the shuttle. Kissinger directed that the special line connecting his office to the Israeli embassy should be removed. All of Dinitz's calls to Kissinger were referred to Sisco or other aides. When they met at Washington gatherings it was no longer "Simcha" but "Mr. Ambassador."

The Kissinger line on the negotiations was very simple. Israel was to blame because it had misled him into thinking that if he made the shuttle it would give up the passes and abandon the demand for nonbelligerency. All of this was never said for direct attribution, but off the record in a backgrounders for reporters and members of Congress.

There is no doubt that Rabin's statements did not help the negotiations. But Kissinger's accusations were baseless. For Israel did make concessions—the demand for an end to belligerency was dropped and "nonuse of force" was substituted for it. In addition the retreat line was moved back to the middle of the passes. Furthermore, it is a fact, and Allon reminded Kissinger of it when the two met in New York in April, that Allon had invited Kissinger to the area only for an exploratory visit. It was Kissinger who decided on his own then to try another shuttle. Kissinger acknowledged that Allon had not misled him, but he kept pointing the finger at Rabin. But when Kissinger talked to others about being misled, it was just by "the Israelis."

President Ford was also visibly annoyed with Israel. With Vietnam collapsing, Ford needed a success in the Middle East. To people close to him he said, "All my life I fought for Israel and now when I need understanding from them I get a refusal."

In both Israel and the United States the new heads of state were gray, insecure men needing visible political victories. The irony was that the success of one would be interpreted as the failure of the other. Temporarily at least it was Rabin who scored. In Israel his political stock went sky-high. He had said no to the United States and that was enough to make him a national hero in most circles. "A national leader was born overnight," was the way some reporters began to write of him.

But it obviously couldn't last long. It was one thing to say no to the United States; it was quite another to measure up to the consequences of saying no. And very soon the consequences became apparent.

It started with another Ford telegram to Rabin

bluntly laying the blame for the failure on Israel and saying that Israel would bear the consequences. Then came the announcement in Washington of a "reassessment" of U.S. Middle East policy. The gloves were taken off and the veiled hints were replaced by crude and blunt talk. Peres was due to arrive in Washington for arms talks and was told he might as well stay home. Arms shipments that had been agreed upon simply stopped ariving in Israel.

While all this was going on President Sadat pulled off a briliant propaganda coup by announcing that despite the failure of the talks the Suez Canal would be opened for international shipping on June 5, 1975, the anniversary of the Six-Day War. The whole world, including Kissinger, applauded the enlightened Egyptian president. No one wanted to recall, certainly not Kissinger, that Sadat had undertaken to open the canal as an obligation stemming from the first disengagement accord signed over a year ago. Nor did anyone remember that he had then also pledged (to the United States) to allow Israeli cargo through the canal.

When several weeks later Israel announced a unilateral withdrawal of some of its troops from the canal area, Kissinger let it be leaked to the press that he regarded the Israeli gesture as meaningless.

In Israel, Rabin, Peres, and Allon got the picture. Now they began their own reassessment. They realized they were not going to get political concessions from Egypt. If they were going to be forced to retreat, therefore, they determined at least to extract the heaviest possible price from the United States. Instead of political steps leading to peace they would get American help in strengthening their security in case of war.

It was actually President Sadat who made the first new proposal. In his Salzburg meeting with President Ford in May 1975, Sadat said he would not back down on allowing an Israeli electronic warning station at Umm Hashiba, but he would consent to it being manned by the Americans.

When the compromise proposal was transmitted to Israel the cabinet divided sharply. Peres was firmly opposed to having Israel rely for its intelligence gathering on a foreign power—even if it was the United States. Instead he came up with a substitute proposal: Israel would keep the early-warning station, but next to it an American military unit would be stationed. An American military presence in the passes, he explained, would reduce to a minimum the dangers of war. It would be much more difficult for Sadat to kick out the Americans than to kick out the UN force. In any event it would be an additional early warning for Israel of Sadat's aggressive intentions. After considerable debate Peres managed to convince the other ministers and the proposal was sent to Washington.

After the trauma of Vietnam, sending American troops into the dangerous Middle East was just too much for the administration to contemplate. The proposal was rejected in Washington and put on ice, to reemerge later in a different form.

In June 1975 Rabin left again for Washington. Ford and Kissinger were still "reassessing" and wanted to hear what Israel had to offer. Ford warned Rabin right away that the aproaching American elections would not get Israel off the hook. If there was no agreement with Egypt, Ford said, the United States would go to Geneva with a plan of its own, even if it lost him votes and stirred up opposition in Congress.

Rabin did have something to offer but again he blundered so badly in presenting it that he came close to provoking another crisis with the United States. When Ford asked about the line of retreat, Rabin told the president that Israel was willing to give up a strip of land in the south near Abu Rodeis that Egypt had demanded in March. Ford was pleased but wanted to know if the Israelis were willing to give more on the passes. He asked Rabin to show him the proposed Israeli line on a map.

Rabin left the room and together with his aides he penciled in a line on the map and brought it back to the president. Ford didn't notice much of a difference, but Kissinger realized that the Israeli line had been moved back several kilometers. He didn't think it would amount to much but said he would send it on to Egypt anyway. Rabin neglected to inform Ford and Kissinger that he had no authority to draw lines.

Back in Israel, when the full cabinet heard Rabin report on his trip to Washington they were furious. They reminded him that he had no authority to move the line back. Rabin, on the defensive this time, did not claim it was his prerogative as prime minister. His excuse was that he had made a mistake in drawing the line too far to the east. He compounded his blunder by promising to correct it.

Two days later an Israeli messenger arrived in Washington. It was the prime minister's military adjutant, Colonel Ephraim Poran, who for the purpose of his secret mission had changed into civilian clothes. In his briefcase he carried a map which he gave to Dinitz, along with a message from the prime minister. Poran returned to Israel immediately.

Dinitz brought the new map to Kissinger, who asked the Israeli ambassador if he was serious. Dinitz shrugged. The line on the map was back where it had been in March—halfway across the passes. How could they conduct negotiations like this? Kissinger demanded of the helpless Israeli ambassador. The United States had already sent the previous map to Sadat. What were they supposed to tell him now?

Ford was also aghast, wanting to know if Rabin was trying to mock him. The result of the whole farce was another tough, no-nonsense telegram to Jerusalem from Kissinger saying he was waiting for new proposals and that Washington's patience was wearing thin.

In the meantime, inside the government Minister of the Treasury Yehoshua Rabinowitz was sounding the tocsin about coming disasters to the economy if there wasn't massive help for the United States—and soon.

All these pressures finally forced Rabin and the others to face their moment of truth. They knew if there was going to be an agreement with Egypt it was now or never. And then, contemplating the stark alternatives, they simply caved in.

The chief of staff was informed there was no way out of retreating from the passes and was directed to prepare a plan for a new defense line east of the Mitla and the Gidi. And an interministerial brain trust was set up to formulate the aid and political commitments that Israel would ask from the United States in return for the total retreat.

The government simply couldn't allow it to appear that they were now saying yes to the same deal they had bravely said no to a few months earlier. True, there would be the heavy American aid and political commitments, but they also needed some face-saving arrangements in the field.

Kissinger, always anticipating, had already provided one of the gimmicks. He knew the trauma that giving up the passes would create in Israel because of their strategic importance. Looking at the Sinai map, he came up with an idea that would allow Israel to say that it had not completely abandoned the passes. He saw that the passes were essentially a route through the peaks of a chain of hills. Though Israel would evacuate the passes running through the hills, he would allow Israel to put its forward defense line at the bottom of the eastern slopes of the hills. Egypt would be allowed to bring its troops to the western slopes of the hills, and the UN buffer zone would be at the peaks of the hills proper. Then Egypt could claim it had forced Israel to retreat from the passes, and Israel could say it had not evacuated completely.

The other face saver would be the presence of the Americans in the hills, near the passes. Peres came up with a plan for getting around the American reluctance to commit troops to the area. The gimmick was to give the Americans something that did not seem like a military mission. He suggested that the Israelis keep the early-warning device at Umm Hashiba in the UN buffer zone, but that in compensation the Egyptians also be given an early-warning device in the same zone. Then six more early-warning devices would be built and manned by American "technicians." The Americans would now have a constructive, nonmilitary function. Furthermore, they would be neutral, providing information for both sides. For those in America fearful of the beginnings of another Vietnam, the argument could be made that, unlike in Vietnam, the Americans are there at the explicit request of both sides.

With some modifications Kissinger basically went for the idea. And the truth is that for all the eventual controversy over whether the idea for the American technicians was Peres's or Sadat's or Rabin's, it was Kissinger who had seen it coming. As far back as the end of 1974 he realized that further progress in his step-by-step diplomacy would involve an American presence. Since there was no apparent Arab willingness to make significant political concessions in return for Israeli retreats, the United States would have to compensate Israel with active American involvement. But in the post-Vietnam atmosphere it was not something that an American secretary of state could propose on his own initiative. The way it would come, he saw clearly, was a request by Israel and the Arabs—and he definitely encouraged the tendency.

The signal that the big breakthrough on the negotiations had come was given from the Virgin Islands, where Kissinger was vacationing at the beginning of August 1975. Ambassador Dinitz came down with the whole package of Israeli proposals and requests to the United States. Kissinger looked them over, consulted with Ford several times on the phone, and then basically agreed.

The Israelis would retreat to the eastern "slopes" and give up their demands for nonbelligerency. In addition to agreeing to the technicians, the Americans would give Israel something in the neighborhood of $2 billion in military and economic aid with some new military hardware. In the political field the Americans would agree to forget about an interim agreement with Jordan. (There would only be a final peace agreement with Jordan.)

As for Syria, the situation was left more ambiguous. In a previous conversation with Ford, Rabin said he didn't see much room for another interim agreement with Syria, but he accepted the possibility of "cosmetic" changes in the cease-fire line with the Syrians. For the moment that was enough for Kissinger. He thought that later the nature of the cosmetic changes could be argued about.

The most far-reaching U.S. political commitment was in anticipation of possible Soviet military intervention. The wording that was agreed upon in the Virgin Islands was that in case of involvement of a foreign power there would be active counter involvement by the United States.

All the American political and economic commitments were given after consultation with Sadat so that in the Virgin Islands Kissinger knew he had an agreement in hand. The last shuttle would be the easiest of all.

When Kissinger went through the ritual of the 12-day shuttle in late August the only real problem that came up was in the joint Israeli-American group that was drafting the formal proposals and commitments that would be exchanged. All of a sudden the Israelis discovered that the Americans were modifying the wording of many of the political undertakings that had been agreed upon in the Virgin Islands. When Kissinger was confronted with this by Rabin he explained that there had to be changes because of the administration's fear that the agreements would be toughly scrutinized by Congress. If Congress concluded that the United States had overextended itself with commitments in the Middle East, there might be a significant backlash that would hurt Israel, Kissinger argued.

The Israelis argued that they also had a Knesset to worry about which had to ratify the agreement, and they needed the commitments to justify the agreement to the Israeli public. Kissinger consulted with Ford and they agreed to restore most of the language that had been agreed upon in the Virgin Islands, with one important exception. Kissinger insisted that Congress would never agree to a commitment of the United States to take automatic military action in the case of Soviet intervention. He said the undertaking had been made in the Virgin Islands without giving enough thought to the implications, and it had to be changed.

The Israeli ministers, with little choice at this late date, gave in. The commitment on foreign (i.e., Soviet) intervention was now worded so that if it occurred the United States and Israel would "consult."

The agreement was initialed in the prime minister's office on Tuesday, September 2, 1975, in front of members of the government, the Knesset, and dozens of journalists. It was accepted without happiness but with a sense of relief and resignation in Israel. The general consensus was that the document had to be signed because there was no alternative, and in the given circumstances it was the best agreement that could be gotten. But it was not the agreement the people had been led to believe they might achieve just a few months before.

There was the absence of an end to belligerency that earlier had seemed an essential quid pro quo for giving the Egyptians the great prize of the passes. Far more depressing was the easy way in which the government had given up another of its sacred negotiating principles—the principle that any territory given up was to be demilitarized. If that principle had been applied, there would have been a large, significant buffer zone in the Sinai separating the two armies. It would have made it very difficult for Egypt to open a war, certainly with a surprise attack. The abandonment of the principle was also a dangerous precedent for possible future agreements in the area, especially in the Golan Heights, where it would be even more vital to Israel's security.

Explaining all this inevitably forced the ministers into considerable verbal contortions. Rabin, for example, gave a background briefing for reporters several days before the agreement was signed. When asked about the end of belligerency, he said he wanted someone to explain to him what that meant. Ask the legal experts, he argued, and they will tell you it is meaningless. This from the man who was the father of the formula "the passes in exchange for an end to belligerency"—just months before on television.

When he was asked about the principle of demilitarization, Rabin dismissed the whole business. No one really expected the Egyptians to agree to it, he said. And if there were another agreement and Israel retreated halfway across the Sinai, he asked rhetorically, did anyone expect that Egypt would agree to have all of the Sinai demilitarized?

Rabin's statement was extraordinary because he himself had practically made demilitarization an ultimatum at the beginning of the negotiations. Furthermore, it was the one element that was probably achievable if the government had played its cards right—that is, if Rabin hadn't blundered with his early statement about giving up the passes. Once he indicated they could be given up he killed the chance that they would be given only at the end in exchange for something significant like demilitarization.

But such are the ways of propaganda and in the days to come the government would try to convince the people that its series of diplomatic blunders had led to a good agreement.

Even the Egyptian agreement to open the canal to Israeli cargo—which the government kept trumpeting as an achievement—was a pathetic joke. As we have seen, it was a concession already made by Sadat at the time of the January 1974 disengagement agreement. Thus it was cargo for which Israel paid twice.

Three months before, Israel had taken satisfaction from being able to say no to the United States. Even this psychological boost was stripped from the Israelis. The world now knew that the "no" in March had no political meaning—it was merely a prelude to the "yes" in August. It was clear that Israel could not stand up to U.S. pressures, even the threat of those pressures, for more than a few months. The consequences of this perception by the Arabs and the United States (whether it is completely true or not) are very ominous for the future of diplomatic developments in the area.

Rabin touched something of the problem in his parting words to Kissinger. "Mr. Secretary," the prime minister said, "now that you have experienced the difficulties of the system of negotiating by shuttle, perhaps in the future you will support direct negotiations between Israel and the Arab states."

It was Israel's oldest dream, and yet the one sure consequence of Henry Kissinger's step-by-step diplomacy was that it had forestalled the dream indefinitely.

A Concluding Note

Statecraft being the art of the possible, one ought not to expect personal sincerity to be one of the virtues of an American secretary of state. Still, nothing the Israeli leaders had been through quite prepared them for their two-year whirlwind relationship with Henry Kissinger. The record of the discussions reveals a pattern of deception and broken promises that would have made even Kissinger's heroes, Metternich and Castlereagh, blush.

It started with Kissinger's devious handling of Ambassador Dinitz over the arms supplies. It continued with the string of broken promises beginning with the cease-fire agreement signed by Kissinger in Moscow. It persisted right up to the most recent disengagement with Egypt in which Kissinger promised the Israelis that there would be no pressure for another interim agreement with Jordan and then turned around and assured King Hussein that he would get precisely such an agreement.

Even as these words are written it has been revealed that Kissinger again violated a specific commitment to the Israelis, made in the course of the negotiations for the second Egyptian disengagement. He had promised to submit to Congress an aid bill which gave Israel two-thirds of the total in outright grants and one-third in repayable loans. The bill actually sent to Congress by the administration reversed these proportions.

Despite the ever-mounting record of broken promises, Kissinger was always able to get something more out of the Israeli negotiators through his extraordinary talent for creating dazzling illusions. Just one more concession, just one more agreement and Israel would be in a better position, the Arabs would begin to show their moderation, and Israel would solidify its friendship with the United States.

His most seductive technique was in convincing the Israelis he was talking to that he was really on their side and taking them completely into his confidence. For this purpose he had a seemingly endless supply of stories about their protagonists. He told them crude jokes about Assad, about the stupidity and backwardness of the Saudis. He was even willing to tell tales that reflected rather poorly on his own character as long as his hosts were properly fascinated. Thus there was his story of how King Faisal had once launched into a lecture about the worldwide Jewish conspiracy. As Kissinger told it, he listened intently as Faisal told him how the Jews had been responsible for the Russian Revolution, how after they were kicked out of Russia they moved to take over the pinnacles of power in the Western countries, including the United States. Kissinger had no compunction about telling this incredible story first to Sadat and then to the Israelis.

To convince the Israelis of how big a confidant of theirs he was, he was not above boasting irresponsibly about how easily he handled the Soviet Union in negotiations, characterizing Soviet diplomacy to the Israelis as "cowardly and inept." Of course, all of Kissinger's talent for personal manipulation would not have carried the Israelis along time after time if it had not been for Israel's desperate dependence on the country he represented. With no reasonable alternative to continuing support by the United States, Israel could not afford to stand back and make a critical judgment of U.S. policy as expressed by Kissinger.

The historians will have to make that judgment. When they come to consider Kissinger's policy, they will not be so moved by temporary successes or his diplomatic talents. They will have to answer the question whether, after the Yom Kippur War, he was able to affect the relations between the Arabs and Israel in any fundamental sense.

What is often said in favor of Kissinger's step-by-step diplomacy is that each partial agreement, in addition to improving America's relations and influence with the Arab world, creates new and unprecedented opportunities for breaking the chain of hatred between the two sides. Specifically, it is argued, the partial agreements force the Arabs to get used to the idea of Israel's existence, and thus build blocks for an eventual peace agreement.

But anyone familiar with the history of the Arab-Israeli conflict should be able to recognize that the interim agreements are not unprecedented. Every war between Israel and its Arab neighbors has led to some sort of partial agreement. Indeed the most detailed and elaborate agreement was concluded directly between Israel and Egypt at Rhodes after the War of Independence in 1948. That agreement included words that came close to defining an end to the state of belligerency. After the 1956 and 1967 wars there were further agreements which included disengagement of forces, demilitarization arrangements, and UN truce forces in buffer zones.

But each of the agreements was followed by another war. There is little evidence that the three recent disengagement agreements have created all that much of a change in the Arab world. Jordan, the one country that has not had an interim agreement, is still the one closest to accepting Israel's existence. On the other hand, Syria, Saudi Arabia, Libya, and certainly the Palestinians voice the same desire to rid the area of the Jewish state. It is Egypt, or, more precisely, Anwar Sadat, which is the only living testimony for the thesis of Arab moderation produced by Henry Kissinger's step-by-step diplomacy. Undoubtedly Sadat has made many statements concerning Israel that are moderate by the standards of the Middle East. But if Kissinger's step-by-step diplomacy has to rest on Sadat, it is a thin reed. Perhaps Golda Meir put it most succinctly when, after one of Kissinger's statements extolling Sadat's moderation, she asked, "And what happens after Sadat dies?" It is not an academic question. Egypt remains a backward, single-party dictatorship with grave economic problems and with the potential for much internal turmoil. Against this there is nothing in the agreements between Israel and Egypt which begins to institutionalize a process of accommodation, however slow, between two peoples. We have only the statements, however promising, of Sadat. Thus Kissinger's personal diplomacy is doubly compounded—depending in large measure on the personal fate and fortunes of Sadat.

What is missing from the interim agreements is precisely the kind of small steps, exchanges, and interactions between the two sides that might begin to affect the deep psychological roots of the hatred. If, as Kissinger kept telling the Israeli negotiators, their dream of an "end to belligerency" was an empty slogan, then where are the practical steps in the agreements? The fact is that after two years of interminable haggling, and thousands of miles logged on the Boeing 707, there is nothing concrete to show. No trade, no exchange of educators or journalists, no joint committees to supervise any aspect of the agreement, no exchange of tourists, no open borders.

Nor has there been any manifestation of an end to hostile propaganda that Kissinger once suggested as one of the practical components of an end to belligerency. To the contrary, the ink on the second Sinai agreement was hardly dry when Egypt was in the forefront of the drive in the United Nations to have Zionism branded as "racist." This was more than mere "hostile propaganda." It was a clear challenge to Israel's legitimacy and right to exist. And it was Sadat himself, upon whom so many of Henry Kissinger's hopes ride, who personally identified himself with this campaign while he was in the United States trying to impress the Americans with his moderation.

If, despite all the indications, Kissinger's step-by-step diplomacy does lead to a new era between Israel and the Arabs, historians will not take much notice of the double-dealing and deception of the last two years. Unfortunately, it now seems that his diplomacy has run its course without having laid any foundations upon which to build a new structure of peace in the region. What the historians will be left with then is only Henry Kissinger's perfidy.

Appendix

TEXT OF DISENGAGEMENT AGREEMENT SIGNED BY ISRAEL AND EGYPT JANUARY 18, 1974

[A]

Egypt and Israel will scrupulously observe the cease-fire on the land, sea and air called for by the U.N. Security Council and will refrain from the time of the signing of this document from all military or paramilitary actions against each other.

[B]

The military forces of Egypt and Israel will be separated in accordance with the following principles:

1. All Egyptian forces on the east side of the canal will be deployed west of the line designated as line A on the attached map. All Israeli forces including those west of the Suez Canal on the Bitter Lakes will be deployed east of the line designated as line B on the attached map.

2. The area between the Egyptian and Israeli lines will be a zone of disengagement in which the United Nations Emergency Force will be stationed. The U.N.E.F. will continue to consist of units from countries that are not permanent members of the Security Council.

3. The area between the Egyptian line and the Suez Canal will be limited in armament and forces.

4. The area between the Israeli line, line B on the

attached map, and the line designated as line C on the attached map, which runs along the western base of the mountains where the Gidi and Mitla passes are located, will be limited in armament and forces.

5. The limitations referred to in paragraphs 3 and 4 will be inspected by U.N.E.F. Existing procedures of the U.N.E.F., including the attaching of Egyptian and Israeli liaison officers to U.N.E.F., will be continued.

[C]

The detailed implementation of the disengagement of forces will be worked out by military representatives of Egypt and Israel, who will agree on the stages of this process. These representatives will meet no later than 48 hours after the signature of this agreement at Kilometer 101 under the aegis of the United Nations for this purpose. They will complete this task within five days. Disengagement will begin within 48 hours after the completion of the work of the military representatives, and in no event later than seven days after the signature of this agreement. The process of disengagement will be completed not later than 40 days after it begins.

[D]

This agreement is not regarded by Egypt and Israel as a final peace agreement. It constitutes a first step toward a final, just and durable peace according to the provisions of Security Council Resolution 338 and within the framework of the Geneva Conference.

For Egypt:

MOHAMMED ABDEL GHANY EL-GAMASY
Major General

For Israel:

DAVID ELAZAR
*Lieut. Gen., Chief of Staff of
Israel Defense Forces*

TEXT OF AGREEMENT ON DISENGAGEMENT BETWEEN ISRAELI AND SYRIAN FORCES SIGNED ON MAY 31, 1974

A. Israel and Syria will scrupulously observe the cease-fire on land, sea and air and will refrain from all military actions against each other, from the time of the signing of this document, in implementation of United Nations Security Council Resolution 338 dated October 22, 1973.

B. The military forces of Israel and Syria will be separated in accordance with the following principles:

(1) All Israeli military forces will be west of the line designated as Line A on the map attached hereto, except in the Kuneitra area, where they will be west of Line A-1.

(2) All territory east of Line A will be under Syrian administration, and Syrian civilians will return to this territory.

(3) The area between Line A and the line designated as Line B on the attached map will be an area of separation. In this area will be stationed the United Nations Disengagement Observer Force established in accordance with the accompanying protocol.

(4) All Syrian military forces will be east of the line designated Line B on the attached map.

(5) There will be two equal areas of limitation in armament and forces, one west of Line A and one east of Line B as agreed upon.

(6) Air forces of the two sides will be permitted to operate up to their respective lines without interference from the other side.

C. In the area between Line A and Line A-1 on the attached map there shall be no military forces.

D. This agreement and the attached map will be signed by the military representatives of Israel and Syria in Geneva not later than May 31, 1974, in the Egyptian-Israeli military working group of the Geneva Peace Conference under the aegis of the United Nations, after that group has been joined by a Syrian military representative, and with the participation of representatives of the United States and the Soviet Union. The precise delineation of a detailed map and a plan for the implementation of the disengagement of forces will be worked out by military representatives of Israel and Syria in the Egyptian-Israeli military working group who will agree on the stages of this process. The military working group described above will start their work for this purpose in Geneva under the aegis of the United Nations within 24 hours after the signing of this agreement. They will complete this task within 5 days. Disengagement will begin within 24 hours after the completion of the task of the military working group. The process of disengagement will be completed not later than 20 days after it begins.

E. The provisions of paragraphs A, B and C shall be inspected by personnel of the United Nations comprising the United Nations Disengagement Observer Force under this agreement.

F. Within 24 hours after the signing of this agreement in Geneva all wounded prisoners of war which each side holds of the other as certified by the ICRC will be repatriated. The morning after the completion of the task of the military working group, all remaining prisoners of war will be repatriated.

G. The bodies of all dead soldiers held by either side will be returned for burial in their respective countries within 10 days after the signing of this agreement.

H. This agreement is not a peace agreement. It is a step toward a just and durable peace on the basis of Security Council Resolution 338 dated October 22, 1973.

PROTOCOL TO AGREEMENT ON DISENGAGEMENT BETWEEN ISRAELI AND SYRIAN FORCES CONCERNING THE UNITED NATIONS DISENGAGEMENT OBSERVER FORCE

Israel and Syria agree that:

The function of the United Nations Disengagement Observer Force (UNDOF) under the agreement will be to use its best efforts to maintain the cease-fire and to see that it is scrupulously observed. It will supervise areas of separation and limitation. In carrying out its mission, it will comply with generally applicable Syrian laws and regulations and will not hamper the functioning of local civil administration. It will enjoy freedom of movement and communication and other facilities that are necessary for its mission. It will be mobile and provided with personal weapons of a defensive character and shall use such weapons only in self-defense. The number of the UNDOF shall be about 1,250, who will be selected by the Secretary General of the United Nations in consultation with the parties from members of the United Nations who are not permanent members of the Security Council.

The UNDOF will be under the command of the United Nations, vested in the Secretary General, under the authority of the Security Council.

The UNDOF shall carry out inspections under the agreement, and report thereon to the parties, on a regular basis, not less often than once every 15 days, and, in addition, when requested by either party. It shall mark on the site the respective lines shown on the map attached to the agreement.

Israel and Syria will support a resolution of the United Nations Security Council which will provide for the UNDOF contemplated by the agreement. The initial authorization will be for 6 months subject to renewal by further resolution of the Security Council.

THE EGYPTIAN-ISRAELI ACCORD ON SINAI (SEPTEMBER 1, 1975)

The Government of the Arab Republic of Egypt and the Government of Israel have agreed that:

ARTICLE I

The conflict between them and in the Middle East shall not be resolved by military force but by peaceful means.

The agreement concluded by the parties January 18, 1974, within the framework of the Geneva peace conference constituted a first step towards a just and durable peace according to the provisions of Security Council Resolution 338 of October 22, 1973; and they are determined to reach a final and just peace settlement by means of negotiations called for by Security Council Resolution 338, this agreement being a significant step towards that end.

ARTICLE II

The parties hereby undertake not to resort to the threat or use of force or military blockade against each other.

ARTICLE III

(1) The parties shall continue scrupulously to observe the cease-fire on land, sea and air and to refrain from all military or paramilitary actions against each other.

(2) The parties also confirm that the obligations contained in the annex and, when concluded, the protocol shall be an integral part of this agreement.

ARTICLE IV

A. The military forces of the parties shall be deployed in accordance with the following principles:

(1) All Israeli forces shall be deployed east of the lines designated as Lines J and M on the attached map.

(2) All Egyptian forces shall be deployed west of the line designated as Line E on the attached map.

(3) The area between the lines designated on the attached map as Lines E and F and the area between the lines designated on the attached map as Lines J and K shall be limited in armament and forces.

(4) The limitations on armament and forces in the areas described by paragraph (3) above shall be agreed as described in the attached annex.

(5) The zone between the lines designated on the attached map as Lines E and J will be a buffer zone. On this zone the United Nations Emergency Force will continue to perform its functions as under the Egyptian-Israeli agreement of January 18, 1974.

(6) In the area south from Line E and west from Line M, as defined in the attached map, there will be no military forces, as specified in the attached annex. B. The details concerning the new lines, the redeployment of the forces and its timing, the limitation of armaments and forces, aerial reconnaissance, the operation of the early warning and surveillance installations and the use of the roads, the U.N. functions and other arrangements will all be in accordance with the provisions of the annex and map which are an integral part of this agreement and of the protocol which is to result from negotiations pursuant to the annex and which, when concluded, shall become an integral part of this agreement.

ARTICLE V

The United Nations Emergency Force is essential and shall continue its functions, and its mandate shall be extended annually.

ARTICLE VI

The parties hereby establish a joint commission for the duration of this agreement. It will function under the aegis of the chief coordinator of the United Nations peace-keeping missions in the Middle East in order to consider any problem arising from this agreement and to assist the United Nations Emergency Force in the execution of its mandate. The joint commission shall function in accordance with procedures established in the protocol.

ARTICLE VII

Nonmilitary cargoes destined for or coming from Israel shall be permitted through the Suez Canal.

ARTICLE VIII

(1) This agreement is regarded by the parties as a significant step toward a just and lasting peace. It is not a final peace agreement.

(2) The parties shall continue their efforts to negotiate a final peace agreement within the framework of the Geneva peace conference in accordance with Security Council Resolution 338.

ARTICLE IX

This agreement shall enter into force upon signature of the protocol and remain in force until superseded by a new agreement.

The U.S. Proposal for Early-Warning System in Sinai

In connection with the early-warning system referred to in Article IV of the agreement between Egypt and Israel concluded on this date and as an integral part of that agreement (hereafter referred to as the basic agreement), the United States proposes the following:

(1)
The early-warning system to be established in accordance with Article IV in the area shown on the attached map will be entrusted to the United States. It shall have the following elements:

A. There shall be two surveillance stations to provide strategic early warning, one operated by Egyptian and one operated by Israeli personnel. Their locations are shown on the map attached to the basic agreement. Each station shall be manned by not more than 250 technical and administrative personnel. They shall perform the functions of visual and electronic surveillance only within their stations.

B. In support of these stations, to provide tactical early warning and to verify access to them, three watch stations shall be established by the United States in the Mitla and Gidi Passes as will be shown on the agreed map.

These stations shall be operated by United States civilian personnel. In support of these stations, there shall be established three unmanned electronic-sensor fields at both ends of each pass and in the general vicinity of each station and the roads leading to and from those stations.

(2)
The United States civilian personnel shall perform the following duties in connection with the operation and maintenance of these stations:

A. At the two surveillance stations described in paragraph 1A, above, United States personnel will verify the nature of the operations of the stations and all movement into and out of each station and will immediately report any detected divergency from its authorized role of visual and electronic surveillance to the parties to the basic agreement and the UNEF.

B. At each watch station described in paragraph 1B above, the United States personnel will immediately report to the parties to the basic agreement and to UNEF any movement of armed forces, other than the UNEF, into either pass and any observed preparations for such movement.

C. The total number of United States civilian personnel assigned to functions under these proposals shall not exceed 200. Only civilian personnel shall be assigned to functions under these proposals.

(3)
No arms shall be maintained at the stations and other facilities covered by these proposals, except for small arms required for their protection.

(4)

The United States personnel serving the early-warning system shall be allowed to move freely within the area of the system.

(5)

The United States and its personnel shall be entitled to have such support facilities as are reasonably necessary to perform their functions.

(6)

The United States personnel shall be immune from local criminal, civil, tax and customs jurisdiction and may be accorded any other specific privileges and immunities provided for in the UNEF agreement of February 13, 1957.

(7)

The United States affirms that it will continue to perform the functions described above for the duration of the basic agreement.

(8)

Notwithstanding any other provision of these proposals, the United States may withdraw its personnel only if it concludes that their safety is jeopardized or that continuation of their role is no longer necessary. In the latter case the parties to the basic agreement will be informed in advance in order to give them the opportunity to make alternative arrangements. If both parties to the basic agreement request the United States to conclude its role under this proposal, the United States will consider such requests conclusive.

(9)

Technical problems including the location of the watch stations will be worked out through consultation with the United States.

Annex to the Sinai Agreement

Within five days after the signature of the Egypt-Israel agreement, representatives of the two parties shall meet in the military working group of the Middle East peace conference at Geneva to begin preparation of a detailed protocol for the implementation of the agreement. In order to facilitate preparation of the protocol and implementation of the agreement, and to assist in maintaining the scrupulous observance of the cease-fire and other elements of the agreement, the two parties have agreed on the following principles, which are an integral part of the agreement, as guidelines for the working group.

1. DEFINITIONS OF LINES AND AREAS

The deployment lines, areas of limited forces and armaments, buffer zones, the area south from Line E and west from Line M, other designated areas, road sections for common use and other features referred to in Article IV of the agreement shall be as indicated on the attached map (1:100,000—U.S. edition).

2. BUFFER ZONES

(a) Access to the buffer zones shall be controlled by the UNEF, according to procedures to be worked out by the working group and UNEF.

(b) Aircraft of either party will be permitted to fly

freely up to the forward line of that party. Reconnaissance aircraft of either party may fly up to the middle line of the buffer zone between E and J on an agreed schedule.

(c) In the buffer zone, between Line E and J, there will be established under Article IV of the agreement an early-warning system entrusted to United States civilian personnel as detailed in a separate proposal, which is a part of this agreement.

(d) Authorized personnel shall have access to the buffer zone for transit to and from the early-warning system; the manner in which this is carried out shall be worked out by the working group and UNEF.

3. AREA SOUTH OF LINE E AND WEST OF LINE M

(a) In this area, the United Nations Emergency Force will assure that there are no military or paramilitary forces of any kind, military fortifications and military installations; it will establish checkpoints and have the freedom of movement necessary to perform this function.

(b) Egyptian civilians and third-country civilian oil-field personnel shall have the right to enter, exit from, work and live in the above-indicated area, except for buffer zones 2A, 2B and the U.N. posts. Egyptian civilian police shall be allowed in the area to perform normal civil police functions among the civilian population in such numbers and with such weapons and equipment as shall be provided for in the protocol.

(c) Entry to and exit from the area, by land, by air or by sea, shall be only through UNEF checkpoints. UNEF shall also establish checkpoints along the road, the dividing line and at other points, with the precise locations and number to be included in the protocol.

(d) Access to the airspace and the coastal area shall be limited to unarmed Egyptian civilian vessels and unarmed civilian helicopters and transport planes involved in the civilian activities of the area, as agreed by the working group.

(e) Israel undertakes to leave intact all currently existing civilian installations and infrastructures.

(f) Procedures for use of the common sections of the coastal road along the Gulf of Suez shall be determined by the working group and detailed in the protocol.

4. AERIAL SURVEILLANCE

There shall be a continuation of aerial reconnaissance missions by the United States over the areas covered by the agreement following the same procedures already in practice. The missions will ordinarily be carried out at a frequency of one mission every 7 to 10 days, with either party or UNEF empowered to request an earlier mission. The United States will make the mission results available expeditiously to Israel, Egypt and the chief coordinator of the U.N. peace-keeping mission in the Middle East.

5. LIMITATION OF FORCES AND ARMAMENTS

(a) Within the areas of limited forces and armaments the major limitations shall be as follows:

(1) Eight (8) standard infantry battalions.

(2) Seventy-five (75) tanks.

(3) Sixty (60) artillery pieces, including heavy mortars (i.e., with caliber larger than 120 mm.), whose range shall not exceed 12 km.

(4) The total number of personnel shall not exceed eight thousand (8,000).

(5) Both parties agree not to station or locate in the area weapons which can reach the line of the other side.

(6) Both parties agree that in the areas between

Lines J and K, and between Line A (of the disengagement agreement of January 18, 1974) and Line E, they will construct no new fortifications or installations for forces of a size greater than that agreed herein.

(b) The major limitations beyond the areas of limited forces and armament will be:

(1) Neither side will station nor locate any weapon in areas from which they can reach the other line.

(2) The parties will not place anti-aircraft missiles within an area of 10 kilometers east of Line K and west of Line F, respectively.

(c) The U.N. Force will conduct inspection in order to insure the maintenance of the agreed limitations within these areas.

6. PROCESS OF IMPLEMENTATION

The detailed implementation and timing of the redeployment of forces, turnover of oil fields and other arrangements called for by the agreement, annex and protocol shall be determined by the working group, which will agree on the stages of this process, including the phased movement of Egyptian troops to Line E and Israeli troops to Line J. The first phase will be the transfer of the oil fields and installations to Egypt. This process will begin within two weeks from the signature of the protocol with the introduction of the necessary technicians, and it will be completed no later than eight weeks after it begins. The details of the phasing will be worked out in the military working group.

Implementation of the redeployment shall be completed within five months after signature of the protocol.

Index